The Javanese Way of Law

The Javanese Way of Law

Early Modern Sloka Phenomena

Mason C. Hoadley

Routledge
Taylor & Francis Group
LONDON AND NEW YORK

First published in 2019 by Amsterdam University Press Ltd.

Published 2025 by Routledge
4 Park Square, Milton Park, Abingdon, Oxon OX14 4RN
605 Third Avenue, New York, NY 10158

Routledge is an imprint of the Taylor & Francis Group, an informa business

ISBN: 9789462989337 (hbk)
ISBN: 9781041188315 (pbk)
ISBN: 9781003706700 (ebk)
NUR 820

Cover illustration: *Sima bangga* (Classic Sloka, no. 1), detail of *Paksi Naga Liman* batik, Kraton Kanoman, Cirebon

Cover design: Coördesign, Leiden

DOI: 10.5117/9789462989337

For Product Safety Concerns and Information please contact our EU representative:
GPSR@taylorandfrancis.com
Taylor & Francis Verlag GmbH, Kaufingerstraße 24, 80331 München, Germany

To the Memory of Daniel S. Lev

Table of Contents

List of Tables

Preface

The present work has its roots in the author's research into the alterations in Java's legal institutions brought about by the expansion of Dutch East India Company political dominance on the island. For the late seventeenth and entire eighteenth centuries the character of the era's source material invited the application of an approach generally at odds with the historical tradition. As a type of 'history of the losers written by the winners', it views the displacement of indigenous legal institutions through the eyes of the same foreigners who were responsible for that change. Although reliance on primarily Dutch sources did not distract from tracing the process of colonial takeover, it lacks the depth necessary to understand more precisely what constituted pre-colonial Javanese law and how it functioned. With few notable exceptions, the foreigners were not interested in the legal system that they were transforming through the introduction of rules and regulations more congenial to Company norms and aims.

In turning to research based on indigenous sources it became clear that the subject was considerably different from that suggested by the sporadic references to Javanese law in Company records. The problem is not so much in the quantity of sources as their quality. Unsurprisingly, subjects adequately covered in the Dutch records are those of interest to Europeans. These include price, quantity, and availability of saleable tropical commodities, methods of producing them, political conditions of the natives to be encouraged or discouraged, often by armed intervention, and the like. This means that only a small amount of information concerning the interface between the alien company and local traditions has been recorded, and that tempered by considerations of furthering the former's goals. Little of it provides the necessary information for a deeper understanding of traditional Javanese law.

The present study rests almost exclusively on Javanese language sources from the time and place under discussion, that is, as near as possible under the circumstances. Autonomous sources from the 'Independent Kingdoms era' are supplemented by sporadic European observations only when appropriate to the narrative. It is felt that this provides a more Asian-centric approach by recognising that the basis of Javanese law does not necessarily tally with that of Europe. As a result, addressing Euro-centric questions to the sources provokes answers that may not fit with reality. John Crawfurd's observation quoted in Chapter 1 provides a telling example. Another would be to pose the question of how Javanese law differentiates civil from criminal justice. Yet it presupposes that the 'civil' and 'criminal' concepts are translatable into Javanese reality, which they are not. A response to what (to local ways of thinking) are meaningless questions, will most likely be answered in kind.

The reverse side of the coin, i.e., what is important for traditional Java, may grate on European sensibilities. 'Traditional Javanese law is proverbial? You must be joking!'. Yet such is literally the case. Many pre- or early-colonial Javanese texts deal at length with what is termed here the *sloka* phenomena consisting of *sloka* proper (roughly = proverbs), *aksara* (legal precepts), *sinalokan* (that made of a *sloka*), *prakara* (cases, instances), set in vignettes. As these have a special character within Javanese society, the challenge for scholarship is to discover the nature of that character and communicate it to a wider public, in a nutshell the purpose of this book.

Introduction

For those unfamiliar with the *sloka* phenomena as the epitome of early modern Javanese law some explanation is in order. Three points seem particularly relevant, namely the role of the *sloka* phenomena within traditional Javanese law, their contribution to placing the law they serve in time and space, and their potential as a tool for investigating legal systems.

Characteristic of the Javanese law least influenced by European impositions is the apparent lack of binding precedent. None of the modest number of documented legal contests – textual, didactic, or actual – resolved by local tribunals refer to preceding decisions under similar circumstances or specific paragraphs from standard legal titles. At first glance, this seems to indicate that traditional Javanese law lacked a concept of precedent, one ensuring that legal decisions in some manner take note of prior manners of handling equivalent affairs. In early modern Java, wisdom of the past as a form of precedent has been distilled into what are termed the *sloka* phenomena, namely *sloka* proper, *aksara*, *sinalokan*, and *prakara* commonly communicated in vignettes. The *sloka* phenomena are not merely adjuncts of law in an *ex post facto* manner implied by translation of *sloka/saloka* as 'proverb'. They were much more. In tune with their Sanskrit predecessors, they constituted the essence of the law to be followed in specific instances.

A second characteristic touches on the historical context. *Sloka* phenomena not only dominate the period's legal texts but also serve to place them in time and space. Expectations of textual continuity from Old Javanese law as preserved in texts filtered through the scribes of Bali are belied by the results of the present study. Absence of the *sloka* phenomena in what is known of the legal titles of Old Java/Bali effectively distances them from the contents of the younger Javanese law texts analysed here.[1] The latter embraces primarily eighteenth-century law prevailing in the Central Javanese kingdom of Mataram, one whose legal principles extended as far

1 In an earlier work the author has implicitly accepted the commonly held assumption that Javanese law of the pre-colonial period was an extension of the contents of texts preserved on Bali written in 'middle' or 'old' Javanese, Hoadley and Hooker, *The Agama*, under 'Date' p. 68ff. and 'Provenance' p. 73ff. Whether these texts – most of the manuscripts are younger than those employed in this study – reflect the legal heritage of, say, fourteenth-century Majapahit remains to be established, see Creese, 'Old Javanese legal traditions'.

west as Priangan Regencies, Jakarta/Batavia, and even the kingdom of Banten on the island's western-most tip.[2]

Even the incorporation of Islamic themes into legal texts of the period left the *sloka* phenomena unchanged. Prominent examples are seen in the names/titles of Islamic-Javanese texts. These include the *Surya Alam*, from a mythological ruler of the Muslim Middle East, the 'Jimbun texts' as the *Undhang Senapati Jimbun* and *Jimbun Slokantara* after Senapati Jimbun (aka Radèn Patah) the semi-mythological vanquisher of the Hindu-Buddhist Majapahit empire of East Java and founder of the region's first Islamic kingdom of Demak in the late fifteenth century, as well as the *Arya Dilah*, after his trusted companion. Despite Islamic trappings, the texts rely upon the *sloka* phenomena as the primary vehicle of traditional Javanese law.[3]

Pre-eminence of the *sloka* phenomena in early modern Javanese law also raises the issue of its relation to *adat* (custom). That which would develop into the academic discipline of *adatrecht* (the study of *adat* law) grew out of rulings by the Dutch East Indies government in the middle of the nineteenth century. By governmental decree, all previous laws were invalidated and *adat* recognized as the legal norm for the island's inhabitants, that is in so far as they had not voluntarily or otherwise already been placed under the colony's European norms. Common sense argues that customary prescriptions had existed since the inception of legal process, yet it is first recorded for Java in the beginning of the twentieth century, mainly through the efforts of Cornelis van Vollenhoven and his disciples leading to the publication of *De Ontdekking van het Adatrecht* (The discovery of the *adat* law) in 1928. Short of some sort of unchanging *adat* defying normal historical developments, research into the past is limited to information contained in the extant legal titles. The fact that texts, as well as actual and didactic or normative legal cases were dominated by the *sloka* phenomena

2 Just how much of those principles found their way into East Javanese legal developments in, say, the kingdom of Balambangan, is not known due to a paucity of texts, which either are no longer extant or undiscovered.

3 As argued in the Chapter 8. 'Character', that the contents of the Independent Kingdoms' law differed sharply from traditions preserved on Bali-Lombok is only secondarily the result of the spread of Islam. Legal tracts brought to Java, as the *Muḥarar* and *Kitab Toepah*, are written in classic Arabic to which have been added translations or paraphrase in Javanese. Their Islamic form and content have thus been retained, even in Dutch translation as, for example, in the *Semarang Compendium* of 1750, van der Chijs, *Plakaatboek*, also discussed under the rubric 'Mogharaer Code' by Ball, *Indonesian Legal History*, pp. 68-70. See also Mahmood Kooria, 'The Dutch Mogharaer, Arabic *Muḥarar*, and Javanese Law Books'.

provides a window of access for reconstruction of the (more) traditional law of the island.

The sheer volume of references to custom within Javanese legal texts obligates one to consider them as a potentially rewarding field of research. In this respect, the present work's contribution lies in the obvious; the only way to reach the past earlier than the span of human memory is to consult sources that have survived, namely datable written texts. The existence of the *sloka* phenomena embodying contemporaneous local custom adds a retrospective dimension to sources otherwise limited by the living memory of its practitioners. Since the *sloka* phenomena are quoted, not created, by the transmitters of the tradition, they must pre-date them. Should one find a way to determine how much so, then we would have a research tool of considerable historical significance. That there is some belief in this direction is indicated by the tag 'Old Javanese' appended to *sloka* and *sloka*-like phrases in modern compilations of such terms. Basically, the term refers to language employed in order to differentiate it from present-day Javanese. However, because Old Javanese was used on the island throughout the period up to the fifteenth or sixteenth centuries, it can be interpreted as indicating that the phrases in question originate from a period pre-dating the sources used in this inquiry. Again, the postulate cannot simply be written off because the form and contents of the law used in the fourteenth century and earlier is far from clear. Looking in the opposite direction, the contemporary renaissance of interest in Javanese tradition, including the *sloka* phenomena, attests to their longevity in the eyes of contemporary Indonesians.

A final point touches on the intellectual debt owed to scholarly predecessors for the data made available by their work, despite that it was not always directed to the same end. A special place is held by C.F. Winter's prodigious collection of 'proverbs/maxims, adages, sayings, and other subjects' (*salokas, paribasans, wangsalans en andere onderwerpen*) found in *Javaansche Zamenspraken* (Javanese Dialogues), as does the observation of its editor, Salomon Keyzer, concerning the close relationship existing between such phrases and Javanese law in the Forward to the second edition of 1858. Other contributions include G.A.J. Hazeu's edition of the Cirebon law book, the *Pepakem Tjerbon*, and Mijnheer van der Hout's translation of the Kartasura *Surya Alam*. Regrettably, neither scholar followed up on these projects. A more modern debt is owed to Peter Suwarno for his comprehensive *Dictionary of Javanese Proverbs and Idiomatic Expressions*.

Present work

Focus of the present work can be summarised in four points. The first stems from the observation that the legal tradition of the Independent Kingdoms era is dominated by *sloka* phenomena contained in various *pepakem* and expressed in vignettes. Either as derivatives of or dependent upon *sloka* for their authority, *aksara*, *sinalokan*, and *prakara* are integral parts of that tradition. This is true if for no other reason than their sheer numbers. Of the fifteen-hundred phrases presented and explained in *Javaansche Zamenspraken*, most of them are directly connected with legal affairs. A typical connection is expressed as 'this is a *sloka* [as contrasted to those of a *paribasa*, etc.] of one having legal suit concerning [its subject]' It also reflects their dominance in the contents of titles identified as providing the main source of information for understanding Javanese law.

The second point is that Javanese law is highly fragmented. 'Texts' in the usual sense of the word implying equivalent contents as, for example, those of the *Babad Tanah Jawi* or equivalent literary works, are exceedingly rare. A given title only to a limited degree shares its contents with titles of the same name, be they from other manuscripts or even the same one. Here titles and textual traditions designate the contents of relevant sources which are similar, but by no means congruent. The similar part comes from the fact that most commonly titles are built around a recognisable core to which variations on that theme are appended.

The third point is that the *sloka* phenomena were functional as opposed to decorative. 'Classic *sloka*' define sovereign rights, obligations, and attributes. They also pre-date the textual tradition in that they are quoted, not created, by ministers, or in the case of the *Surya Alam*, the sovereign himself. *Aksara* provided legal categories of chastisement and instruments of resolving legal contests, *sinalokan* employed parts of *sloka* in order to authenticate cases, and *prakara* summarised them all. In those rare examples of case law preserved in the sources, *sloka* phenomena also define the nature of the affair as well as assess its seriousness.

The fourth point is whether the *sloka* phenomenon as defined here are antiquarian relics from a vaguely understood past or relevant concepts for the present. Anticipating the work's conclusion, it can be noted that *aksara* and *sloka*, as well as the vignettes in which they are embedded, are alive and well and living in the Republic of Indonesia today. Thanks to modern media they are discussed and interpreted as never before. This contrasts with the modern (European) legal transplants, comprising by far the largest part of the Republic's laws. These seem to lack acceptance as measured by their failure in providing a guide to behaviour for the majority of Indonesians. How else does one explain the Republic's rampant corruption if not by conscious ignoring of the alien laws and rules inherited from the colonial government. In contrast, the message of traditional written texts in harmony with those of the *adat* have become increasingly important in present-day Indonesia with its concern over the apparent lack of public morality. This has reached the extent of reinterpreting age-old Javanese traditions within the context of modernising Islamic ones.

The work's organisation roughly follows the demarcation between vehicles of traditional law and its contents. Section I. 'Law, *Sloka*, and Sources' opens the work. Tradition and its expression are found in Chapter 1. 'Traditional Law. *Sloka* in *pepakem*', which is built around an early eighteenth-century Dutch source providing unique information on the composition of indigenous law. Of special interest is the *pepakem* genre or 'written law in general'. Chapter 2. '*Sloka* in Javanese titles' opens with a consideration of available Javanese source material before turning to an in-depth discussion of the individual *sloka* phenomenon and their relationship to specific titles. Subsequently the chapter turns to the contents of titles identified as key sources of information. Section II. '*Sloka* Phenomena in Vignettes', Chapters 3-7 – respectively '*Sloka*', '*Aksara*', '*Sinalokan*', '*Prakara*', 'Vignettes and Practice' – constitute the work's substantive contribution. They draw upon a range of titles for discussion of these key elements and hence provide the textual context of the *sloka* phenomena from which they take their significance.

Section III. 'Character, Apparent Demise, and Context' summarises the basics of traditional Javanese law (Chapter 8. 'Character') and relevant developments taking place after the period under scrutiny (Chapter 9. 'Context'). More specifically, the first half of Chapter 9 traces the fate of traditional law and particularly its formal disenfranchisement by the 'New Legislation' introduced by the Dutch East Indies government between 1846 and 1848. The radical step was facilitated by the legal vacuum during the Cultivation System era (1830-c.1870), a gap paralleled by the reformulation of law in the region which would become the Kingdom of the Netherlands. Despite such measures, sources of traditional law continued to be copied, edited, and revised, raising the possibility that the perceived cleft between banished and presumably forgotten Javanese written law and the living oral *adat* is overemphasized. The last half of the chapter documents the longevity of the *sloka* phenomena into the present as seen in modern references, both written and on the Internet, and even a tendency to merge with contemporary Islamic ideas of public morality. Section IV supplements the presentation through discussion of the *Pepakem Tjerbon*, analysis of two dozen Classic *Sloka*, consideration of important titles not directly relevant to the present work, and presentation of diverse components only touched upon in the narrative.

Section I

Law, *Sloka*, and Sources

Section I introduces the work's subject, advances its thesis, and evaluates the original source material available for accomplishing its objectives. In reconstructing traditional Javanese written law, the focus is upon the key indigenous principles of customary law, the *sloka* phenomena of the title. Understanding such principles renders comprehensible the contents of hundreds of Javanese manuscript folios comprising that law. Despite a well-informed colonial administrator describing it as a jumble of disorganised and incompatible elements, the fact that the individual *sloka* phenomena tend to be concentrated in separate sets of texts allows organisation of the available materials into a body of information composed of a reasonably consistent matrix of related components.

1 Traditional Law. *Sloka* in *Pepakem*

If a single entity could stand for the contents of traditional law, it would be paragraph four of a text called the *Wadigun Wangkara*.[1] The article opens by citing the Hindu concept of *yuga* (epochs) in the world's cosmic decline. In it the original four Sanskrit *yuga* are rephrased in the form of five Javanese terms representing stages of decreasing validity in legal claims. Highest on the scale is the *Krţa/Satya Yuga*, which becomes Javanese *Tirta* assuring victory; lowest, the *Kali Yuga* becoming *Sengara*, dooms a case to defeat. More important, explanation of the term marking the final epoch describes the king's efforts to counter the *Kali* era of darkness and deceit by creating rules communicated through the *sloka* phenomena. The extraordinary step of introducing innovations into the body of law customarily regulated by experience (*drigama*) was necessitated by ministerial evasion of their moral and professional duty in the face of the unexpected death of a high official's son. Unacceptability of 'passing the buck' through each minister deferring to the opinion of the others prompted the *patih* (prime minister, king's chief counsellor),[2] Gajah Mada Amongpunggung, to reveal a *sloka* (proverb, maxim containing a simile, metaphor [esp. as a legal term]) constructed from the names of the five irresponsible *mantri* (palace officials). The result is a particularly damning description of their actions as 'clearly smelling of evil' (*gandaning nyata*), constituting punishable negligence based on the 'crime of silence' (*sidhem pramanem*). Pronouncement of the legal *sloka* was accompanied by the imposition of large fines levied from the errant ministers. This in turn established a *sinalokan* (a phrase composed of *sloka* elements), which became the custom of the realm. Not to be outdone, His Majesty Wijayang Sastra created (*adeg*) a reprimand in the form of two affairs (*prakawis/prakara*). These were *aksara* (legal precepts), which constitute

1 The *Wadigun Wangkara*'s catholic character is established by reference within a single article, itself a narrative vignette, to all four *sloka* phenomena, the subject matter of this work. Characteristic of the era's legal titles, three versions of the text are found in one manuscript, namely, British Museum [*sic* British Library] Additional Manuscript (hereafter Add) 18 398, ff. 55r-56v, 60_r-62r, and 62v. Parallel versions are found in Leiden Oriental Manuscript (hereafter LOr) 7440, ff. 181-188, as well as part of § 7 of the *Cacad*, also from LOr 7440, ff. 184-188 and LOr 7410, f. 15. In addition, it forms the combined title, termed in this work the *Jimbun Slokantara II*, namely: 'This is the *Slokantara* [*Raja Niscaya*] [and] *Wadigun* [*Wangkara*] composed by Senapati *Jimbun* for *dursila* (criminal) cases (LOr 7440, f. 132ff.)'. The *Slokantara* tradition is discussed in Chapter 2.

2 Unless otherwise stated translations into English marked by parenthesis come from Robson and Wibisono, *Javanese-English Dictionary*. Otherwise the term/phrase is marked with quotation marks and a note provided.

categories of royal chastisement. As part of the standard dozen or so *aksara*, the two created by Wijayang Sastra were *aksara geni* 'the order of a king who punishes' and *aksara bumi* 'the loyalty/steadfastness (*kukuh*) of the court'. The article closes with the statement: 'End of the reading of the *Wadigun Wangkara* taken from Patih Gajah Mada'.

Javanese written law

More than just an anomalous reference to Hindu cosmology in an era assumed to be Islamic in character, the components singled out by the *Wadigun Wangkara* dominate traditional Javanese written law. As the subject of this inquiry it is traditional by virtue of stemming from an era characterised by semi-independent kingdoms, successors of earlier Hindu-Javanese kingdoms modified through accumulative internal developments and the island's conversion to Islam. The latter is usually understood as having taken place from the fifteenth century onwards marked by the rise to prominence of the Demak federation centred on the eastern Pasisir (Java's northeast coast). This took place under the leadership of Radèn Patah (aka Kyai Senapati Jimbun). Radèn Patah by tradition is seen as the vanquisher of the Hindu-Javanese Majapahit Empire, the greatest figure of which was Patih Gajah Mada (c. 1290-1364). Albeit with decreasing authority, the Javanese kingdoms continued to function throughout a period in which the island's legal institutions were successively inundated by rules, regulations, and practice resulting from the growing political hegemony exercised by the Dutch East India Company. Although a period of transition extended over a relative long period of time, it is best documented for the eighteenth century, which saw the kingdoms of Banten-Lampung, Cirebon, those of the Priangan region, Mataram (after 1755 Yogyakarta and Surakarta), and Balambangan brought under Dutch authority. As a result, 'Independent Kingdoms' has been coined for the period under consideration, one felt to be more appropriate than an unwieldy 'Semi-Independent Kingdoms' or a deterministic 'Pre-Colonial Period'.

Traditional law is Javanese in two respects. The first lies in the medium of transmission. Its texts are written in common or *ngoko* (the basic speech style of Javanese) using the ha-na-ca-ra-ka alphabet, the twenty *aksara* or more accurately the *den-taywajana*.[3] An exception is the Kartasura *Surya Alam* written in '*pégon*' (Javanese language written with Arabic script), but subsequently copied in ha-na-ca-ra-ka. The second aspect is that Javanese

3 Winter, *Javaansche Zamenspraken*, vol. II, pt. 1, pp. 1-2.

texts of a legal nature are by no means confined to the linguistic areas designated as Javanese speaking, namely Central and East Java. A type of chancellery Javanese characterised administrative documents, mostly legal texts and treaties, from Banten-Lampung in the west to Balambangan in the east; it may even include Bali-Lombok. Complemented by the striking similarities in contents between traditions originating from Sundanese, Javanese, and Madurese speaking regions, the wide-spread use of an official Javanese style argues for a common, Java-wide usage, a 'Greater Java' in its legal tradition.[4]

That this traditional law is written is obvious. Less so is the implication that the veracity of conclusions reached from its contents is dependent not only on the quantity of sources but also on the quality of interpretation. Because the period lies beyond the scope of human memory, of necessity data concerning its contents must be drawn from extant texts originating from that era or, failing this, as near to it as possible. Unfortunately, there are few serviceable texts with uncontested pedigrees of provenance and date. What lies to hand are textual traditions that can be screened in order to make provisional judgments on the eldest and most reliable. Inevitably, such an evaluation is bound to raise questions. One of them concerns the practical necessity of concentrating on a relatively limited number of manuscripts out of the many extant examples held in European and Indonesian collections. Since an acceptable canon is lacking there seems no alternative. Another concern is the challenge of deciphering the sources' contents. This applies to both determining what the manuscripts say – due to unclear or botched copies, irregularities in grammar and spelling, as well as apparent omissions – and interpreting what they mean in terms of the law of which they are a part. Here the existence of a limited number of published works, mostly in Dutch, provides invaluable assistance when used with caution. Despite the inherent challenges, the source material provides a reasonably consistent picture of the law under consideration.

A final point concerns the inquiry's definition of law. A common assumption (or pious hope) of colonial officials was that Javanese law did not differ too greatly from positive law in the European sense. The danger

4 Hoadley, 'The Role of Law in Contemporary Indonesia'. Parenthetically it can be noted that the commonality of titles considered here suggests that the subsequent division into four *adat recht* 'circles' – Lampung, West Java, Central Java and Madura, and 'The Principalities' of Yogyakarta and Surakarta – by the Dutch East Indies government in the twentieth century seems to be a misinterpretation of traditional Javanese law. A shared written tradition and a differing oral one defining separate geographic and ethnic entities is unlikely. See ter Haar, *Adat law in Indonesia*, pp. 6-10 and maps on the inside cover.

of equating Javanese sources of law with those of Europe is illustrated by a negative judgment on the former by one of the more knowledgeable of later European officials, namely:

> all of them display a remarkable character of rudeness and barbarism. Institutions so imperfect, indeed, have never, in all probability, been, among any other people, committed to writing. No attempt is made in them at arrangement or classification, but the most incompatible matters are blended together, and the forms of judicature, criminal and civil jurisprudence, maxims of morality, and commercial regulations, are incongruously intermixed.[5]

Despite its negative tone, Crawfurd correctly identified traditional Javanese written law's most characteristic features. These include a lack of consistency between titles, the apparent mixture of different modes of law, and admonitions of what 'ought to be'. Of the mainstream titles – *Jugul Muda, Jaya Lengkara, Luwangan Undhang-Undhang, Raja Niscaya,* and *Surya Alam* – only the last named has been published in translation, and then in less-than-useful forms (Chapter 2). Thus, any inquiry into the contents of the law is dependent on manuscript versions. Familiarity with the contents of these texts confirms the veracity of Crawfurd's observations. This is with the qualification that they are negative only in terms of European expectations. Further study of their contents brings out the positive contribution. The essence of law is not dependent upon Euro-centric prejudices, but on what is seen as important by Javanese practitioners. This was recognized a century and a half ago in Keyzer's preface to the second of edition of C.F. Winter's monumental *Javaansche Zamenspraken.*

> The possibility of understanding the old[er] Javanese law books is above all opened through the utilization of expressions, couched in a few words

5 Crawfurd, *History of the Indian archipelago*, pp. 78-79. John Crawfurd (1793-1868) was a Scottish physician, colonial administrator, diplomat, and author best known for his work on Asian languages and his role in the founding of Singapore. During the British interregnum 1811-15 Crawfurd not only acted as Resident of Yogyakarta, by that time reduced to a semi-independent princedom, but also traveled widely in the archipelago. His interest in law is attested to by the relatively large number of legal manuscripts in the British Library's Crawfurd collection. Among them is Add 12 303 owned by Hamengkubuwana II, the source of several titles used in this work. In addition, Add 12 277 is the (more original) copy of the *Agama* law book presented to Crawfurd by the Raja of Buleleng, Bali, see Hoadley and Hooker, *Agama*, p. 52. Many of the Crawfurd collection manuscripts are being digitalised by the British Library under the 'Archive of Yogyakarta' project, after the publication of Carey & Hoadley of the same name.

> sometimes in a single word, which serve to give knowledge of whole suits/causes.[6]

Emphasis on these expressions is a logical conclusion born of familiarity with the contents of C.F. Winter's work. Even a cursory reading of the second section of *Javaansche Zamenspraken* reveals the terms' intimate involvement in legal affairs.[7] Tuan Anu, Winter's straight man in the didactic dialogues comprising that work, shows a re-occurring interest in connecting the *sloka* under discussion with phrases from the contents of literary works, mainly the *Ramayana* and *Mahabharata*. This probably reflects the texts available at the time, as there is little else to connect the phrases with the preceding period of Javanese history. Another field in need of updating is that of providing nuanced definitions of the expressions. In *Javaansche Zamenspraken* they are too often subsumed under the general rubric of *saloka*. According to the titles drawn upon in this work many of them fall into the category of *prakara*.[8]

6 Keyzer, Preface to *Javaansche Zamenspraken*, vol. II, p. iii. Salomon Keyzer (1823-1868) was lecturer in Islam and Indigenous Law at the Royal Academy, Delft. His scholarly contributions include publication of a textual edition of the *Kitab Toepah*, an article entitled 'Javaansche Spreekwoorden', as well as his early recognition of the importance of the British Museum's collection of Javanese manuscripts. This is in addition to capacity as editor of the *Bijdragen tot Taal-, Land- en Volkenkunde*, the major vehicle of scholarship on the Indies.

7 It is difficult to avoid the conclusion that Winter was aware of the connection between *sloka* and legal affairs. The titles chosen as sources – the *Salokantara*, *Jugul Muda*, and *Surya Alam* – are clearly legal texts. With the addition of the *Jaya Lengkara*, whose contents are very close to the two versions of the *Jimbun Slokantara*, they duplicate the sources used for the present work. However more precise information on the written sources drawn upon by Winter and expressed in *Javaansche Zamenspraken* by his alter-ego, Radèn Kawitana, is not available. Although the Yogyakarta *kraton* archive was plundered in 1812 by Raffles and company, in Winter's time there remained texts held by the Surakarta *kraton* archive and private collections. Although their contents are not known, judging from his interpretation of the *sloka* cited in this chapter they do not seem to have differed greatly from those found in extant European collections.
Carel Fredrick Winter (1799-1859) was official translator at the Institute for the Javanese language, Surakarta, from 1832 to 1843, becoming its director in 1834. A Eurasian educated in Dutch schools, he had an uncommonly deep understanding of all aspects of Javanese life, especially of its literary and legal tradition as attested to by several key publications, *Javaansche Zamenspraken* being the most cited. The fact that the dialogues comprising that work were made up by Winter himself has provoked criticism. Yet here his multiethnic background enabled him to compose the dialogues of Tuan Anu (Mr. What's name), a European straight man, played against the knowledgeable *mantri*, Radèn Kawitana. In any event, E.M. Uhlenbeck, Professor of Javanese, Leiden University, felt that this 'seems to be not quite justified: in the first place because it [does] not take into account that Winter's command of the language came near to that of a native speaker' (*The Languages of Java and Madura*, p. 49).

8 Most of the '*Thirty Prakara*' listed in Table 6.1 are cited in Winter's *Javaansche Zamenspraken* as '*saloka*'.

Dealt with in Volume 2, part 1-3 of that work, the quantity and consistency of such expressions is truly impressive. Drawing on contents of the major textual traditions, as well as his near encyclopaedic knowledge of things Javanese, Winter brought together with succinct explanations roughly fifteen-hundred such generic terms. Many of them appear in modern collections of proverbs and idiomatic expressions.[9] Moreover, these pithy phrases are legal in nature, being identified as such in the entries' explanation of the individual terms or phrases. According to Winter, they come from recognized titles of the period 'all of them taken from the *Surya Alam* and the *Salokantara* (*Slokantara* in this work) as well the *Jugul Muda*'.[10]

In contrast to the heterogeneous nature of the titles in which they are found, the *sloka* phenomena are consistent in terms of form and contents. In this respect there exists an 'arrangement or classification', although not one to which Europeans were accustomed. Through use of apophthegms or aphorisms judicable acts are brought into relative hierarchies. Valid cases are separated from those declared invalid (*tan dadi, boten lampah*), those deserving to win (*menang*) and lose (*kalah*) are indicated, meritorious solutions are given by way of examples, and legal consequences of losing are specified in the form of restitution, single or double compensation, and fines payable to winner and/or the sovereign. In addition, such phrases also indicate those situations surrendered to private retribution or demanding capital punishment by sovereign authority. A corollary is that the specific paragraphs, phrases, and terms cited constitute the germ of law, the texts the chaff.

Legal texts as *pepakem*

If the Javanese titles accepted and classified as such by generations of scholars, librarians, and archivists are not law books in the European manner, what are they? In a nutshell, they are (*pe*)*pakem* ('a type of manual of *wayang* stories, legal rules, etc'.).[11] An often-quoted contemporaneous observation provides the clearest description of how such *pepakem* fit into the basic tenets of Javanese law. Dating from 1716, well into the period of Dutch East

9 Consulted in this study are those of Suwarno, *Dictionary;* Darmasoetjipta, *Kamus Peribahasa*; Ngafenan, *Paribasan*; and Hariwijaya, *Kamus Idiom*.

10 Winter, *Javaansche Zamenspraken*, vol. II, pt. 3, p. 143. It must be acknowledged that not all the terms and phrases can be linked to the relevant texts. They may have been part of an undocumented oral tradition of the mid-nineteenth century.

11 Pigeaud, *Javaans-Nederlands Woordenboek*.

India Company hegemony,[12] three sources of the Javanese legal tradition are identified. According to Resident Gobius of Cirebon (1714-1717), criteria for the 'old original laws' valid for the *jaksa* (assessors-at-law) were:

1. That they conform to the true contents and meaning of the *pepakem*, being written law in general.
2. That they heed the edicts and ordinances of the state (*oebaya ing nagara*).
3. That they observe the custom of the land and the manner of procedure as such has been practiced from olden times, which has thus become custom and law, comprehended under the phrase: 'The *adat* practiced by the *jaksa*' (*adat kang sampun kalamphan déning jaksa*).

Thereto have the judges been strictly held on pain of nullity of their judgments.[13]

Gobius' third point is the least controversial. It has been interpreted as providing one of the earliest references to *adat* made so popular in the beginning of the twentieth century.[14] Supplementing the dictionary meaning of *adat* (traditional patterns of behaviour), it is more commonly termed 'customary law'. In theory there can be no objection to the observation that adherence to customs hallowed by time and usage constituted a binding obligation for those responsible for legal settlements. In practice, however, complications arise. The most serious of these is that there are no contemporaneous sources revealing the specific contents of the *adat* at that time, that is, if it was an exclusive or near-exclusive oral form of law.

The second point concerning '*oebaya*' (*ubaya*) is revealing. Gobius' interpretation of the term seems to be wishful thinking, namely of the imposition of centralised governmental institutions felt by Dutch officials as a necessary adjunct of political hegemony. 'Edicts and ordinances' of the state would become characteristic of the mature colonial system of the nineteenth century. They were an anomaly in reference to the institutions of Java's semi-independent kingdoms. During the period under consideration *ubaya* (1 promise, agreement (regarding time); 2. summons to appear before a court at a certain time) retained its original meaning. As seen in the three

12 The Dutch East India Company had been ensconced at Batavia/Jayakarta since the early 1600s. By the end of the seventeenth century its authority had expanded to the Cirebon-Priangan region in the aftermath of the break-up of the Central Javanese kingdom of Mataram resulting from the Truna Jaya revolt of 1677.

13 'Gobius on Priangan *Jaksa*', cited in Hoadley, *Selective Judicial Procedure*, p. 53; Hoadley and Hooker, *The Agama*, p. 242, and, among others, Ball, *Indonesian Legal History*, pp. 47-48 quoting Kern, *Javaansche Rechtsbedeeling*', pp. 344-372.

14 Ball, *Indonesian Legal History*, pp. 166ff.

translated examples from the Cirebon-Priangan region promulgated in the first quarter of that century, *ubaya* were agreements between parties, that is, among Javanese potentates and between them and the Dutch East India Company.[15] As a result, we can turn to Gobius' first point, namely that concerning *pepakem*, a characteristic feature of the eighteenth-century law books.

The *Undang Nitih Cirebon* of 1723-1725 documents the place of *pepakem* in the period's legal system. According to the Introduction and §§ 3, 5, and 12, procedure should conform to the contents of *pepakems* (*saraket saungelé pepakemé*).[16] Most of the period's legal titles are identified either by themselves or by contemporary texts as '*pepakem*'. Those qualified to interpret *pepakem* were *jaksa*. Contrary to common assumptions, *jaksa* did not function as judges; as masters of traditional Javanese law – assessors-at-law in Pigeaud's felicitous phase, albeit for the Majapahit *upapatti* – their task was to provide those deciding cases, the sovereign or his ministers, with textual basis of law as found in *pepakem*. These contained the customary norms. 'In agreement with the *adat* of old shall be their decision (§ 8)'. No single handbook contained the entire corpus of law. Each contained a portion of that law, apparently brought together according to interests or priories of the individual *jaksa*. Their contents contained examples of acceptable legal solutions. These were multiple in the sense that there existed more than one acceptable alternative for a given situation. The sovereign or his surrogates chose that which best fit the circumstances'.[17]

15 Hoadley and Hooker, *The Agama*, pp. 258-269. In this respect they are precursors to the *prajanjian* (agreement, contract) or 'treaty, accord', Pigeaud, *Javaans-Nederlands Woordenboek*, and '*angger-angger*' (rule, regulation) of a younger date in Central Java. Parenthetically, form and contents – i.e., numbered paragraphs with concise and internally consistent contents, reference to their validity in time and space, and a statement of the issuing authority – show them to have been strongly influenced by Dutch models of positive law, see Hoadley, *Islam Dalem*, pp. 291-296. With reference to the titles drawn upon for this work *ubaya* stands for 'agreement of the court' as the ninth of the ten *andhih-andhihan* or hierarchically arranged methods of establishing legal proof (*aksara bener*). It is overridden only by *parusa,* 'the written word of the sovereign', see Chapter 4. '*Aksara*'.

16 Showing the compatibility between written and oral sources of law, the *Undang Niti Cirebon* contains a unique reference in § 8 to '*adat* of old', reproduced in Hoadley & Hooker, *The Agama*, p. 264.

17 For this reason, they were also taxonomic. Claims were classified in advance as to whether they could or could not be handled by a recognized tribunal and, if so, to which legal category they belonged. Criteria for such a judgement came from the *aksara* (legal precepts) of the right (*aksara bener*) and wrong (*aksara salah*) (Chapter 4. *Aksara*). The negative aspects constituted by far the greatest part of the legal tradition. These were negative in that they defined a claim's

Generic *pepakem* and the *Pepakem Tjerbon* of 1768

By focusing on *pepakem* it is all-too-easy to substitute one unknown for another. *Pepakem* can embrace many things. These can range from a formal legal tract to a 'miscellany book',[18] including letters (*serat*/*surat*), and even the random notes found in several of the textual traditions. Formal definitions of *pepakem* are many, but relatively consistent. In addition to that of Pigeaud a recent version is found in Robson and Wibisono. They confirm the handbook's nature as a 'summary, concise version of a story used as a guide by a *dhalang* (narrator and puppeteer of traditional shadow-plays)'. Prawiroatmaja emphasizes its function as a 'basic guide or compass, the original story (*wayang*, law, etc)'. In short, a *pepakem* was an aid to memory. But this was only for those possessing an understanding of legal custom necessary for an acceptable interpretation, namely, those functioning as *jaksa*. Moreover, *pepakem* law books were inclusive, in that they provided multiple solutions for like issues, and random in that their contents varied from title to title or even within the same title.

Easily the best known is the *Pepakem Tjerbon* published as the '*Tjeribonsch Wetboek van het jaar* 1768'.[19] Although claimed to have been compiled from selected parts of several legal titles, the contents of the published work contrast with those of the manuscript titles, or at least those available for this study. Promulgated on the authority of the Dutch East India Company, and therefore valid from a set date and applicable to a specific geographical area, the compendium was intended as a guide for its officials to supervise local courts. Its contents were exclusive, specific, and consistent. Thus, it supplied much of what Crawfurd felt was lacking in Javanese law. Because the *pepakem* genre of the manuscripts is easily confused with the *Pepakem Tjerbon* compilation, their relationship needs to be clarified, if only summarily.[20]

As a Javanese-Dutch project involving the Cirebon princes, their *mantri*, and officials of the East India Company, the *pepakem* of *pepakem* was promulgated by the Dutch East India Company via 'a Resolution taken by

circumstances which either precluded it from due process (*tan dadi*) or led to defeat (*kalah*). Thereby weak or superfluous cases were kept from the court docket.

18 *Memorie van Overgave* 1717, Johan Fredrik Gobius, cited in Hoadley & Hooker, *The Agama*, pp. 241-242.

19 Hazeu, '*Tjeribonsch Wetboek*'.

20 Appendix I. 'The Problematic *Pepakem Tjerbon*' provides an analysis of the shortcomings preventing it from being automatically accepted as representing traditional Javanese law.

the Sultans and Resident at Cirebon Monday the 18th of April 1768'.[21] The *pepakem* project was brought to completion under the auspices of Meester Pieter Cornelius Hasselaer, the Cirebon Resident between 1757 and 1765, who was trained in the Roman-Dutch law then practiced in the United Provinces. The *Pepakem* drew upon of a half-dozen titles known from manuscript sources stemming from West and Central Java specifically named in the opening rubric.

> A *pepakem* or law book of Cirebon extracted and compiled from diverse *pepakem* by name the Raja Niscaya, the Undang-Undang Mataram [aka *Luwangan Undhang-Undhang*], Jaya Lengkara, Kontara Manawa, and Adilulah [aka *Surya Alam*].

In addition, the contents of the published text refer to the rules of a *Jugul Muda*.

The *Pepakem Tjerbon*'s strength lies in identifying Javanese titles valid in the Independent Kingdoms era. Seen in hindsight, its weakness comes from failure to recognize that Javanese legal titles, themselves *pepakem*, are rarely consistent and almost never congruent. For example, there are two fundamentally different versions of the *Surya Alam*, three if one counts the Raffles translation for which the original Javanese text is not available, and four if one includes the just-named *Adilulah* as the title's prototype. The *Jugul Muda* has a standard first half, but is followed by very different endings; a manuscript source of the *Undang-Undang Mataram* has yet to be identified, hence the stand-in of the *Luwangan Undhang-Undhang*; and the *Kontara/Kuntara Manawa* title seems to be more a catch-all term rather than a specific name.[22] In contrast, examination of the titles reveals that the actual contents built around the *sloka* phenomena are not only consistent but also almost identical between manuscripts.

If it could be shown that the *Pepakem Tjerbon* was an authentic, acceptable, and autonomous law book reflecting the era's legal practice, then traditional Javanese law could be equated with the contents of the published work in eighteenth-century Dutch. By lack of alternatives this approach comes close to that employed in studies of pre-modern Javanese law. Despite its reputation, the *pepakem* is an artificial creation motivated by aims foreign

21 Reproduced in Hazeu, '*Tjeribonsch Wetboek*'.

22 The *Jimbun Slokantara* I § 24 characterisies various exemplars in stating 'This is the meaning of the *Kontara Manawa*, many are the names [of *manawa*] as evil *manawa*, good deeds *manawa*, etc.

to the spirit of that law. The artificial nature comes from the fact that Dutch East India Company officials and servants, i.e., 'team Hasselaer', selected from the entire corpus of written law those provisions useful for governing the 'natives' through reference to local law. Anything falling outside these aims or those considered too complicated were simply ignored. Clearly the *sloka* phenomena fell into this category. They are conspicuously absent from the compilation despite the fact that they dominate the individual texts of which the *Pepakem* was composed. As argued in Appendix I. 'The Problematic *Pepakem Tjerbon*', specific shortcomings are seen most clearly in its late date, innovations which break with local tradition, and a lack of correspondence between cited paragraph sources and those found in the published work bearing the same name.

2 *Sloka* in Javanese Titles

In analysing Javanese manuscripts relating to law some hard realities must be faced. A gap between what is needed and what is available is the most obvious. The ideal would be access to an authoritative text with an authentic date and provenance placing it in the time and space under consideration. Such a paragon would include a recognizable beginning, middle, and end; possess a reasonable degree of internal consistency; and show congruence or at least close similarity with the contents of other texts bearing the same name. Within the parameters of the present discussion such would come to pass if the list of the titles contributing to the Javanese legal tradition as found in the *Pepakem Tjerbon* were texts in the accepted meaning of the term.

Warned by Crawfurd's observations, it comes as no surprise that matters are not as straightforward as one might wish. The concept of text as a defined entity seems to be alien to traditional Javanese law. As noted earlier, there are several variants for most of titles contributing to our understanding of the subject. Even exceptions are challenging. These are titles found in a single manuscript whose unclear contents cannot be deciphered through reference to other exemplars. Another challenge is raised by the titles said to constitute the *Pepakem Tjerbon*. Study of their contents shows that there seems to be scant congruence between the compilation's contents and titles cited as its sources (see Appendix I, Table 1, 'Literal authenticity'). Were it not for the titles' self-identification it would be hard to recognize the various exemplars with the same name as a single text.

It is generally accepted that sources of information consist of those titles identified by nominal catalogue entries for manuscript packages. The latter are presently housed in archives and libraries in The Netherlands and Germany, the United Kingdom, and Indonesia.[1] Such entries are nominal in that they draw upon criteria for identification deriving from internal information or contextual clues. Subsequently such identification has been transformed into definitive titles by curators, collectors, and scholars. Such can be embarrassingly short sighted. *The Archive of Yogyakarta* describes a text from The British Museum's Additional Manuscript collection (Add 12 303) as 'a heterogeneous collection of some twenty-eight separate

1 Respectively: Pigeaud, *Literature of Java* and *Javanese and Balinese manuscripts* and Ricklefs and Voorhoeve, *Indonesian manuscripts in Great Britain*. Indonesian collections can be divided into those at Bandung, Ekajati, *Naskah Sunda*; Yogyakarta, Behrend, *Katalog induk*, and Surakarta, Florida, *Javanese Literature in Surakarta manuscripts*.

paragraphs', which was assigned the name *Cacad* after the term found in the first sentence.[2] Further study, however, revealed it to be a large part of one of the better examples of the standard Yogyakarta *Surya Alam* considered below. Another example comes from LOr 1832's third section. Following the title's name, the catalogue identifies it as a '*Salokantara by sénapati Jimbun*'. However, on folio 44 the text turns into a copy of the first two-thirds of the Kartasura *Surya Alam* found in the Berlin 402 manuscript.

Inescapably information for this study derives from bundles of writing brought together in ways unknown and given a name. Seldom is there any indication of how the entities took their present form or whether this took place before or after they were acquired by the present owners. They have been catalogued from what can be gleaned of them as separable entities, with whatever information is available concerning date, provenance, calligraphy, paper, etc. Such crucial, if often thankless, tasks constitute the invaluable first steps for any serious research based on the contents of original manuscripts. This results in considerable uncertainty.

> When the catalogues do designate the provenance of a given manuscript, it is often a conjecture based on paleographical features that are themselves never described.[3]

Accepted usage calls such bundles manuscripts. They are designated by the abbreviation of the respective collections. For the present work the most relevant are the British Library Additional manuscripts (Add), including the Crawfurd collection, the India Office Library (IOL) and the Mackenzie collection of the former British Museum; Leiden University's Oriental Collection (LOr); the Royal Asiatic Society Raffles collection (RAS); and the Berlin Staatsbibliothek Oriental Manuscript (Berlin). These are followed by the catalogue number. Examples used here include the often-mentioned Add 12 303, containing the *Jaya Lengkara*, *Surya Alam*, and minor texts; RAS 6 and 33, containing the *Jugul Muda* and others; and Berlin 402 containing the Kartasura *Surya Alam*, along with other texts. LOr 7440, 7410, and 7442 contain, among others, all three traditions, namely the *Jugul Muda*, *Jaya Lengkara*, and *Surya Alam*, while LOr 6423 is synonymous with Yasadipura I's verse rendition of the *Surya Alam*. The special case of bundled or compiled texts resulting in the *Pepakem Tjerbon* of 1768 is discussed in some detail in Appendix I.

2 Carey and Hoadley, *The Archive of Yogyakarta*, vol. II, pp. 87-89.
3 Behrend, 'Small collections', p. 24.

Practical experience with unpublished sources of a legal nature reveals the variation of manuscripts' contents. In some title and manuscript coincide, as the just-mentioned Yasadipura *Surya Alam* (LOr 6423). As a rarity, its introductory paragraph also identifies author and provenance, thereby minimising the range of possible dates of composition, which is not provided. If it was the original manuscript, things would be considerably easier. As it stands, this best identified text is, according to the information provided by Soeripto, a copy transcribed into European letters of a manuscript from the Surakarta *kraton* (palace complex) archive.[4] It was most likely originally written in the ha-na-ca-ra-ka Javanese alphabet or possibly *pégon*. A second complication comes from the fact that the introductory paragraph designates as author Yasadipura I (1729-1803). This must mean that it took final form sometime before his death in 1803 and the emergence of a second Yasadipura.[5]

More commonly manuscripts contain several titles. In addition to the legal titles, Add 12 303 contains a medley of texts ranging from horse cures through land tenure documents, lists of arms and accoutrements, and a great deal more.[6] While LOr 7440 and 7410 used extensively in this study tend to be somewhat more specialised with regard to legal texts, they also include Islamic prayers, land and produce registers (mainly coffee), and others less easy to identify. The diversity of such sources can be seen in the list of the contents of these manuscripts appended to the study of the *Agama* law book.[7]

Manuscripts v. titles

The fact that several texts have been gathered into a single manuscript is convenient. It also complicates determining date and provenance of the individual titles. Many of the manuscripts from the Yogyakarta *kraton* contain titles copied by the same hand, presumably at roughly the same time.[8] Whatever process of copying, transcribing, and editing that took

4 Soeripto, *Ontwikkelingsgang*, p. 190, n 1.

5 Ricklefs, 'The Yasadipura problem', p. 281.

6 Carey and Hoadley, *The Archive of Yogyakarta*.

7 Hoadley and Hooker, *The Agama*, pp. 256-257.

8 More specifically this includes Add 12 303 containing the *Jaya Lengkara*, *Raja Niscaya*, and most of the *Surya Alam*. Others include RAS 6 with the *Raja Kapa-kapa*, *Jugul Muda*, and *Surya Alam* and Add 18 398, which Keyzer identifies as the manuscript underlying the *Pepakem Cirebon* of 1768, Ricklefs and Voorehoeve, *Indonesian Manuscripts in Great Britain*, p. 54. Add 18 398 also contains a variant *Jaya Lengkara*, a *Sunduk Prayoga*, several versions of a *Slokantara*, as well as a *Wadigun Wangkara*, and an *Arya Dilah*.

place before taking their present form has effaced information concerning the original date and provenance. By default, the only certain date is the *terminus ante quem* set by that of the entire manuscript package in which they are now found. Common sense argues that all the titles must be earlier than the umbrella manuscript, although how much is anyone's guess.

For this reason, the London collections housed in the British Library and Royal Asiatic Society are singled out as some of the more important collections of Javanese manuscripts. They all must date from earlier than June 1812 when most of them were taken from the Yogyakarta *kraton* to become respectively the Crawfurd collection of the British Museum, the Mackenzie collection of India Office Library, and the Raffles collection of the Royal Asiatic Society.[9] They contrast with most Javanese manuscripts, which tend to be collections of various writings in different hands datable only by that of the collection, usually in the late nineteenth or even the early twentieth century. For example, LOr 7440, 7410, and 7442 were acquired by the Leiden University Library, after the death of Snouck Hurgronje, the previous owner, in 1936; LOr 2215 (the manuscript of the Jonker translation of the *Kuntara Manawa* [*sic Agama*]) in 1876; and so on. This, of course, does not automatically mean that the contents of the texts or paragraphs are not older, sometimes much older. LOr 7410 contains the date written in the margin of A. J. 1736 or 1809 (f. 129) and LOr 7440 that of 1219/1804 (f. 72). However, internal criteria argue that the titles must have been in circulation from the beginning of the eighteenth century as they were apparently owned by a Sumedang *jaksa* active in the 1720s.

More problematic is whether the seemingly random dates appearing within a given manuscript apply to a specific title or its entirety. At one extreme stand the *angger-angger* texts of Add 12 303. They all contain dates expressed in the Javanese calendar, which can be re-calculated into Common Era dates. At the opposite extreme are the legal titles as the *Jugul Muda*, *Jaya Lengkara*, *Surya Alam* (aka *Adilulah*), and the minor texts, the *Cacad*, *Arya Dilah*, and *Wadigun Wangkara*, which are likely to have been in circulation before the beginning of the colonial era, even though they are not dated.[10] In point of fact, none of the titles used here can be assigned

9 Even this is not entirely certain. A telling example is provided by RAS 33, which contains a *Gajah Mada*, a *Raja Niti*, and a '*Saloka*, legal text'. A note on the front of this manuscript reads 'Sumenep, 4 Febr 1814'. This means that it cannot have been collected from the Yogyakarta *kraton* two years earlier.

10 That they preceded the Javo-Dutch *angger-angger* texts rests on the assumption that date, division of the text into definitive paragraphs, and numeration of those paragraphs stem from European practice, unknown for purely Javanese legal tracts.

specific dates. An exception is the '*Saloka* [of] Kyai Mrata, Rajya', with a date calculated from the Javanese chronogram (*sengkala/sangkala*) of A.D. 1726.[11]

A further challenge is provided by ambiguous cases. For example, the date and ownership of the entire Add 12 303 manuscript is unproblematic. As the personal property of Hamengkubuwana II (r. 1792-1810/1811-12/1826-28), it was put together sometime before 1812 and its acquisition by the British Expeditionary forces. Yet its component parts as individual titles are considerably older. Several of the *angger-angger* date from the mid-to-late eighteenth century, although the legal titles of concern here are undated. Another example comes from LOr 7440. In the colophon (folio 37) to one of the additional texts, namely a *Niti Sruti*, is found the statement 'the end of the writing of *kawula* (royal servant) Candra Yuda (*titi tulis kawula Candra Yuda*)'. On folio 72 following a *Niti Praja* is penned in another hand:

> [*K*]*itab* [book or religious tract] descended from the elder royal servant Candra Yuda, *jaksa* of the country of Sumedang.

This is followed in still another hand by a note that this *kitab*, which must apply to the entire manuscript, comes from the palace official Adipati Suriya Nagara from the royal servant Nyatanu [?] on Wednesday the 8th of the month Jumadigul [*Jumadilawal*] in the year 1219, over which is written '1804'. The Dutch East India Company records attest to the fact that Candra Yuda was a Sumedang *jaksa* active in the 1720s. But does this mean that the preceding text was written or owned by him? Adipati Suriya Nagara, apparently the last owner of the manuscript before it was acquired by Snouck Hurgronje, has not been identified. The crucial question is whether the attribution applies all the texts in LOr 7440 or some of them and, if so, which ones? What does one then make of the other, seemingly random dates of '1829, Sumedang', found on folio 74 directly following the attribution to Candra Yuda? A similar problem comes up with Berlin 402. The colophon of one text (f. 14) contends that the title/text was copied in AJ 1661/AD 1736-1737 and owned by Pangéran Aria Purbaya (aka Radèn Demang Urawan), who was exiled by the Dutch to Sri Lanka in 1738. Does this then mean that all the titles in Berlin 402 date from before 1738 or only some of them? Several bear dates

11 Ricklefs and Voorhoeve, *Indonesian Manuscripts*, p. 82. That title also lacks numbered paragraph divisions, a feature characteristic of all the titles utilized here. Exceptions are limited to the early nineteenth century published versions of the Raffles and Yasadipura *Surya Alam*. Generally, the paragraph numbers cited in this work in order to identify the precise source of information have been imposed by the present author for ease in reference.

in the 1720s. This seems reasonable. Many of them reflect a strong Islamic flavour that characterised Kartasura between 1726 and 1749.[12] Nevertheless, in both cases there remains an element of uncertainty. A moderate position is taken here, namely that we are indeed dealing with texts utilized, if not produced, during the period of Java's Independent Kingdoms.

What emerges from a close reading of the legal titles used in this work is an impression of traditional Javanese written law. 'Impression' seems appropriate because only a relatively small number of the extant legal texts have been examined. As a group those investigated show the island's legal tradition to have been diverse and ambiguous, which departs from the unity and consistency expected of law books. If the challenge lies in ascertaining their characteristic features, then its crux is how the sources have been packaged into their present form. Sources range from individual terms and phrases through paragraphs; to 'texts' i.e., the entities associated with a specific title; to manuscripts, usually, but not always containing several titles; to archival bundles. In the latter various paragraphs, texts, and titles, as well as miscellaneous notes and jottings, have been assembled together posthumously, as it were, by Javanese chancelleries or European archivists.

Titles of the *Sloka* phenomena

The contents of the available titles would appear to constitute nearly insurmountable barriers to better understanding of traditional Javanese written law. Manuscripts contain a mixture of titles, single title manuscripts are a rarity, and titles with the same name usually differ in contents. Yet, a unique feature of the *sloka* sources also shows a way of meeting the challenge. Information with which to analyse individual *sloka* phenomenon – *sloka, aksara, sinalokan,* and *prakara* – tends to be concentrated in separate textual traditions. This greatly simplifies utilizing the materials at our disposal. As we have seen, the first layer of the phenomena consists of *sloka* proper. They are introduced and clarified in the *Jugul Muda* whose core they constitute. The title accounts for by far the largest number of *sloka* identified as 'Classic *Sloka*' analysed in Appendix II. A second layer consists of *aksara*. In the legal literature of the Independent Kingdoms era the terms usual meaning (1 letter of an alphabet; 2 written character) has been overruled by three functional modes. These include a descriptive and functional mode topped by that of the *askarâji*

12 Ricklefs. *Seen and Unseen Worlds*.

(*aksara* + *aji*), the 'science of kings'.[13] This is in addition to *aksara* as providing instruments for resolving quarrels, civil disputes, and criminal process. From the examples cited from the *Rangga Lawé*, the 'science of kings' must refer to the sovereign's legitimate use of force. Constituting what can be understood as constituting its dedicated text, the *Jaya Lengkara* law book is specifically aimed at expounding the *aksara* within *drigama* ('experience, custom'). A third layer of the *sloka*-phenomenon consists of *sinalokan* ('that made from a *sloka*') introduced in the second half of the Leiden *Jugul Muda* manuscripts (LOr 7440, 7410, and 7442). Their subject matter consists of vignettes summing up exemplary cases closed by *sinalokan* in which the actors' names have been woven into the resolutions' *sinalokan*. *Sinalokan* are also found in 'didactic vignettes', as well as in actual cases handled by the joint Dutch-Javanese local courts of the early eighteenth century. Yet most productive of *sinalokan* is the dedicated title, the late Mataram *Luwangan Undhang-Undhang*. Its fifty or so paragraphs focus solely on *sinalokan*. They are often multiple, one for winners, another for losers, and even one for those who were in some manner responsible. To these titles must be added the *Jaya Lengkara*.

A fourth layer is composed of an even more general concept, that of *prakara/perkara* (matter, case). These are almost exclusively found in the *Surya Alam* tradition. The Combi *Surya Alam* (Add 12 303 plus RAS 33 discussed below) is its dedicated text. Sporadic references are found in other titles. King Surya Alam as spokesman for the tradition is said to have reduced the number of *prakara* to the standard number of 144 from the original of a thousand or more. A fifth and final layer is not, strictly speaking, composed of *sloka* phenomena. Rather it consists of a complementary collection of vignettes as common components of Javanese law. *Sloka*, along with its derivatives, are embedded in and often take their meaning from a vignette. Those considered here come from the three major titles of the *Jugul Muda*, *Jaya Lengkara*, and *Surya Alam*, supplemented by information contained in the minor texts.

Sloka

Yet, it is the abstract concepts contained in the *sloka* phenomena that are the focus of this work. Texts/titles in manuscripts provide the concrete wherewithal to reconstruct their nature and function. These are the *sloka* proper supplemented by its derivatives in the form of *aksara*, *sinalokan*, and *prakara*. Despite the conventional definition of *sloka*, the term is much broader. Simile,

13 Zoetmulder, *Old Javanese-English Dictionary*.

metaphor, and the like correctly describe the *sloka* function only when used as an *ex post facto* explanation 'held to embody a general truth'.[14] Within the context of Javanese legal texts of the period *sloka* and its derivatives not only existed prior to the action/behaviour in question but also sanction punitive response to them. They provided textual authority for punishment and/or for determining defeat in legal affairs. This applies to all *sloka* derivatives.

However, before showing how individual titles focus on specific phenomena, we must dispense with the notion that *sloka* of the Independent Kingdoms era were identical to or even dependent upon foreign historical models in anything but name. Unlike the remainder of the phenomena, the term '*sloka*' (alt. *saloka* or Sundanese *siloka*) has both a long and foreign history. The original meaning and function emphasize the uniqueness it has taken on as the key legal concept of the Independent Kingdoms era. *Sloka* is defined by Zoetmulder as '... (Skr) a stanza, esp. two lines of 16 syllables each'. Moreover, they are inseparable from *smrti,*

> the whole sacred tradition (*dharma*) as remembered by human teaching (in contradistinction to *sruti*), what is directly revealed and heard by *risis*.

Lingat contends that in testing Max Müller's hypothesis with respect to the *Manava-dharma-sutra* it has been established in classic Hindu law that:

> there existed from a very ancient period a floating mass of adages or precepts in verse form from which [were] formulated a rule of law or a moral duty. These precepts, *dharma-slokas* analogous to the maxims (*brocards*) of Europe but in a popular and spontaneous style, are found in the *sutras*.[15]

Legal texts are prose compositions mostly secular in nature. Partial exceptions are found in the younger versification of the *Surya Alam* by Yasadipura and parts of the Kartasura text. A clue as to when the term came to take on its characteristic meaning may be found in J. Gonda, *Sanskrit in Indonesia*.

> [The *sloka* stanza] has been preserved in Sundanese, where *siloka*, which is no doubt the identical word, denotes apophthegm, metaphorical sayings, especially when dealing with esoteric or religious lore.

14 *The Concise Oxford Dictionary*.

15 Zoetmulder, *Old Javanese-English Dictionary*, under '*saloka*' and Lingat, *The Classic Law of India*, p. 89.

Tellingly, Gonda adds that:

> it seems, however, to apply in a more particular way to texts composed in the pantun style, i.e., in that king of literary form which is neither prose nor poetry, but historically speaking both, consists of shorter or longer series of free rhythmic units.[16]

By the period under consideration *sloka* had lost *smrti* law associations and strict rules of meter.

Slokantara tradition

Logically one could expect to find clarification of *sloka* in a text bearing the title of '*salokantara/slokantara*' or the like.[17] However, the expectation is punctured by the contents of available textual traditions. The most obvious candidate should be the *Salokantara* edited and translated by S. Rani. Yet its form and contents are alien to the legal literature of the Independent Kingdoms period. According to its editor, the work consists of:

> 83 Sanskrit slokas followed by their Old-Javanese prose explanations [...] In general the *Salokantara* corresponds to the *niti* texts of Sanskrit

16 Gonda, *Sanskrit in Indonesia*, p. 188. See also Eringa, *Soendaas-Nederlands Woordenboek* under '*siloka*'.

17 The ambiguous relationships existing between *sloka* and *Slokantara/Salokantara* titles of the period is confirmed by a survey of relevant manuscript catalogues. British collections contain only two *Slokantara* manuscripts. More accurately these are a mix of different titles. Add 12 323 is cataloged as: 'A: ff. 1r-30v *kagungen-dalem Serat Surya Ngalam kalih Salokantara* (property of the palace, a *Surya Alam* [mixed] with a *Salokantara*)'. It is, in fact a *Surya Alam* variant. The other reference, Java 33, is listed as: '[...] C: pp. 176-251. *Saloka*, legal text with a possible date in the early eighteenth century', Ricklefs and Voorhoeve, *Indonesian Manuscripts in Great Britain*, p. 82. As noted earlier, this is not a *Slokantara*, but contains among others a core *Jugul Muda* text. Dutch collections are equally unhelpful. 'Judicial Literature [...] Compendiums of jurisprudence of Old Javanese Origin', Pigeaud, *The Literature of Java*, vol. I, p. 305, lists two relevant manuscripts, namely 'Slokantara, collection of originally 1044 cases by Senapati Jimbun', LOr 1832 and 6203, f 20a. The latter is Brandes' transcription of the former, *Ibid.* 310. The last thirty folios (223-253) of LOr 1832 contain what the cataloger terms a '*Slokantara*'. However, only the first third belongs to a *Slokantara* tradition, which turns out to be a variant version of the title. As noted above, the last two-thirds (ff. 22-67 written in the text) of LOr 1832 comprise the first fifty paragraphs of the Kartasura *Surya Alam*.

literature, though there are a few items which would strictly form a part of a smrti text.[18]

In other words, *sloka* in the published *Salokantara* text lack the characteristic Javanese 'expressions [...], which serve to give knowledge of whole suits/causes' identified by Keyzer a century earlier. More concrete objections come from the fact that the contents of the *Salokantara* are almost exclusively concerned with matters of Hindu ethics, rights and duties of caste, the order of cosmic decline, etc. As a product of Bali, it is of considerable interest.[19] Yet, excluding the name, it would seem to have little or no direct connection with the *sloka* phenomenon of the time and place under consideration.

As befitting the primary focus of this work, texts of the era that convey the meaning and function of *sloka* fall into three separate textual traditions with similar contents. They include the *Jimbun Slokantara* with supplementary titles, the *Jugul Muda* tradition with which we have already met, and the *Surya Alam* tradition. For clarity's sake, they can be sketched separately.

Jimbun Slokantara

In the absence of a textual cannon for the *sloka* genre, the present work draws upon a *Slokantara* contained in LOr 7440, ff. 100-117, seconded by a variation in LOr 1832, and a possibly more original version in Add 18 398. Noteworthy here is that the first two are consistent in their identification with Kyai Senapati Jimbun, which the British Library exemplar lacks. The opening rubric of LOr 7440 is quoted in connection with the *Wadigun Wangkara* text (p. 23n1). Referred to as the *Jimbun Slokantara I*, it consists of some thirty-two paragraphs, whose contents touch on *sloka*-related affairs consistent with those in other titles of the period.[20]

A second version of the title, *Jimbun Slokantara II* is contained in LOr 1832 (ff. 1-67 [alt ff. 220a-253a]) dated 1843, which appears to be a younger re-working of the text. While the first fifteen paragraphs match those of LOr 7440, §§ 14-21 differ, the last named being the first paragraph of the *Wadigun Wangkara* which with this work opened. Paragraphs 27-37 follow LOr 7440, while the last six (28-44) again depart from the pattern. Curiously

18 Rani, *Salokantara*, p. 5.

19 Hoadley & Hooker, *The Agama*, p. 19.

20 These include the *astha corah* (§§ 1, 16), the *sad-atatayi* (§§ 2, 28), *uger-uger* (§ 9), *saksi* (§§ 10-13, 17), and the *ikral/andhih-andhihan* (§§ 14, 15). Just before the '*Titi*' ending the text, § 32 mentions a request of the Susuhunan to Kyai Ngabehi Wirantaka. The latter is sporadically cited as a *jaksa* in the legal literature.

§ 41 is composed of four *sloka*, the first used in the Dutch East Indies in 1717 (Chapter 8).

> This is the law court [*pangadilan*] of His Majesty Senapati of Jimbun received by His Majesty Senapati of Mataram, which became the jewel of the palace (*sotyaning pura*), the nail of the universe, and the pillar of the land (f. 230). [As for] the *tirta* and *pratonggapati*, *tirta* is the [holy] water which gives clarity, cleansing all the people of the world; *pratonggapati* is the sun, which enlightens, lighting up the people of the whole world.

A third version of the *Jimbun Slokantara* is found in Add 18 398 (ff. 90-92). It differs from the former two as variations of one another. It is also exceptional in that it lacks any expressed connection with Senapati Jimbun. The introductory paragraph also brings it in direct connection with Javanese usage.

> This is the sound of the *Slokantara pepakem*, which regulates behaviour on the island of Java, [namely] the decisions of the 'eight affairs'

As expanded in § 1 and referred to by at least one other of its seven paragraphs, the 'eight affairs' are the *uger-uger* or *aksara* of the right/true whose presence furthers a suit (see Chapter 5. 'Aksara'). Paragraph 2 deals with steps in legal process, § 3 the actions of the court, and § 4 repeats that the 'eight affairs', i.e., the *uger-uger* considered in Chapter 3, which

> decide (*megat*) *padu* (1 *ng*, *paben kr*, to quarrel) cases which are applied on the island of Java, following the *pepakem* for all, which has been valid from of old.

Paragraphs 5-7 deal with the manner of losing a suit.

Combi *Slokantara, Raja Niscaya, Wadigun Wangkara*

What has been termed a combi (= combined) version of the title is found in LOr 7440 (ff. 131-140), LOr 7410 (ff. 18-15), and Add 18 398 (ff. 55r-57r). The first two versions consist of eight paragraphs, the last only four. Noteworthy the title contains a relatively great number of Classic Sloka. Paragraphs 2-4 include a *sloka dursila* (*sloka* of criminality) *kusuma* [...] *tawasa*, Classic *Sloka*, no. 17, a *sloka Raja-gama*: *andriyoga* [...] *sadarana*, no. 12, and a *sloka* of the court *srengéngé pine*, no. 19. Coming from the *Jaya Lengkara*, they reflect later developments on those cited in the *Jugul Muda* considered below. The title also reflects the overlapping nature of the texts under consideration. As indicated in the titles, it shares several paragraphs with the *Raja Niscaya*. The final paragraph reads:

> These are the good intentions (*trapsila*) of *jaksa* in handling quarrels (*padu*) and civil (*pradata*) cases. Do not pronounce out of spitefulness! Do not pronounce out of favouritism but stick to the just (*adil*)! *Agama* [here Islam] in its speech takes priority over *drigama* (experience, custom) as it comes from The Prophet. [Some titles give the reverse priorities] The *jaksa* who apply the teaching of this writing/*sloka* will be admitted into the highest Heaven; if not [they will be] cast into Hell to become a worm or snake.

The admonition to avoid spitefulness against enemies and favouritism for toadies, to which could be added the key criteria of not altering one's decision (*tan gingsir*), are often repeated in the introductory paragraphs of the *Surya Alam* tradition. However, the last sentence seems closer Hindu nature of the Java-Bali *Salokantara* contained in Art. 33.

Jugul Muda tradition

Javanese tradition traces the origin of *sloka* back to the semi-mythical era of Medhang Kamulan. Creation of the first ever *sloka* is attributed to Aji Saka. However, the essence of *sloka* is most clearly captured in the *Jugul Muda* law book, which is seen as the eldest layer of the Independent Kingdoms legal traditions.[21] The title takes its name from the *patih* (prime minister, king's chief minister) Jugul Muda from 'the land of origin' (*bumi tulén*) called 'The Old Story' (*purwaning carita*), Medhang Kamulan ruled by King

21 The earliest version of law associated with Patih Jugul Muda of Java comes from a creditable seventeenth century tradition, the *Kitab Musarar*, compiled by Sunan Giri Perapen, the third Sunan of Giri (Ngampel-denta near Surabaya) in c. 1618. From it was subsequently distilled the prophecies of Jayabaya (*ramalan Jayabaya*), attributed to the twelfth-century king of Kediri (see Chapter 9). This was the work of Pangéran Wijil I of Kadilangu (near Demak) in 1741-1743, who was the immediate predecessor of Yasadipura I as Surakarta court *pujangga* until his death in 1747. From the *Kitab Musarar* (alternative *Kitab Asrar*) was derived the *Serat Jangka Sech Subakir*. In Canto I, verse 1 of the latter it is related that King Mahapunggung and his *patih* Jugul Muda 'wished to order the realm by creating the king's justice (*adil ing Narapati*).' The information is contained in LOr 6606.

Mahapunggung, successor of King Anyakrawati, and a descendant of Aji Saka who had seized it from the man-eating ogre Dewa Cengker.

The present study draws upon two versions of the *Jugul Muda* tradition. The first comes from LOr 7440 and 7410, supplemented by a fragment from RAS 33 and a book published at Surakarta in 1929, the *Serat angger: Jugul Muda,* written in the ha-na-ca-ra-ka script. They open with a short introductory vignette stressing the need for (written) law followed by a much longer one citing and clarifying the first dozen Classic *Sloka*. A final section shows how *sloka* are applied to 'crimes', as for example theft (*corah*), violence (*tatayi*), assault (*walat*), etc. via the process termed *sinalokan*. A second version of the *Jugul Muda* title comes from RAS 6 (ff. 22-71), which is bound together with a *Surya Alam* (ff. 72-119) and a *Raja Kapa-Kapa* (ff. 1-21). It repeats the first two vignettes of the Leiden manuscripts. The final section turns into a collection of disjointed paragraphs with references to Islamic themes.

> These are the steps of His Majesty in extending his hands over [to sooth] the troubles/disturbances of his subjects. In sheltering from famine His Majesty recites the Quran (*tilawat*). In sheltering by prayers (*salat*) His Majesty does not sleep at nights [with appropriate references to Allah] (f. 52).

The remaining folios are a mixture of animal parables called here '*sloka*', some *sinalokan*, and references to several unknown titles. This section is repeated almost verbatim in a fragment within a title calling itself '*Saloka*' found in RAS 33.[22] After providing the date and author, 1726 written by Kyai Mrata Rajya, the text opens with paragraphs parallel to those of the *Surya Alam* (ff. 177-208) before turning to a copy of the *Jugul Muda* (ff. 208-234). It repeats the first two vignettes of both the Leiden and RAS versions, turning in the final section to one very close to the RAS 6 'Islamic' paragraphs. The final source of the *Jugul Muda* is a published book in verse and ha-na-ca-ra-ka script claiming to be a reproduction of an unnamed Surakarta manuscript.

With the general structure of the *Jugul Muda* as background, we can turn to a consideration of its content vis a vis *sloka*. After a short introductory paragraph providing the title's pedigree, the core of the *Jugul Muda* revolves about the two interrelated vignettes named earlier. The first is limited to a few paragraphs. It relates the course of a dispute between a person named Dora ((to tell) a lie), i.e., duplicity and another named Sangkara (from *sengara* = curse; solemn oath) over pawned land on which a quantity of gold was

22 Folios 176-251, where it is preceded by a *Gajah Mada,* ff. 1-84, and a *Raja Niti,* ff. 86-175.

found. According to the Javanese tradition gold that is dug up (*dhudhuken*) constitutes a cache of hidden loot, by implication stolen, which automatically belongs to the sovereign. The quarrel between Dora and Sangkara over whether the owner or the leaseholder had the strongest claim, ultimately resulted in the death of both. Ominously, the incident precipitated the coming of the *dvapara* epoch (RAS 6 '*dupara*', LOr 7440 '*dopara*', and LOr 7410 '*dwapara*') equivalent to the final age in the cycle of Hindu cosmic decline. It brings the beginning of all human suffering. The Leiden titles relate that the onslaught of the *dopara/dwapara* age of lies and deceit was marked by inauspicious natural phenomena as rainfall out of season, blood rains, earthquakes, flashes of lightning, and ominous rainbows.

Continuity with the second, more important vignette of the *Jugul Muda* is provided by the cache of gold. As the cause of the quarrel between Dora and Sangkara, it was seized by the king and made into a golden image (*anak-anakan emas*). In the vignette's continuation the golden image was stolen by a gang of eight miscreants (*duratmaka*) under the leadership of a man called Dustha, an anthropomorphic representation of the concept of the *astha dustha* ('Eight Thieves').[23] The golden image, referred to as '*embanan*' or that carried in a shawl as a baby, implicitly stands for the load of sins as the wages of greed. It had already caused the death of Dora and Sangkara at each other's hands, thereby precipitating the era of deceit. It continued to plague their descendants.[24]

According to the LOr 7440 version, the nefarious activities of the eight miscreants were brought to the king's attention by the wives of their leader, Dustha. Dissatisfaction over distribution of the spoils between older and younger wives motivated them to 'blow the whistle' for which they were rewarded. Dustha and his eight accomplices were arrested and bound. At this juncture, the king turned to Patih Jugul Muda for counsel as to whether he could or should execute the nine for stealing royal property. The *patih* defers his answer until the other ministers have been heard. Consequently, the *Tumenggung*, *Demang*, *Jaksa*, *Rongga*, and *Pandelgan* (royal astrologer) each quote a *sloka drigama* ('a *sloka* of experience/custom') followed by an explanation. Still following LOr 7440, this was elicited by the king himself. Patih Jugul Muda caps the other minister's *sloka* by quoting two *sloka drigama* and two *sloka ratu* (royal *sloka*). The latter describes the

23 These, along with the *sad-atatayi* and *astha corah* are explained in Appendix IV.

24 In the apparently younger *Gajah Mada* law book found in RAS 33, ff. 1-84, the golden image very likely was the source of conflict between Patih Gajah Mada, who owned it, and the king of Majapahit, who coveted it. This resulted in the *patih*'s banishment to a hollow tree (alternatively a cave) where he was tutored in Javanese law by his grandfather, Begawan Sukerti. The motif provides the title's frame story.

king's position in relation to criminal process. The counsellors' advice was unanimous; all demanded that the king impose the death penalty on his own authority. At the same time, Patih Jugul Muda's *sloka ratu* emphasized the dire consequences for a king if his judgment was not just. This presented a dilemma for King Mahapunggung. Despite the demand of the pre-existing *sloka* quoted by his ministers, he declined to sentence the culprits out of fear of divine retribution should his judgment lack righteousness. Consequently, responsibility was delegated to Patih Jugul Muda, who handed out monetary fines (*raja-dhendha*). In addition, the *duratmaka* were declared slaves (*ulun*) of the king. As chief instigator, Dustha was ordered to become head of the *duratmaka* with special duties to guard the king's palace. The vignette closes with the king withdrawing to the palace and the ministers returning to their respective residences. The core text ends with 'Such is the story of *dustha*'.

The *Surya Alam* challenge

Correspondence between *sloka* phenomena and a specific title, or titles, does not always exist in a one-to-one relationship. As mentioned above, *sloka* phenomena cluster around certain titles, but are not restricted to them. The most striking example of this is the ambiguous relation prevailing between *sloka* and the *Surya Alam* tradition. The latter has two regional variants. The Kartasura/Berlin *Surya Alam* contains numerous citations of *sloka*, one in nearly every other paragraph. This provides a welcomed supplement to the *Jugul Muda*'s dozen or so Classic *Sloka*. In contrast, the Yogyakarta/Combi version counts only a half dozen *sloka*, being dominated by *prakara*. Thus, the *Surya Alam* tradition is split by concentration on *sloka* respectively *prakara*. Greatly simplified, the Kartasura version belongs to present discussion of *sloka;* the Yogyakarta/Combi version to the one on *prakara* presented in Chapter 6.

The general tone of the Kartasura *Surya Alam*'s can be obtained from a translation of the opening paragraphs characteristic of all versions.

> In the name of God, the Beneficent, the Merciful.
> These are the exhortations of King Surya Alam speaking before all his *bala* (here = subjects). 'All of you shall be obedient and believing, accepting the fortunes and misfortunes granted by Allah the sublime (*Allah ta'ala*). Do not be immoral (*zina*). Do not plague (*siya-siya*) [other creatures]. Commit yourselves to the religion of Islam, accepting fortunes and misfortunes brought by Allah the sublime [in order to avoid] the hellfire that is predestined. Do not commit heresy (*shirk*) but hold fast

to the exhortations of Allah the sublime. Do not become irritated, do not become apprehensive, but continually pay respect [to Allah]. If one does not follow the exhortations of Allah, your body will waste away. [One must] repent to Allah for one's cursedness (*siku*) before Allah and furthermore repent for [sins = *asaylatim*?] and show piety before Allah as a form of freeing oneself from one's transgressions (*dosa*)' [the paragraph ends with demands on purity of food and drink].

The following paragraphs contain specific legal instructions. This orientation continues throughout the remainder of the seventy-four paragraphs comprising the title.

1. And thus instructed Sultan Ngarip [Surya Alam] the two *jaksa:* 'When a dispute rises it must be thoroughly investigated. If one party will not submit to the court (*karta*) the case is lost and all his possessions forfeited to the crown. And should the winner out of his own free wish to honour judge, minister, or even the king with a monetary gift, such can be accepted, upon which the looser is given forgiveness.
2. Where there is formal litigation and one party does not appear [within the stipulated three sittings], the case is lost and a fine of *triguna* levied.
3. If one has been robbed by night (*bégal*) or stolen from (*maling*) by day and neglects to suit formally (*pisaid*) before the *jaksa*, the case is dismissed. If one subsequently presses [the original claim], then the *jaksa* decides against the plaintiff and the case cannot be brought up again'.

In keeping with the character of Javanese law, the title portrays King Surya Alam as the transmitter of pre-existing legal traditions. Kings could give orders on behalf of religion or morals but could not make law in the sense of binding legal or moral precepts valid for all time. The rules they make and agreements they enter into (*ubaya, angger-angger, prajanji*) are valid only to the extent and for as long as the specific ruler commands the necessary force to back his claim of authority. Traditional law exists; even kings must obey. The contribution of this version of the *Surya Alam* to an understanding of traditional Javanese law lies in confirming the shared nature of terminology and meaning of the *sloka* phenomena. The text's contribution, however, is uneven. Its strongest suit lies in citations of Classic *Sloka*. Of the various examples of the *Surya Alam* genre, the Kartasura version accounts for six identifiable *sloka* out of the two-dozen singled out in this work as typical of the era's legal texts (Appendix II. 'Classic *Sloka*'). Although the number seems modest in an absolute sense, it is relatively high in that it surpasses all the Yogyakarta examples and is seconded only by the Yasadipura verse version of the early nineteenth century. This includes the consistent use of the term *sloka* for all short phrases by Berlin 402, even those accepted by most sources as *sinalokan* or *prakara*. As we shall see, the *prakara* constitute the subject matter *per se* of the *Surya Alam* genre.

The Kartasura *Surya Alam* and the van der Hout translation

To make matters more complicated the most accessible version of the Kartasura *Surya Alam* has been published in Dutch by the *Bijdragen tot Taal- Land- en Volkenkunde.*[25] At first glance the text seems to verify Crawfurd's unfavourable opinion of Javanese law books. Yet with facet in hand – knowledge of the early eighteenth-century *Surya Alam* from Berlin 402 – the van der Hout *Surya Alam* (after the translator) contributes to a better understanding of the source of information. A note at the article's beginning by the editor, S. Keyser, is marginally helpful.

> This piece was forwarded to me from Batavia by a *Meester* (of law) van der Hout, who earlier had completed his studies at the Delft Academy in an excellent manner and subsequently has acted in a variety of capacities in the service of the Indies. Notable are the differences between the text and the first line, through which various works are identified. The piece seems to me a mixing of both, as well as being of importance for those who would make the acquaintance with this section of Javanese literature.

The date and provenance of the title are added in a note on p. 57.

> Copied on Saturday Kliwon the 18th of the light of the fasting month, Puwasa, in the year Be 1728, corresponding to 20 March 1801. Translated at Surakarta the 27th of April 1816 by ...

Re-creation of an authentic reading of the Kartasura *Surya Alam* from the van der Hout's translation would be a substantial undertaking. Its contents must be separated from those of several other titles, among others an *Ambiya* or 'Stories of the Prophets', which is mixed with the core text in addition to shorter or longer examples of 'colloquial *shari'a*', that is, rules, regulations, and rites from the *Sunna* expressed in translated Javanese scattered

25 Van der Hout *Surya Alam*.

throughout the title. Key to such a reconstruction comes from the Berlin *Surya Alam*.

But if an authentic version of the title in Javanese exists, why go to the trouble of reconstructing it from a seemingly younger Dutch translation? There are several reasons. First, Berlin 402 is written in *pégon* (Arabic script without vowel marks) in what can be described as a 'cramped' hand. Thus, to the challenge of translating the title's contents comes a prior one of deciphering what it says. While the manuscript's readings are clear enough to enable matching its contents with the corresponding parts of the Dutch translation, they are insufficient to provide the basis of an acceptable translation. By drawing upon the van der Hout publication one gains a 'second opinion', one of a copyist(s) writing a century closer to the text owned by Pangéran Urawan/Purbaya of Kartasura.[26] Second, in the Dutch translation the contents are available to those who could come with insights or viewpoints potentially contributing to a better understanding of the text. Third, the core text's contents in comparison with the apparent additions of 'colloquial *shari'a*' provide a concrete example of how some features of Islam were grafted onto traditional law. The following discussion of the Kartasura *Surya Alam* is based on the present author's reading of the Berlin title tempered by the contents of the van der Hout translation, as well as that of LOr 1832,[27] a younger a copy of the first two-thirds of that title.

With this background to the core Kartasura *Surya Alam* – folios 414-376 (*pégon* texts are written back to front) of the Berlin manuscript – we can turn to the contents of the van der Hout publication. Its contents fall roughly

26 As with most of the works considered here, the text is included as one of a dozen titles, this one in a manuscript held by the Berlin Staatsbibliothek MS Or. fol. 402 [hereafter Berlin 402]. The individual texts include notes on Islamic law dated 1737, as well as such titles as a *Paniti Sastra, Caraka Basa, Dasa Nama, Jaya Lengkara Wulang, Sewaka, Serat Angling, Johor Sah*, etc. Several are dated between 1736 and 1737. Yet it is the tenth title which is of interest here, namely the 'Kartasura *Surya Alam*'. Moreover, on folio 14 it is claimed that the title was at one time owned by Pangeran Purbaya/Urawan. Logically it must have been existence before 1738 when the *pangéran* was exiled by the Dutch to Sri Lanka. This reasonable assumption follows the lead of Ricklefs in *The Seen and Unseen Worlds in Java 1726-1747*, which draws upon several of the manuscript's titles to clarify the socio-religious environment surrounding Pakubuwono II at Kartasura before its destruction in the Java War (1740-1742).

27 Folios 44-54 of LOr 1832, dated 1843 contain a text calling itself the '[Senapati] Jimbun Salokantara'. In fact, it reproduces the first fifty or so paragraphs of the Kartasura *Surya Alam*. Although LOr 1832 dates from three decades after van der Hout's work, the fact that it is written in legible ha-na-ca-ra-ka script confirms the title's significance to Javanese literati. More practically, it can be used to confirm the reading of the first fifty of the seventy-four paragraphs comprising the Kartasura *Surya Alam*.

into three parts. The first part is identified by the opening lines, namely 'Translation of the Javanese *Kitap Ambio* [*sic Kitab Ambiya,* i.e., stories of the prophets] beginning as follows'. The text then goes on to describe the creation of the world, the heavenly tree *Saya-ratil-moentaka*, the four original angels, the beginning of the Faith with *La-illa-ha-ille-lat* (There is no God but God), termed *isti-geno*, the five daily prayers, etc., in most of the first seven pages. The *Ambiya* contains the introduction to King Surya Alam, who is:

> renown in war, who continually without discomfort or fatigue waged war, which is why he also became immovably the 'Nail of the Realm' (*pakubuwana*[?]), having in his entire realm only three counsellors who maintain justice, the headman, the chief minister, and a judge [with the king they comprise the *catur manggala* (four commanders)] (p.5).

In a change of pace, the next folio and a half revert to the subject of fasts in the 'temple'. These are described in terms of *tapa* (asceticism) ending with The Prophet's exhortation that the king and his three counsellors ensure welfare throughout the realm so that the inhabitants become pious and righteous and hence can enter Heaven.

The second part of the text constitutes a translation of Kartasura *Surya Alam*. It starts in the middle of page seven – corresponding to folio 408 of Berlin 402 and folio 44 of LOr1832 – with the standard opening phrase shared by most versions of the *Surya Alam*. 'This [writing] is King Surya Alam speaking before his army/subjects'. Immediately following the quotation come some thirty folios, which by drawing upon the usual markers of subject breaks – *maka, lamon*, and *punika* – can be divided into seventy-four paragraphs. Comparison of the first fifty or so paragraphs transcribed from the *pégon* with the Javanese text of LOr1832 in ha-na-ca-ra-ka script confirms the paragraph divisions.[28] The Javanese text of Berlin 402 ends on folio 377 with '*tammat*' (The End).

The third part of the van der Hout text begins directly after Berlin 402's '*tammat*'. This is followed by what appears to be a colophon dedicating the title to the memory of The Prophet. The colophon asserts that it has drawn upon both precepts of *agama* ('religion, more specifically Islam') and *drigama* ('experience', or a form of written *adat*). No date is given.

28 Further comparison of the two reveals commonalities to the extent of being able to conclude that the relevant part of LOr 1832, ff. 44-54, is an incomplete copy of the Kartasura *Surya Alam*. This leaves the question unanswered of why the first fifty paragraphs were copied into a title identifying itself as 'Senapati Jimbun *Slokantara*'. This seems to be a later interpretation implying that the historical Senapati Jimbun (aka Radèn Patah, the first ruler of Demak), can be identified with the semi-mythological King Surya Alam.

These thirteen pages (pp. 57-44) appear to be a translation of another law book or possibly several. Many of the legal and religious terms and phrases given in transcription followed by a Dutch explanation are recognisable as authentic terms from the era as witnessed in the contents of Berlin 402 and the texts drawn upon by this work, although identification of the specific title(s) from which they originate remains unknown.

Aksara

As the second layer of the phenomena, '*aksara*' is used by the texts under scrutiny in a manner at variance with accepted wisdom. Standard reference to *aksara* indicates the twenty letters of the Javanese script, dubbed ha-na-ca-ra-ka after the first five letters, ultimately deriving from India's Devanagari alphabet. More accurately, the unadorned twenty characters of the Javanese alphabet, the actual letter plus 'a', are termed *den-taywajana*.[29] These are subsequently 'clothed' (*pasangan*) with diacritical marks to indicate the remainder of the vowels – i, é, o, u – the 'r', and the punctuation marks employed. In the texts of the Independent Kingdoms era, *aksara* are normally the name for a set of legal precepts associated with sovereign rights and duties, as well as for setting priorities of proof in settling legal conflicts.

The dedicated text for *aksara* is the *Jaya Lengkara*. In contrast to the modest number of *Jugul Muda* and Kartasura *Surya Alam* exemplars, there are numerous examples of the *Jaya Lengkara*. Moreover, their contents are relatively consistent, being built around a standard frame story with near identical beginnings in all versions and endings in most. For present purposes the most accessible version of the *Jaya Lengkara* is that of Add 12 303 from the Crawfurd collection. *Jaya Lengkara* texts are also found in RAS 38, as well as those of the often-named Leiden manuscripts LOr 7440 and 7410. Notwithstanding the standard contents of manuscripts from both West and Central Java, a significant variant is found in LOr 7440's middle section. As an addition to the standard frame story, it consists of paragraphs nearly identical to §§ 1-14 of the *Jimbun Slokantara I* discussed earlier. Another variant is found in LOr 2125. It follows the standard introduction of the *aksara* and *drigama*, but then turns to legal paragraphs following the 'utterances' or *tatrapan* (*sic trap-trapan* = arrangement, application)

29 Winter *Javaansche Zamenspraken*, vol. I, pp. 1-2.

of Senapati Jimbun.[30] The first few lines of all exemplars leave no doubt as to the title's intension.

> *Om awignam astu nama sidhem* (Skr. 'May there be no hindrances')
> This is to know/disseminate via literature (*ngawikan*) and explain (*mirsaken*) the *aksara* [legal precepts] termed the glue of the universe, the nail of the world, the jewels of the *aksara* [written word].

The frame story turns about a great durbar of kings and ministers from the lands 'above and below the winds'. This was held at Aji Saka's kingdom of Medhang Kamulan, traditionally identified with Java's northern *pasisir.* The durbar was convened by King Jaya Lengkara. In time-honoured Javanese fashion the assembly discussed and collectively approved (*musawarat–mupakat*) the principles of Javanese law.

> All were there, the kings and ministers of ancient times at the Great Audience Hall of Medhang Kamulan. That considered by the ministers, one and all, were the prohibitions (*waler*) of *drigama* ('legal precepts based on experience received from Sang Niti Jagat') and the prohibitions of the *aksara* (*aksarâji?*), which become the basis for the courts (*kerta*).

Thus, are introduced the *aksara* in the meaning of legal precepts consistently employed as such in the Independent Kingdoms' legal texts. The dedicated nature of the *Jaya Lengkara* comes from its focus on the specific meanings of the *aksara*. In the paragraphs following the introduction, the chief ministers of the assembled kings take turns expounding for the assembled dignitaries the meaning of the ten-to-twelve *aksara.* Appropriately, the *Jaya Lengkara* closes with a dialogue between Kerta Bangsa from the lands above the winds and the *patih* of Medhang Kamulan, Madana Sraya. The exchange re-confirms the purpose of the tradition.

> 'Èh, Patih Madana Sraya what is the origin of His Majesty of Medhang Kamulan renown in the world of human beings; what is being taught'?

30 Kyai Senapati Jimbun of the legal texts would not seem to be identical with the historical Senapati Jimbun/Radèn Patah of the late fifteenth century, who became the first ruler of Demak after overthrowing Majapahit ruler. More likely he is a retrospective projection by a younger generation of scribes apportioning sections of the Independent Kingdoms' legal tradition to a recognized Islamic cultural hero.

> Patih Madana Sraya's answer, 'The teachings of the *Adigama* [*drigama*] and the contents of the world is what is being taught [...] thus, we have investigated the utterances of the *aksara* in the light of the midday and fixed their intention'.

Just before that dialogue, Patih Madana Sraya praises the noble character of worthy sovereigns as conveyed in a *sloka* of rulers (*slokaning ratu*) *adriyoga* [...] *bramacara*. The *sloka,* Classic *Sloka,* no. 12, echoes Patih Jugul Muda's final advice to King Mahapunggung as related in the LOr 7440 *Jugul Muda.* In any event, the frequent citations in most of the other texts considered here establishes the place of the *aksara* in this meaning within the Javanese legal tradition.[31]

Sinalokan

The third layer of the phenomena consists of *sinalokan*. Grammatically *sinalokan* are direct derivatives of *sloka*. They are formed by the addition of the passive suffix '*-in-*'plus the causative '*-aken/akan*'. The resultant meaning is something like 'to be formed of/from *sloka*'. Although sometimes mistakenly mixed by copyists, the two are conceptually separate. *Sloka* predate the affairs to which they are applied; *sinalokan* are cited or occasionally coined at their conclusion, often incorporating parts of existing *sloka*. As noted above, the last section in the Leiden manuscript versions of the *Jugul Muda* turns into short vignettes summed up in *sinalokan*. Along with the published Surakarta book they present nearly fifty short vignettes. The first half dozen deal with major criminal acts in the form of miscreants named Ki Corah (theft), Ki Tatayi (evil doer), Ki Walat (violence), Ki Sangraha

31 Even in this short consideration of the titles dealing with primarily *aksara*, as well as that of the other *sloka* phenomena to come, raises the question of how the *aksara* could have been missed when working with the titles cited by the *Pepakem Tjerbon*. With the exception of Zoetmulder's comment on the '*aksarâji*' the alternative has been ignored. This is as true for 'team Hasselaer' as for subsequent scholarship. The voluminous manuscript traditions containing titles as *Jaya Lengkara*, *Arya Dilah*, *Raja Niscaya*, and the like simply have not attracted scholarly attention. This may be due to the assumption that the *Pepakem Tjerbon* contains the true essence of Javanese law. In fact, it constitutes a highly selective version of that law. Yet, once the reality is accepted, it opens up possibilities of re-interpreting a number of titles, among others the introductory paragraphs of the *Surya Alam*, where *aksara* as 'letters, characters' simply does not make sense. The manuscript originals of virtually all the titles so named contain one or more paragraphs directly relevant to *aksara* as legal precepts.

(sexual assault), etc.[32] Whereas those of the *Jugul Muda* describe crimes and misdemeanours, the *Jaya Lengkara* vignettes, a secondary source of the phenomena, relate the consequences of actionable behaviour, followed by cryptic *sinalokan*. *Sinalokan* are also contained in related texts as the *Adilulah*, *Arya Dilah*, and the *Cacad* fragment. The fact that these are totally different from those of the *Jaya Lengkara* suggests that *sinalokan* by nature are either one-off affairs or *ad hoc* compositions made up of fragments of existing *sloka*.

Luwangan

The dedicated title for *sinalokan* is the *Undhang-Undhang Luwangan*. Despite the Central Javanese attribution, it is contained in two West Javanese manuscripts, namely LOr 7440 (ff. 264 -315) and LOr 7410 (ff. 47r -57r). The former is the most complete. It also has the best credentials in terms of date and provenance. The text's preamble and first paragraph can be translated as follows.

> This is letter of legal precedents observed in the land of Mataram which has been collectively agreed upon by the honourable *jaksa*, Kyai Ja[ya?] Manggala and Kyai Subamuhita, as well as by the *jejeneng* (assistants) Kyai Tumenggung Sasmita Sastra and Kyai Tumenggung Mangunrana, along with the honourable scribe, in harmony with the greater and lesser officials (*mantri*) in the land of Mataram, who have agreed upon it with the lesser officials of the North Coast, the outlying provinces, as well as the officials from the West [the Cirebon-Priangan region].

Its counterpart in LOr 7410 is almost identical. Three shorter *luwangan* texts – LOr 7440 (ff. 164-174), LOr 7410 (ff. 10_r-14_r), and LOr 7442 (ff. 56-69) – contain a much longer list of officials and a much shorter substantive text. In the latter two names and titles are those re-cycled from highly placed Mataram officials from the seventeenth and eighteenth centuries.

The paragraphs open with *yèn ana wong* 'If a person [does so and so]' and then describe concrete circumstances. These include dealing with fees and court costs (§ 1), accusations of adultery (§ 2), murder and highway robbery

32 These are followed by an indefinite number of seemingly spurious topics, apparently without relation to the contents of the vignette. There are vignettes concerning a Pun Lebu (dust), Pun Kebo (water buffalo), and Pun Tikus (mouse), as well as some that suggest violence as *pangpang-pungpung*.

(§§ 3, 4), theft (§ 5), stabbing (§ 6), nobles (§ 8); the 'Six Tyrants'(§§ 7-12), crimes against women (§§ 14, 15, 26-30), *sidhem pramanem* (§ 6), fighting (§§ 17, 24), seizing lands (§ 20), false procedure (§§ 21-23, 25), and debt and repayment (§§ 31-35, 38). In addition, LOr 7440 contains some six paragraphs on procedural starting with *lokika-tidarsa* (§ 39), steps of the judge (§§ 40-41), *andhih-andhihan* (*aksara* of the right) (§ 42), *cacad padu* (§ 43), and *uger-uger* (*aksara* of the wrong) (§ 44). In LOr 7410 the subjects are further indicated by key words written in the left-hand margin of the manuscript, much as the case in the *Agama* manuscript, Add 12 277.[33]

Each paragraph first sets the condition. This is followed by further specification before naming the consequences in the form of a fine, compensation, or, rarely, corporal punishment. At the paragraph's close there is found a *sinalokan* in archaic Javanese. Paragraph 20 on default of land can serve as a typical example.

> A civil legal decision from of old. In a suit concerning appropriation of land the fee for the plea is 1.5 *laksa*. If the land has been cultivated for four years and the owner has not suited before the *patih*, not to speak of assertions, it is authorized for that land to be taken over by the new-comer. If there have been assertions [by the original owner], then it remains with he who owned it earlier. If it has continued for as long as a *windu* (a period of eight Javanese years) and he who owns it suits before the *patih* he must pay 1.5 *laksa* to be confirmed in his ownership in perpetuity. If he does not apply to the *patih* it becomes the property of the newcomer. This is termed *kadalu-warsa*.

The paragraph is followed by two *sinalokan*, one for the looser and one for the winner. Both have defied translation.

Each paragraph in the *Luwangan* focuses upon a specific, albeit negative, condition and supplies the appropriate response. The *Luwangan* assigns neither punishments nor remedies. It only identifies what would be fitting under the specified circumstances. The passive, or self-fulfilling and self-enforcing, character of Javanese law is underscored by the text itself.

> This is the measure of the *jaksa* in handling of *padu* and *pradata* affairs: it is not the *jaksa* who cause persons with such suits to be defeated; defeat comes from the utterances of those suiting (§ 50).

33 Hoadley and Hooker, *The Agama*, pp, 51 ff.

Thus, determination of one's guilt can be said to be *tekèk mati ing ulahé* or 'a gecko dies because of its own voice' or 'to suffer or fail because of one's own words',[34] a common *sloka* in the literature under discussion.

Didactic *sinalokan*

A final textual source of *sinalokan* comes from 'didactic *sinalokan*'. They provide a bridge between the written tradition and legal practice in that *sinalokan* were appended to the *kukudung* and *salaran*, the documents awarded respectively a winner and a loser in a law case. The centre of attention here is two literary cases actively employing *sinalokan*. The first, the Ki Awas v. Ki Samar affair, is related in a *salaran* contained in LOr 7440 (ff. 201 -208). In describing legal procedure, including the formulation of a *sinalokan* at the end of an affair between two or more parties, the *salaran* is indistinguishable from the, albeit few, authentic documents as found in the Dutch East India Company archives. In addition to being included in a manuscript containing primarily legal titles, what ensures that the affair is a didactic one is that it was handled by the *jaksa* court of Wiranata, a well-known figure of the semi-mythological kingdom of Medhang Kamulan.

The Ki Awas v. Samar affair turned on a controversy over a pair of water-buffalo which were claimed by Samar (vague, obscure) after borrowing them from Awas (3 alert, on the lookout). Samar could not describe the animals, which brought him under two of the *uger-uger* (*aksara* of the wrong), namely *anir yukti arah* (to accuse someone without providing any evidence)[35] and *toyamarta* (untruthfulness in testimony). Ki Awas was able to provide these facts in some detail. As a result, Ki Samar was felled with a losing *salaran* containing *sinalokan*, which provides a supplementary source of information. The case also turns up in the *Pepakem Tjerbon*, complete with a well-known *sloka/sinalokan: adedamar tanggal sapisan kapurnaman* ('while using the dim light of the moon on the first day of a Javanese month, suddenly the full moon shines brightly').[36] A more useful interpretation of the *sloka* used as a *sinalokan* is 'something hidden during the dim light of a waxing moon', i.e., the ownership of the *kebo*, becomes fully illuminated by the full moon's bright light, namely Ki Awas pointing out identifying marks of the animals.

34 Suwarno, *Dictionary*, no. 1527.

35 Mentioned also in *Ibid.*, no. 143.

36 *Ibid.*, no. 6.

Similar circumstances apply for the other case, Kartiguna v. Japlak. It is the centre of focus in the middle of a text called the *Serat Arok*, which deals at length with the conflict between Surabaya's ruler and the hinterland. Although it is supposed to have taken place in Majapahit times, it seems more likely that it reflects the campaigns of Sultan Agung against the *pasisir* in the early Independent Kingdoms period. In any event, the manuscript as paraphrased by Robson[37] originates from Cirebon and hence reflects the legal usage of the West Javanese manuscripts LOr 7410, 7440, and 7442. At the end of the trial between Kartiguna and Japlak a *kukudung* and *salaran* are awarded to respective winner and loser, each finalised by a *sinalokan*. The narrative of the preceding trial makes references to several legal instruments of the time, some of which directly touch on the *sloka* phenomena. The Japlak affair, along with the Ki Awas case, has been dealt with elsewhere.[38]

Prakara

The fourth and final layer of the *sloka* phenomena are *perkara/prakara* ([legal] matters, case [...] lawsuits, cases). The *Surya Alam* can be said to provide the dedicated text in that it monopolises enumerations followed by terse clarifications. As indicated above, the title can be divided into elder Kartasura and younger Yogyakarta versions, a division reinforced by differences in presentation, degree of religious influences, and, most important, orientation to *sloka* phenomena. The Kartasura version comes from Berlin 402, dating from no later than the 1730s. It is narrative in nature, a collection of some seventh-four paragraphs each concerned with a single legal issue. Their order seems random, in that they are not grouped together by subject or any discernible logic.[39] Because the Kartasura *Surya Alam* contributes almost exclusively to our knowledge of *sloka*, subsequent discussion concentrates on the younger version, which is overwhelmingly concerned with *prakara*.

37 Robson, '*Serat Arok*'.

38 Hoadley, 'Literature as Law'.

39 Despite this, its contents were copied verbatim into both the van der Hout version of 1806/1816 and a partial copy of the first 50 paragraphs in ha-na-ca-ra-ka script in LOr 1832 from 1843. The contents were thus seen by subsequent scribes as a text worth reproducing.

The Yogyakarta/Combi *Surya Alam*

Standing close to the published translation found in Raffles, Appendix C, is the Yogyakarta/Combi *Surya Alam*. The descriptive rubric 'Combi' comes from the fact that the title is composed of two manuscripts differing only in the lacuna of Articles 1-8 in the Add 12303 version.[40] Since the contents of this version are repeated in several manuscripts from Yogyakarta,[41] the 'Yogya *Surya Alam*' is used as a synonym. In comparison with the Kartasura version, the Yogya *Surya Alam* is faintly religious and, except for the first eight paragraphs, tabular in construction. This is literally so for the lists of *prakara* found in §§ 9-15, which as the core of the title contain the ideal number of 144 *prakara* of which the text claims it is composed.

Its frame story turns about the allegoric kingdom 'Righteousness' (*Adi-lulah*), implicitly set in the Muslim Middle East. The fame of its king, Surya Alam rests on among other things having reduced the traditional number of Javanese legal affairs (*prakara*) from 1507 to 144. The resultant *prakara* are composed of two to three cryptic terms making a phrase. This is followed by an explanation (*tegesé, artiné*) in compact modern Javanese. The 144 *prakara* are consistently listed in groups of respectively Ten, Thirty, Eight, Twenty, Eighteen, Seventeen, and Fifteen *prakara* (Table 2.2). King Surya Alam's other claim to excellence comes from his identity with Titi Jagat. He alone commands the attribute '*sang*' (honorific maker applied to exalted persons or things). Only a king who behaves in an exemplary manner can be accepted as a Sang Titi Jagat. Such a ruler fulfils his sacred duties by

> watching over the realm [and] causing to be narrated a *pepakem* (hand-book) composed of *aksara* for [bringing forth] (*tirta,* lit. water; *tirta marta* the water of life, drink of the gods) i.e., truth.
> As for the one thousand [five hundred] seven *padu* cases, the *pepakem* resolves them into one hundred and forty-four [...] Yea, this is the king

40 For reasons unknown, the Add 12 303 exemplar (ff. 4v-18v) starts with § 10 of the standard text. The missing paragraphs 1-9 are supplied by the identical text of RAS 6, ff. 72r-75r, in order to complete the text termed here the Combi *Surya Alam*.

41 Those examined for this work include Add 12 323, Add 12 329, and IOL 99, all of which are equivalent to the Combi version. Ricklefs and Voorhoeve cite at least six *Surya Alam* manuscripts in the British collections and Pigeaud four in those of The Netherlands. By rights they should be similar in contents to the *Surya Alam* published in Raffles' *History of Java*. Yet the latter's explanations of *prakara* transcribed into Roman script followed by what are supposed to be translations rarely agree with the Javanese equivalents in other texts. However, when the translations can be identified with the original Javanese terms, they provide welcomed insights, standing as they do closer in time with the original.

> who punishes righteously, even to the point of his right hand cutting off his left one if it offends [and vice versa]. He thus is the one who is called righteous (*adilulah*), a Sang Titi Jagat carrying out the obligatory duties (*titi sywara*).

In the Yasadipura verse rendition of the *Surya Alam,* apparently drawing more upon the Yogyakarta than the Kartasura tradition, it is claimed that the text has

> become valid in the land of Java [...] The acceptable truths of the past being selected, continuing without impediment [...] the raiment of law, the rules of Demak, Pajang, Mataram (Canto I, verse 6).

A more fundamental problem concerns the texts' contents. Excerpts from the sole English translation, that found in Raffles' *History of Java,* can be cited in order to give an idea of the extent to which the text lists these *prakara* expressions. A typical example, provided by Article XVI, reads:

> The following are thirty different cases of lawsuits, viz.
> 1, *Amra Kadang* (sic *jamur amét kadang*), here one who is accused of theft points at either another person or the accuser himself,
> 2, [...]
> [...]
> 30, *Kasabda malicha permana* (sic *sebda malecha*) when a person denies what he has once publicly disclosed.
> With respect to the thirty foregoing cases, it will be for the Jaksa to consider and determine when a lawsuit can, and when it cannot be instigated.

The title's composition conforms to the *Surya Alam* pattern of succinctly worded, if obscure, phrases followed by an explanation. An overview of the major manuscripts summarised in Table 2.1 provides an idea of what the text is all about. For comparison sake the corresponding paragraphs from the Raffles, Yasadipura, and Kartasura manuscripts are included.

Table 2.1 represents the core *Surya Alam.* The reduction from 1507 to 144 cases cited by most titles is followed by additional paragraphs as repetitions, additions, etc, which have not been included. Diverging from the authorized paragraphs (§§ 8-15), their contents are possibly leftovers from the original 1507 cases. As noted above, the narrative part of the title is limited to the Introduction cited above, plus the first seven paragraphs.

Table 2.1 The *Surya Alam*

RAS 6-Add 12 303 ('Combi'),	Raffles	Yasadipura	Kartasura: Berlin 402
Add 12 323 & 12 329, IOL 99		(LOr 6423)	(van der Hout)
[narrative section]			
Intro: King Surya Alam			
≈ Sang Titi Jagat		I:8	
1507 cases >144	Intro.	I:7-8	§ 39
§ 1. – punishment of unjust judges	§ I		
§ 2. – bad (*sloka*) and good judges	§ IX		
§ 3. – *pangulu, jaksa, patih* =	§ III		§ 46
setting of the jewel (king)			
-*trirasa upaya*			
§ 4. – *force majeure*	§ V		§ 43
§ 5. – *kirya-wikirya*, etc.			
§ 6-7 – *Ikral* (*andhih-andhihan*)	§ VII	II:3-6, VI:9	§ 48, 49
26 cases			
[tabular section]			
§ 8 'Ten affairs'	§ XII	I:11, VII:3-10	
§ 9 'Thirty affairs'	§ XIV	I:9-10	
§ 10 'Eight affairs'	§ XVII	IV:2-10	
§ 11 'Twenty affairs'		V:11-22	§ 49, 72
§ 12 'Eighteen affairs'			
§ 13 'Twenty-five affairs'	§ XXIV		
§ 14 'Seventeen affairs'			
§ 15 'Fifteen affairs'			
143 (*sic* '144') cases			

As for the rest of the 144 affairs starting with § 8, the naming of them the Ten, Thirty, Eight, etc. [number of] *prakara* may at first glance seem too stark. This is especially so in light of the more poetic nuances shown by the *sloka* phenomena. Yet it is a literal reflection of the contents. All Yogyakarta *Surya Alam* manuscripts, thus in contrast to the Kartasura/Berlin text, use this organisation. This is even in cases where individual items are also known under specific rubrics. For example, the 'Eight' affairs of § 8 are, in fact, the '*uger-uger*' or '*aksara* of the left/wrong' and the 'Seven affairs' of § 7 are the '*aksara* or the right' or *andhih-andhihan* setting a scale for determining validity of proof. (See Chapter 4. *Aksara*)

Summary

At a moderate level of generalisation, a correspondence between *sloka* phenomena and their sources of information becomes apparent. *Sloka* proper are formulated by the *Jugul Muda,* with a considerable dosage of *sinalokan* in the text's second half. The most conscious exposition of the *aksara* is found in the *Jaya Lengkara,* many of which are sealed by *sloka* introduced in the *Jugul Muda. Sinalokan* are found in most of the minor texts and all the major texts except the Berlin *Surya Alam.* Yet, it is the *Undhang-Undhang Luwangan* that is dedicated entirely to their exposition. In it more than fifty *sinalokan* are tersely explained in slightly more than one per paragraph. The ostensibly youngest of the *sloka* phenomena are the *prakara* found primarily in the Yogyakarta *Surya Alam.* As part of that tradition is the enunciation of the standard number of 144 *prakara.* Some cases seem to have derived from *sloka*; others incorporate terms from various *sloka* phenomena. As seen in Table 2.2, the dedicated and secondary titles mesh to make a textual matrix for the *sloka* phenomena.

Table 2.2 Dedicated and non-dedicated titles containing *sloka* phenomena

	Sloka	Aksara	Sinalokan	Prakara
Dedicated titles:	*Jugul Muda* (frame story) *Surya Alam*	*Jaya Lengkara* *Jugul Muda* (final section)	*Luwangan*	*Surya Alam* Combi
Number of citations in non-dedicated titles				of:
Raja Niscaya[42]	0	3	5	0 [18]
Adilulah[43]	0	4	1	1 [11]
Cacad fragment[44]	6	6	8	1 [20]
Arya Dilah[45]	1	4	10	0 [13]
Jimbun Sl.	0	3	1	3 [32]
Sloka-RN-Wadi	4	1	0	0 [8]
Wadigun Wangkara	2	2	3	2

42 The *Raja Niscaya* is one of the dominant sources of the *Pepakem Tjerbon*, comprising some 30% of the substantive text. Near identical texts are found in LOr 7410, 2v-8r, and Add 12 303, 35v-38v. Paragraph 1 proclaims it to be the 'critical thoughts (*pangurayangan*) [of the] *Raja Niscaya, Wadigun Wang*[*kara*] and *Slokantara Talaga Ening*'. Classic *Sloka*, no. 23: '*angon-angonaken* [...] *eri*' is cited by § 1, *sloka* by §§ 12, 17, and *sinalokan* by § 16. The *andhih-andhihan* (*ikral*) or *aksara* of the right (§§ 3-4) and uger-*uger* or *aksara* of the wrong are explained in §§ 7-11, as well as *prakara* in § 15.

43 Of the minor texts containing information on the *aksara*, the *Adilulah* is the most ambivalent. As found in LOr 7440, ff. 117-131 and LOr 7442, ff. 1-21, it partakes of the name and some of the contents of both the *Surya Alam* and the *Jaya Lengkara*. Consisting of almost a dozen paragraphs, it opens with the statement that 'This is the story of the righteous (*adilulah*) king of the land above the winds, whose king is named Surya Alam'. Despite the closeness of the introductory paragraphs to the opening of the *Surya Alam* tradition, the remainder of the *Adilulah* deals in summary form with subjects central to the *Jaya Lengkara*. Paragraph 3 mentions *aksara* connection with Sang Titi Jagat, while §§ 4, 7 concern the true (*bener*) and false (*salah*) *aksara* and § 8 refers to the 'jewel of the *aksara*'.

44 By default, '*cacad*' (defect) serves as the title of this 'minor text'. The term comes from the text's first line, which reads 'These are the defects [committed by] people in civil cases' (*Punika cacad ing wong padu iku*). The single title found in LOr 7440, ff. 174-201 consists of some twenty paragraphs. Despite appearing as a fragment, the *Cacad* can be considered as a unity in and of itself. The copyist sets it off from the preceding and following texts by the *pada luhur* mark indicating the close of one and beginning of another. It is also found as an almost identical text in Add 18398, f. 93ff. Although the title opens by listing the 'Twenty *prakara*' identical with § 11 of the *Surya Alam*, it is mainly concerned with *sinalokan*, even citing *sinalokan*, repeated in other texts. It also contains references to *sloka* (§§ 4, 5), which are differentiated from the more common *sinalokan*. Even more important are §§ 12 and 13. Like those of the *Adilulah*, the paragraphs relate the *aksara* of the right and wrong, i.e. *bener* and *salah*.

45 The most striking feature of the *Arya Dilah*, LOr 7440, ff.146-164; 7442, ff. 29-56, is the account of the origins of the *aksara* in § 1, which parallel that of the *Jaya Lengkara*. This is followed up by the more generalised meaning of *aksara*, again emphasising the distinction between correct/true (*bener*) and incorrect/false (*salah*) *aksara*, see *Cacad* §§ 11, 12.

Section II

Sloka Phenomena in Vignettes

The conceptual and source foundation for the substantive part of this work have been laid in Section I. In addition to capturing the general meaning of the *sloka* phenomena, it has outlined the source material available for delving deeper into the key components of traditional Javanese law. Understanding them is facilitated by the concentration of the *sloka* phenomena in separate titles.

According to tradition, *sloka* constitute the oldest layer of the genre, one created Aji Saka dating back to the semi-mythological kingdom of Medhang Kamulan. Their flowering in recognizable form is witnessed by the contents of the *Jugul Muda*, whose reputation as an early stratum of legal titles is substantiated by sources from the early Independent Kingdoms era and communicated by literati from the late Kartasura period onwards. Sources dating from the mature Independent Kingdoms period of the eighteenth-century attest to *sloka* as the font of Javanese law. At a more precise level the phenomena consist of *sloka* themselves, the basis of their authority (*aksara*), recycled parts and additions thereof (*sinalokan*), cryptic summaries of their meanings (*prakara*), and textual context (vignettes).

3 Sloka

The *sloka* genre is introduced by legal texts associated with kingdom of Medhang Kamulan. In addition to the first ever *sloka* formulated by Aji Saka himself, the main source of early *sloka* comes from the *Jugul Muda*. According to Javanese tradition attributed to the sixteenth century,[1] it constitutes the earliest title of the period concerned with law. Hence, the *Jugul Muda* and those texts belonging to that tradition provide the material for capturing the main features of the genre. On the more practical level, *sloka* provide the basis for resolving suits.

Both *sloka* and the means of communication, *aksara,* are common Javanese terms. *Aksara* as the twenty letters comprising the Javanese writing system can be traced back literally to the beginning of time. The ha-na-ca-ra-ka alphabet composed of *aksara* is attributed to Aji Saka, who also invented the Javanese *saka* calendar. In order to relate the tragic story of his two loyal servants, Dora and Sembada, he breathed life into the abstract symbols, through which the *aksara* – here in the standard dictionary meaning of letters of the alphabet – were arranged into stanzas thereby creating the first *sloka*. The story is as follows.

> On the way Java from India, Aji Saka and his retinue landed on the island of Majethi. Once there Sembada was asked to remain and guard the priceless heirloom, a *kris*. On no account should it be surrendered to anyone but Aji Saka in person. Aji Saka continued to the Javanese kingdom of Medhang Kamulan, at that time ruled by a man-eating demon named Dewata Cengker. The latter was bested through the ruse of an ever-lengthening turban wrapping, turned into a white crocodile, and ultimately exiled to the southern sea. Dora was then dispatched to Majethi in order to retrieve the *kris,* which was to become the palladium of the newly-won kingdom. True to his pledge, Sembada refused to surrender the *kris* to anyone other than Aji Saka. Dora stuck by the order to retrieve it. The two were equally steadfast in their commitment to carry out their master's wishes. They were equally matched in fighting prowess. Both perished. Unswerving loyalty was immortalised by Aji Saka through creating the twenty *aksara* to compose a *sloka* of four lines of five letters each to their memory.

1 Chapter 2, note no. 21.

Aksara	Javanese	Translation
Ha-na-ca-ra-ka	*ana utusan*	There were two messengers
Da-ta-sa-wa-la	*padha garejegon*	They were of equal resoluteness
Pa-dho-ja-ya-nya	*padha didayané*	They were of equal strength
Ma-ga-ba-tha-nga	*padha dadi batang*	They both became corpses.

The Dora-Sembada *sloka* is important if for no other reason than utility. Entries in Javanese lexicons, as well as references in *Javaansche Zamenspraken,* are arranged alphabetically following the order of the *aksara* given above. *Sloka* must be learned by everyone studying Javanese letters, thereby repeating it endlessly as a *mantra*.

Realization that a *sloka* is more than a mnemonic device or a curious bit of forgotten lore raises questions. If they are synonymous with the Javanese law pioneered by Aji Saka's kingdom of Medhang Kamulan, then why is the intention of the original *sloka* so contradictory? What would have happened had Dora or Sembada followed common sense instead of their master's conflicting orders? They would have been guilty of *durhaka* (rebelliousness, insubordination), which was punishable by death at the will of the sovereign. The underlying intention of the *sloka* was coupled to the demands of Javanese authoritarianism, a monument to unswerving loyalty (*setia*) and avoidance of disloyalty/treachery (*durhaka*) tempered by mild sovereign concern for subordinates. As we shall see, the authoritarian character of *sloka* is recognized by contemporaneous Indonesians. One well-known culture figure has even attempted to liberate it from the narrow warrior mentality (Chapter 9. 'Context'.).

For present purposes a more important aspect of the first ever *sloka* lies in its illustration of the intimate contextual relationship between *sloka* and function. Unfortunately, in the relevant titles the often cryptic *sloka* phrases are rarely accompanied by more detailed vignettes or supplementary textual explanations from which their meaning and purpose can be determined. Even when such complementary materials are provided, the explanations themselves are often in need of clarification in order to arrive at the intended meaning of the phrase in question. Consequently, the following paragraphs will first consider the bare outlines of the *sloka* introduced by the *Jugul Muda* before turning to an analysis of their context with a view of establishing the basic features of the genre. A more detailed analysis of some two-dozen classical *sloka* is undertaken in Appendix II.

Substance of a *sloka*

It will be recalled that the initial vignette of the *Jugul Muda* revolved about a dispute between Dora and Sangkara over a windfall found on leased land. More specifically, it centred about whether the owner or renter profits from a treasure dug up after agreeing upon a common *tebasan* (sale with payment in advance) leasing arrangement. The cache was jinxed by the presence of stolen goods, especially so because they were of gold. Dora and Sangkara contesting ownership rights of tainted goods revealed deep moral failings. According to the *Jugul Muda,* these led to the onslaught of the sorrowful era of deceit, the Dopara/Dwapara Age. In the more detailed version of LOr 7440 the respective widows of Dora and Sangkara reported the incident to the king for which they were rewarded, thus breaking the bounds of loyalty between husband and wife. King Mahapunggung appealed to his *patih* Jugul Muda for advice, who responded by quoting a *sloka.*

> *Sima bangga rebut mangsa mati katiban taru*
> A deviant tiger seizing prey dies, struck by a falling tree [alt. a falling star].[2]

Dora and Sangkara are the tigers who have deviated from the well-known principle that stolen booty is forfeited to the crown. Blinded by greed, they chose to ignore it and met with unexpected death. The gold taken by the king was made into a golden image (*anak-anakan kencana*), which caused the controversies related in the second vignette of the frame story. This first vignette concludes by re-emphasising that the incident revealed moral backsliding thereby calling down the calamity of *dopara* on the people of Purwa Carita. In broader terms the vignette's lesson is that an era of lies and deceit necessitates laws and law courts in order to counteract human greed. This provides the leitmotiv for the rest of the *Jugul Muda,* whose contents as expressed either in *sloka* or, in the last section, *sinalokan* deal with various criminal acts held to be particularly abhorrent in the Javanese legal tradition.

Taken out of their vignette context *sloka* are to a high degree cryptic. Without further explanation, which is seldom available, they are nearly incomprehensible. In some cases, clarification or partial clarification comes from collections of such phrases. With reference to the *sloka* considered here, the second volume of *Javaansche Zamenspraken* offers a couple of parallels

2 Unless stated otherwise *sloka* translations without parenthesis or quotation marks are mine.

with the just-quoted *sima bangga* phrase. Number 318, '*sloka* of the *Jugul Muda*', reads *sima bangga andurkara amet mangsa*. Thus the 'deviant tiger' seeking prey is also one of bad character. *Andur* means to do bad things and *kara* is a word or affair.[3] According to Winter, the *sloka* concerns theft through killing the owner. It has come down to the present as 'a tiger that struggles to rebel and commits a crime in order to capture its prey', further explained by a modern researcher as 'a person who rebels and commits a crime, such as killing someone, in order to obtain what he wants'.[4] Dora and Sangkara showed themselves willing to kill to satisfy their own greed. As retribution for challenging custom they were struck down. A variant of the *sloka* is '*sima bangga tanpa karana*' (a deviant tiger without reason).[5] Suwarno interprets the phrase as 'a person who goes on a rampage without reason' using the example taken from the *Mahabharata*.

> In an act of *sima* [...] *taru*, Lesmana waited until the Pandawa warriors had left and then entered their compound to kill the women and children who had been left behind.[6]

Despite the information provided by *Javaansche Zamenspraken* and others, within the context of the textual tradition something is still missing. Winter's work aims at 'an understanding of old[er] Javanese law books', in which explanations are descriptive rather than causal. They are thereby reduced to similes lacking the activating clause which renders *sloka* functional in a judicial sense through transforming them into binding behaviour norms. The emphasis in Winter and others falls on the 'what' rather than the 'why'. The existence of persons with evil intentions, figuratively *sima bangga* as dominant/disobedient tigers is obvious. But what should be done with them in society's interest?

Sloka and *sloka* phenomena are about obedience. Obedience is directed to the norms hallowed by time and experience (*drigama*), which can be considered as more or less equivalent to a written *adat*. 'More' because they share a common concern with preserving norms from the past as standards for the present; 'less' because there are fundamental differences between the two. Under traditional circumstances *adat* is continually renewed by press of events. As a Malay *pantun* from the Minangkabau region puts it:

3 Suwarno, *Dictionary*, no. 422.
4 *Ibid.*, no. 1460.
5 Cited by Winter, *Javaansche Zamenspraken*, vol. II, pt. 3, no. 319; Ngafenan, *Paribasan*, p. 124.
6 Suwarno, *Dictionary*, no. 1461.

If the river is in spate, the washing place is shifted,
With a change of *rajah* comes a change of *adat*.[7]

Possibly because it is written, and thus fixed, traditional Javanese law as expressed in *sloka* is seen as eternal. It cannot be legislated or modified by the authority of mere mortals or even of religious commandments. The flexibility necessary to allow it to function under changing conditions comes from multiple, equally authentic prescriptions for the same or equivalent acts. Choice rather than change is its hallmark. It is also what has allowed traditional law to survive over time, of course, valid only within a defined area of accepted core values.

Characteristically, *sloka* phenomena also emphasize limits; stepping outside them brings disaster. In the case of Dora and Sangkara coveting sovereign property symbolically called down retribution in the form of the *Kali-yuga*. The form, but not necessarily the underlying (Vedic) philosophy, was borrowed from the Hindu-Javanese past and applied indiscriminately long after the island's conversion to the monotheistic religion of The Prophet. Even the signs of the *Kali-yuga* were to a high degree Javanese, namely blood rains, unseasonable downpours, excessive displays of lightening, etc.

The message of the Dora-Sangkara dispute is made clear through what seems to be a paraphrase of the message from a slightly later text. Paragraph 18 of the *Luwangan Undhang-Undhang* deals in general terms with disputes over unclaimed riches.

> [The case of] One finding the possessions of another [note *saliring* = 'all', 'any', alt. *seler ing* = stolen, thus any stolen possession], no one knows when they have been cached, and the owner has not reported (*anahid*) the time of the loss to the minister (*kang dados sotya ing nagara*) [but] the finder has. If there arises a quarrel (*pinadhu*) all are losers; the possessions are taken by the king with a punishment for [the actors'] responsibility, a fine of 4 *laksa*. This attributed to the *sinalokan* [*sloka* derivative] *padhu bangga rebut mangsa mati katiban ing taru*, or the disobedient [= wrong] legal claimant by seeking gain dies, struck down by a falling tree (retribution)'.

The *sima bangga* (disobedient or deviating tiger) of the *Jugul Muda*'s *sloka* has become a deviant law suit or claim in the *Luwangan's sinalokan*.[8] The

7 Cited by Holleman, *van Vollenhoven on adat*, p. 24.

8 *Sinalokan* and their relationship to *sloka* proper are explained in Chapter 6. *Karuhunan* as something unexpectedly going wrong, i.e., befallen by misfortune, is common in modern-day Javanese proverbs, see Suwarno, *Dictionary*, nos. 620, 533, 335.

principle of law, in existence prior to the individual quarrel or case, is expressed in generic terms as 'bad character', which with modifications is used to clarify a specific instance, in the *Luwangan* 'a deviant case'. Neither should have been brought to court because the disputed objects fell under sovereign prerogatives. Consequently, both parties were struck down. For Dora and Sangkara this was death at each other's hands, for the loser in the *Luwangan* a sizeable fine. Both the tradition and the title go further than the simile arrived at by Winter. Through the device of adding to the negative role model the threat of being struck down by the king's justice or divine retribution it is confirmed that *sloka* are functional, not descriptive.

The second vignette

The contextual aspect of *sloka* is even stronger in the *Jugul Muda*'s second and much longer narrative vignette.

> The gold seized by the king from Dora and Sangkara was made into a golden image (*anak-anakan kencana*). Subsequently this was stolen by a *duratmaka* (lit abductor; 2 thief) named Ki Dustha. It was taken to the burial grounds wrapped as a baby (*embanan*) with appropriate lamentations, where it was buried. Hearing of the theft, eight other miscreants joined Dustha, each bringing a grave offering. Each is named after one of the individual crimes (*corah*) comprising the *astha corah* (Eight Thieves). These include *codékah* [alternatively *coraka*] (one who gives shelter to a miscreant), *pratingah* (one who accompanies a thief), *bojaka* (one who eats and drinks with an evildoer), and *samudinta* (alternatively *samargananda*, one who shows the way).[9] A ninth miscreant, Ki Makaka, brought no offering, but hid himself among the bodies in the burial grounds. In order to circumvent such a subterfuge Dustha had ordered that all the corpses be counted, sticking each in turn with a *kris*. After they depart Ki Makaka digs up the golden image and limps home with the image wrapped in a shawl. Upon their return the following night the

9 The *astha corah*, along with the related *astha dustha* and *sad-atatayi*, are among the oldest recognized categories of miscreants/evil ones, see Hoadley and Hooker, *The Agama*, p. 209 n 1. In the *Pepakem Tjerbon*, pp. 65-66, the first three of some twenty-one miscreants correspond to those named in the *Jugul Muda* and generally accepted as constituting the category, see Appendix IV.

theft was discovered with suspicion falling on Ki Makaka. The miscreants assembled at his house and persuaded him to reveal its whereabouts, with the understanding that he would receive two shares of the booty. Dissatisfaction with the distribution between wives motivated them to report the theft to the king.

In preparing to sentence Dustha and his eight accomplices King Mahapung-gung again shows his dependence upon his highest ministers. Jugul Muda as *patih* is asked first. He declines to commit himself before the other ministers have expressed their opinion. Each in turn is asked whether the king has the right to execute the nine miscreants on his own authority; each answered in the affirmative by quoting the appropriate *sloka*. To a certain extent the traditions differentiate between an ordinary *sloka* and a *sloka agama* (*ratu*, *dursila*, etc). One assumes that an ordinary *sloka* are general observations, which contrast with the relatively specific ones quoted by the ministers of Purwa Carita.

Deliberations over appropriate sentences for the nine miscreants result in the citation of a dozen *sloka*. Nine come from the *mantri* and three from Patih Jugul Muda. While most are a general response to the charges levelled at the miscreants, two enumerate the qualities of a sovereign, which were also expected of his officials.[10] The first of the 'Classic *Sloka*' has been discussed in connection with the Dora-Sangkara vignette. Hence, focus in the following analysis falls on those for which reasonable translations can be given, namely, nos. 2-6, 8, 9, 10c.[11] To avoid undue confusion only the significant parts of the *sloka* apparatus are analysed.

Interpretation

Inherent to the genre, *sloka* focus on circumstances already in existence. Anticipated by the results of the Dora-Sangkara affair, the dozen *sloka* cited by King Mahapunggung's *mantri* sanctioning punishment of the *duratmaka* are quoted verbatim as advice to the king in the exercise of his

10 A detailed account of *sloka* sources is found in Appendix II. 'Classic *Sloka*'. In them the minister who quotes the *sloka* is first named followed by a translation. Next comes variations, copies found in both manuscript titles and younger compilations, and, if present, a textual explanation, i.e., additional clarification provided by the title as found in LOr 7440. Later interpretations by, among others, Winter in the mid-nineteenth century and Suwarno, Ngafenan, etc. in the late twentieth century are appended by way of clarification.

11 Nos. 7 and 11 have defied translated.

judicial authority. The wording of *sloka* is fixed. Only a limited amount of variation is allowed as shown by examples coming from titles of different origins within the Independent Kingdoms era. Because the intent of a *sloka* is predetermined, interpretation is crucial for understanding the manner of applying them. In turn knowledge of what constitutes *sloka* is dependent upon the contents of the extant titles, including possibilities of scribal errors, earlier copies misinterpreted, and conscious fabrication. Hence the most pressing challenge is that of text, namely the reading of a given *sloka*. For present purposes the LOr 7440 version of the *Jugul Muda* has been chosen as providing the standard. Variations, as those found in the titles cited in Appendix II, are more of degree than kind.

Once the individual *sloka's* reading has been satisfactorily established there remains the challenge of interpretation. What is the intention? Interpretation and translation go hand in hand. A good illustration of challenges met and overcome is that of deciphering arguably the best known *sloka* of the *Jugul Muda* cited by Tumenggung Raja Sasana.

> *Mustika brahmara corah titir penajaraken surak ing ampuhan mati déning ngalun-alun.*
> [The presence of] mice and bees as *corah* [discordant elements] trigger the alarm, [even with] supernatural powers; [miscreants] die due to their own actions (Classic *Sloka*, no. 2).

Repeated in almost identical form by a dozen titles and compendiums, it is known as the '*sloka* of *dustha*'. Only the published *Jugul Muda* book contains minor variations. Just after citing the *sloka,* the book version continues with a textual explanation, namely that

> *Mustika* is the name of a mouse, if this mouse is present (*saba*) in a dwelling (*wisma*) it may be killed; *brahmara* is the name of a bee, if this bee is present in the dwelling it is allowed to be killed.
> This is the utterance of Kyai Tumenggung Raja Sasana [who adds], 'A person who carries out a theft against Your Majesty may be killed at the place (*lungguh* = behest?) of Your Majesty').[12]

Typical for the genre, the significance of an individual *sloka* extends beyond the literal reading or even its textual explanation.

12 *Serat angger: Jugul Muda*, p. 331.

Comparing the wording of the *sloka* with the explanation reveals that something has been left out. The explanation covers only the part concerning mice and bees as unwanted guests famous for being pests, which occasions the sounding of the alarm (*titir*). While this provides motivation for ending their activities by allowing them to be killed, it leaves out a key feature of *sloka* as law. Two supplementary components follow the main clause. The first, '*surah ing ampuhan*', a person 'applauded by a storm', remains unclear, even in light of an alternative, dictionary meaning of 'endowed with supernatural powers'.[13] The meaning of the second component, '*mati déning ngalun-alun*', cannot be derived a literal reading of 'dying by the grassy town square'. Such an interpretation becomes impossible due to the causal conjunction '*déning*' (done by, because of), which links death and the *alun-alun*. The paradox is resolved by information in another title, LOr 7410, whose minor departure in the textual explanation gives 'dying because of his acts'. This is seconded by Winter in the mid-nineteenth century, who adds that a *durjana*'s acts (*alunipun*) are well known for their wickedness.[14]

This must mean that '*alun*' or '*alun-alun*' has an extra-dictionary meaning of 'deeds, behaviour', which seems to be the *sloka*'s intention. As far as can be discovered, '*alun*', '*alo*', '*alon*', etc. are not generally, or even exceptionally, used as meaning 'deeds'. Very likely someone well-versed in the art of legal *sloka* has drawn the functionally correct conclusion and connected the dots despite lack of lexical authority. In the present case this was quite likely done by Winter's source of information, most likely an oral tradition current in the first half of the nineteenth century. The full meaning is then re-reflected in modern times by *sloka* compilations such as that of Ngafenan and Suwarno.[15]

In this instance the gap between literal contents and intent/explanation is filled by another source from roughly the same date. But what happens if there is no supplementary title? In such cases the logical interpretation by default becomes part of the *sloka*. The point is significant for two reasons. First, in the application of *sloka* or *sloka* phenomena to actual litigation interpretations are made by the legal experts possessing the necessary qualifications.[16] Second, the interpretation of *pejah/mati déning*

13 Suwarno, *Dictionary*, no. 948 and Robson & Wibisono under '*ampoh*'.

14 Winter, *Javaansche Zamenspraken*, vol. II, pt. 3, no. 442.

15 Ngafenan, *Paribasan*, p. 88 and *Dictionary*, no. 948, respectively.

16 In the eighteenth-century Cirebon-Priangan region: 'The best and most experienced Javanese [had been chosen] to become *jaksa* [...] It is unthinkable that they [Regents and Princes] should choose un-virtuous people from whom they expect to receive judgments: all the more so because

alun-alunipun conforms to the documented tendency for a relatively great degree of judicial self-enforcement. Like that of the Dora-Sangkara affair, the titles attribute an actor's unfortunate fate (death or a capital sentence) to the result of his own actions rather than an arbitrary ruling of human beings, including *mantri* and kings.

Given the interest in earlier Javanese literature shown by the exchanges between Tuan Anu and Radèn Kawitana, respectively Winter's straight man and alter ego, *Javaansche Zamenspraken* emphasizes the simile character of *sloka* over the moral.

> This is the *sloka* of *durjana*. The meaning of *mustika* is *tikus* (mouse), *brahmara* is *kombang* (bee), *corah*: *misuwur* (famous, widely known). A *durjana* who [is seen as] a mouse continually destroys, as a bee is constantly making its presence known everywhere. [Their] evil deeds are well-known. The meaning of *surak ing ampuhan* or *waraning ampuhan* is to possess supernatural powers, alternatively a gale with mist and rain in the mountains, i.e., a *durjana* who is well-known [causing] much evil can be seized. The meaning of *titir pinajaraken* is the sound of the alarm gong-gong announcing the news [of a *durjana*], which is the essence of the alarm. A *durjana* which has been the object of the alarm may be killed. The meaning of *mati ing alun-alun* is a *durjana* dying because of his *alon* (own actions, own utterances), whose evil deeds are already well-known. Certain is his death.[17]

Despite similarities with the *Jugul Muda* version, there is a critical difference. This lies in the transformation of the act into a causal mode. The punishment is justified 'because they [*durjana*] ruin the people of the entire country' (*karana angrusuk ing wong sa-nagara*). Another variant of the tradition (LOr 7410) states that the miscreants are executed due to their own widespread fame, a self-fulfilling type of justice typical of Javanese law. Further testimony for the *sloka* as a legal rule comes from the contrast between Winter's bland 'may or have the authority to kill' (*wenang kapejahan*) and Tumenggung Raja Sasana's imperative 'must be executed' (*patènana*). The simile-like interpretation and narrative tone chosen by Winter is belied by the earlier tradition, which indicates that the phrase was

[they] [...] continue in their responsibilities for life.' *Memorie van Overgave*, Cornelius Jongbloet cited in Hoadley, *Selective Judicial Competence*, p. 19. It is assumed that judicial personnel in the remainder of the legal community of Java-Bali were equally qualified.

17 Winter *Javaansche Zamenspraken*, vol. II, pt. 3, no. 442.

meant to be utilized in practice. As stated in the textual explanation, the *sloka* goes from the figurative description to actual rules with Tumenggung Raja Sasana's explicit utterances that they are to be applied to human beings. They should be dealt with as the mice or bees!

Verbal symbols

Figures of speech, *tembung kéras* in Javanese, are a characteristic feature of *sloka*. In several examples *sloka* demonize evildoers by equating them with undesirable, even despicable, animals. Gnawing mice and swarming bees descend to jackals and thieving monkeys in the following *sloka* to reach a climax with snakes, worms, and leeches. Only a few examples can be given here by way of illustration.

Senapati Raja Gondala (Classic *Sloka*, no. 3) cites the *saloka agama*: 'snake in the house': *Sarpada awésma adhustem pajaletnam prabem wisésa pakreti* or A miscreant snake in the dwelling *pajaletnan* (?), due to the king's power (*wisésa*) is killed. A textual explanation adds:

> This snake, if inside the dwelling, must be killed, by day or night, [so that] there is no peace for miscreants. Likewise, a miscreant in the jungle [or] in one's house must be killed.[18]

A modern interpretation maintains that 'A snake in the house dies because of the power of the king or of the owner of the house', which is clarified as 'a thief caught committing a crime within a home must be killed, and the owner has the right and power to do so'.[19] In another example Demang Lembu Jawa, cites the *saloka agama* 'a tiger dies' (Classic *Sloka,* no. 4).

> *Sardu pejah dugayem prabu ak dati(?) sadula macan ky (?) macan iku rahina wengi ingalas ing we[na]ng sawenang pinaténan karana durjana.*[20]
> A tiger dies [by his] wickedness [as a result of] the king's virtuous deeds. Any/all tigers by day or night in the forest [or in the town] may be executed because they are miscreants.

18 *Jugul Muda*, LOr 7440, f. 332.

19 Suwarno, *Dictionary*, no. 1415. See also Ngafenan, *Paribasan*, p. 121 and Winter, *Javaansche Zamenspraken*, vol. II, pt. 3, no. 270.

20 LOr 7440, ff. 332-333.

A final example in the *Jugul Muda,* Classic *Sloka,* no. 6, is cited by the *jaksa,* Raja Niti. An interpretation by Winter reads:

> *Kremi sampéka wreki kaka duratmaka wredu ongga sardula wikridita.* This is the *sloka* of thieves. A thief is the same as parasitic worms, intestinal worms, snakes, carrion crows, leeches, and wild tigers. Truly such must be killed.[21]

This demonizing is also reflected in a parallel paragraph from the Yogyakarta/Combi *Surya Alam* tradition, although one standing outside the standard 144 *prakara.*

> These are the scourges for all those who guard the realm
> The scourge of the town, these are the *dustha,* tigers, jackal
> The scourge of the forest, worms
> The scourge of one's own body, the intestinal worms
> The scourge of the grass, snakes
> The scourge of water, leeches
> The scourges of the Crown are many (§ 26).

Telling is the contrast existing between the first part of the *Jugul Muda*'s main vignette concerning the eight *duratmaka* and the just cited *sloka.* In the former a moral judgment is made through reverse anthropomorphism in giving the actors the names of crimes from the *astha dustha.* The later half's *sloka* go further. Miscreants are set outside the pale of ordinary human relations. They are not only criminals in the usual sense of the term. They are even more reprehensible through causing disorder by not conforming to society's behavioural norms. Being identified with distasteful beasts further relegates them to the realm of the non-human.

One hastens to add that this by no means indicates extreme sovereign authority. On the contrary, the exercise of sovereignty is limited. As illustrated by the ministers quoting *sloka* to the king, his authority was dependent upon the application of pre-existing social norms contained in *sloka* as uttered and interpreted by knowledgeable ministers. An example of this sovereign duty monitored by ministers comes as a reaction to what seems to be the king's hesitation to follow their counsel. It is expressed in a *sloka* cited by the *Pandelegen* (astrologer) Titi Mantri as Classic *Sloka,* no. 9.

21 Winter, *Javaansche Zamenspraken,* vol. II, pt. 3, no. 169.

In Winter's version it reads: '*Ashta dusthem durgayem astri, wirodra dulikam dustem rajem wiroda, pejah dustem éstriyem*', which is interpreted as:

> Its meaning is that the eight thieves, the responsibility [of the king], [are] to be executed (*kisas*) together with their wives, because the viciousness of the theft surpasses the sternness of the king's power (*kawisésa*).[22]

In principle this agrees with the *Jugul Muda* text, although the latter makes allowance for Ki Makaka's wife, who was only indirectly involved. By attacking the property of the king, they had become *durjana.*

Crucial here is the fact that the ministers remind the king of the social responsibilities inherent to his position. As the *sloka* specifically states, the nine evildoers – eight plus the leader Dustha – must be executed (*paténana*, in the imperative mood), 'because they have become the scourge of the people of the country' (*karana dadi durgama ning wong sa-nagara*). Authority (*wisésa*) to execute is not exercised as an autonomous attribute of Javanese kingship, but as a demand for conformity to the mores embodied in *sloka.*

Sloka ratu

Some *sloka*, as Classic *Sloka*, nos. 8 and 12, contain a more positive message. From relating harsh duty and demonized perpetrators they develop definitions of sovereign authority. Consequently, they are specifically termed *sloka* of kings (*sloka ratu*) in contrast to the just-quoted *sloka agama.* A couple of them also raise the issue of their relationship to the *aksara* considered in more detail by Chapter 4. In this respect the *sloka* cited by the Rangga is of special interest.

> *Giri suci jaladri pawaka surya sasangka anila tanu*
> [A]n ideal king is firm and just (like a holy mountain [*giri suci*]), caring and forgiving (like the sea [*jaladri, segara, banyu*]), punishing (like fire [*pawaka, geni*]), enlightening (like the sun [*surya, srengéngé*], forbearing (like the moon [*sasangka, candra, wulan*], able to accomplish tasks thoroughly and completely (like the wind [*anila, angin*]), and decisive and unchanging once he takes his stand (like ink).[23]

22 *Ibid.*, no. 65.
23 Suwarno, *Dictionary*, no. 465.

On the general level the king is likened to positive features of natural phenomena. Yet the terms are specific; they embrace six *aksara* (legal precepts) associated with kingly authority, namely *aksara bumi, banyu, geni, srengéngé, wulan,* and *angin.* As we shall see in the following chapter, these constituted half of the ten-to-twelve *aksara* concerning sovereign prerogatives (*aksarâji*) whose origin and specific means of enforcement complement the moral demands of *sloka*.

But let us return to the *Jugul Muda* narrative. In it all the ministers have taken a stand by quoting *sloka* connected to the specific issue of the king's authority and/or duty to impose sentences. In addition, the just-quoted *sloka* of *Rangga* Panjang Sora adds to the general guidelines of Javanese kingship special qualities through the appropriate text. At this point Patih Jugul Muda comes forward with his own *sloka* citations, above and beyond that cited as providing the meaning of the Dora-Sangkara affair in the first vignette.[24]

The title's final *sloka,* Classic *Sloka,* no. 12, applying to sovereign and *bupati* alike, is quoted by Patih Jugul Muda in closing the *Jugul Muda*'s core vignette on *dustha*. It can be reconstructed to read:

> *Anrayoga braca*[*ji*] *karajahit, asura-*[*sura siri*] *widagda pratamḗwira sadarana.*

Tellingly, it also provides the conclusion to the *Jaya Lengkara.* It will be recalled that it took the form of a dialogue between the *patih* of Medhang Kamulan and one of the distinguished guests from the lands above the winds. For once the *Jaya Lengkara* text provides a textual explanation by way of defending the resolutions reached by the great durbar in agreeing upon the prohibitions of the *aksara* as part of *drigama* (worldly law).[25] The repetitions provide opportunity to compare different versions in order to arrive at a more accurate understanding of the *Jugul Muda* tradition. Since the *Jaya Lengkara* version is somewhat clearer than the *sloka* found in the LOr 7440 version of the *Jugul Muda,* it can be used as a framework upon which to add the relevant additions provided by the Leiden *Jugul Muda* manuscripts.

24 In general, the three cited by him are identified in the *Jugul Muda* as '*sloka* of the fixed tradition of kings' (*sloka ning ratu agama*), alternatively *sloka ratu* or *sloka bupati.* All are directed specifically at royal duties and responsibilities. Because these, as well as and the *tataneman* [...] *sinatriya sloka,* constitute part of the *aksara* – in fact their *raison d'être* – discussion of them and related *sloka* is postponed to Chapter 4.

25 *Sloka* of *ratu* and *bupati* are also found in the *Jimbun Slokantara* II, § 4, albeit with little clarification.

In the *Jaya Lengkara*, the *sloka* reads '*adriyoga karahita prasama asura widagdya, anukma bramacari*'. Since the wording of the *sloka* calls for a degree of philological expertise not possessed by the author, discussion here follows the explanation provided by the Add 12 303 version of the *Jaya Lengkara*, filling it out with crucial additions from the *Jugul Muda*.

> The meaning of *adriyoga* [*anrayoga*], a king complete with the character of renown; [*abracha*] *karahita*, a king with good will to his servants and who cares for his kingdom; *prasama*, great and small are equated; *asura widagda*, brave in which none dares to challenge, solid not publicly shame-able, generous not stingy; *bobotan sikara* not doing evil [to his servants/subjects], *anukma bramacari*, handsome, not feminine; *adoh ing raja tamah*, far from evil passions.[26]

To this the *Jugul Muda* adds a couple of key pieces of information. The first is that the king is:

> like the moon (*wulan, candra*) [forbearing in keeping with the *giri* [...] *tanu sloka,* Classic Sloka, no. 8, quoted above] determining the fate of *wong larang* (people breaking the king's prohibitions), and pardoning those who have gone astray.

The king is seen as the ideal role model for his subjects, which he must treat with care and understanding; there is no tyrant, *wisésa ning nagara,* or all-powerful king in this description.

But why should he follow an ideal picture of kingship? In this case the answer lies in the contents of the immediately preceding *sloka ratu* uttered by Patih Jugul Muda. The main initiative comes from the *tataneman astha orem* Classic *Sloka,* no. 10 (not analysed here).[27] This is followed by another *sloka,* Classic *Sloka,* no. 11, *pawatik* [...] *tani,* which again emphasizes the king's duties, even in sentencing accomplices of *duratmaka* as Dustha's wife. After the last *sloka* the king asks Jugul Muda:

26 Add 12303, f. 31r.

27 A preliminary interpretation is: *tatanem astha orem* means that as far as what is planted there are no differences. His Majesty has been created by the gods and there is no difference with the common masses. The difference is only in name and status, which is recognized or not [short phrase to the effect that women cannot be equal]. Not without importance, the *sloka* is the one providing authority to the *aksara bumi*, see Chapter 4.

> Eh, patih, when I receive my servants how do I distinguish between good and evil and how does one avoid the weight of the gods (*botena déning batara*) concerning those who have overstepped the prohibitions of the gods [including the king himself], because I fear their wrath.

Jugul Muda's answer is less than reassuring. He cites still another *sloka*. This is likewise found only in the RAS version, which refers to the contents of the *tatanem astha orem sloka*. In somewhat ambiguous terms the *sloka* lists terrible afflictions, such as blindness, crippling sickness, goitre, leprosy, etc. These could be sent by the gods were one to fail to do justice (*adil*) as described in the preceding half-dozen *sloka*. The burden of the gods moves King Mahapunggung to an unprecedented reaction.

> Patih, I surrender the country of Purwa Carita, the weight of its tranquillity, [judgment of] evil and good, the challenge of meting out life and death, all of this I surrender to you because I fear the retribution of the gods [if not just].

The *patih* accepts the task. The eight miscreants and their leader are subsequently sentenced to non-capital punishments. Noteworthy here, there are no *sinalokan* issued after the sentence. They fall under the authority vouched for by the *sloka* cited by the ministers. Further reminders would have been irrelevant.

A couple of issues raised by the *sloka ratu* are worth noting. First, if the *sloka* influenced the formulation or use of *aksara, sinalokan, prakara,* and the like, where did the original come from? There seems no good answer, except that they are indelibly early modern Javanese with nominal influences from Kawi/Old Javanese and Sanskrit. Crucial here is that they existed outside of and above kingly authority (*wisésa*). Kings must not only respect the legal tradition contained in the *sloka* cited by his ministers but also live up to their demands on pain of divine retribution should they fail to do so. Such criteria only partially apply to the *patih* and other ministers. They are only instruments of His Majesty, who is ultimately responsible for everything that happens in the realm. A second peculiarity of the *Jugul Muda* tradition is that the major culprit, Ki Dustha, is appointed to a position equivalent to the royal house guard. That is, he becomes responsible for arresting just the type of miscreants as himself. Possibly a Javanese version of 'to catch a thief', the phenomenon is repeated in the *sinalokan* section as a continuation of the *Jugul Muda* found in the Leiden manuscripts. This is documentable for the cases of Ki Corah, Ki Tatayi, and Ki Walat. And finally, the *sloka* quoted by Medhang Kamulan's highest ministers turn up, often repeatedly, in virtually all the titles considered in this work.

Sloka authority to punish

In the *Jugul Muda* the lack of specific provisions in the *sloka*'s wording allowing/requiring punishment was unnecessary. Those being sentenced were obviously guilty. However, a similar lack of specific motivation for punishment by *sloka* found in titles not providing contextual certainty of guilt requires explanation. Crucial here is that there existed a link between *sloka* wording and actual punishment, one supplied by an allegoric directive. Miscreants are equated with troublesome beasts. If they are present in the home should be killed by the one in charge, the house owner or, by analogy, the king as ultimate householder. Being identified as malicious animals that must be exterminated transforms the *sloka* into a concrete measure of practical judicial application. More specifically, it authorized imposition of punishments on litigants. This is made easier by an unambiguous juxtaposition of deed and guilt. It will be recalled that Tumenggung Raja Sasana after condemning the unwanted animals/*durjana* added that theft of the king's goods should be punished with death.

In turning to other titles of the period efforts to understand *sloka* are met by a different challenge. The relative straightforward assigning of sentences as, for example, to the nine miscreants, plus the Dora-Sangkara affair triggering the *Kali-yuga*, is replaced by the need to establish general *sloka* authority to punish. While space allows the handling of only a few examples here, it is the contention that *sloka* authority based on interpretation by those entrusted with judicial powers played an important role.

The first example of *sloka* authority to punish as dependent on judicial interpretation is provided by a *sloka-agama* appropriately known as 'the criminal *sloka*' (Classic *Sloka*, no. 15). The main source of information concerning this *sloka* comes from the *Pepakem Tjerbon* citing a *Jaya Lengkara* as the source. In transcription the Dutch text reads: '*Koesoema Witjitra, gierba Sadjie, Awee Trinaragina, Madja rawa, Seewasa*' (Jav. *kusuma wicitra, griba, saja, awéh trinaragina, majarawasé, tawasa*). The last two words of the expression – *majarawase, tawasa* – notwithstanding, the Javanese of the de Nooy manuscript reproduces the original Dutch of the 1768 document. Yet despite repetition in a half-dozen titles, the phrase is conspicuously absent from the compilations of *sloka*-like phrases drawn upon by this work. This includes the numerous phrases analysed by *Javaansche Zamenspraken* and younger compilations. Fortunately, due to the *Pepakem Tjerbon*'s bilingual edition there are not one, but two textual explanations of the 'criminal' *sloka*. A translation of the Dutch reads:

> [O]f which the clarification is that the judges must be experienced in the artifices of *durjana* and *duratmaka*, evil doers and thieves, because they are as pleasant of mien as a flower; their practices are as fine as water which cannot be understood, as the wind so subtle at coming in everywhere, as a *tapa*, or anchorite, who comes begging for alms [but] whose intention meanwhile is the opportunity to spy on one's house, or as clouds or smoke in the mountains, so great and daring. These are the practices of the *durjana* and *duratmaka*. Such with justice are subjected to *jarah-kukud*, confiscation of goods and forfeiture of wife and children's freedom.[28]

As explained in Appendix I. 'The Problematic *Pepakem Tjerbon*', generally there is little difference between the Dutch original and the de Nooy Javanese manuscript appended to the published *pepakem*. What is questionable is the last sentence containing the punishment. On the one hand, explicit punishments are only rarely prescribed by *sloka*. In any event, the clause is suspiciously similar to the Dutch addition to a judgment of a Javo-Dutch court in 1717. In explaining the verdict to Batavia, Resident Gobius after citing an '*astra geni*' [*sic aksara geni*] as its basis, adds that the defendant's goods, as well as wife and children are forfeited 'to the Honourable Company'.[29] In this instance Company officials borrowed local legal concepts for their own ends. Forfeiture of the freedom of wife and children through the criminal actions of husband or father is a well-established rule in traditional Javanese law.[30] But, as we shall see in the following chapter, *aksara geni* is never connected with such a punishment, *aksara lintang* being the closest with enslavement of a guilty minister.

According to the *Pepakem Tjerbon*, the *sloka* originates from the *Jaya Lengkara*. This is confirmed by reference to the LOr 7440 version of that title. To a lesser extent it is supplemented by the *Jimbun Slokantara II* found

28 *Pepakem Tjerbon*, p. 53.

29 The Puspa Nagara case of 1717 is analysed in Hoadley, *Selective Judicial Competence*, pp. 87-94 and summarised below, Chapter 7, p. 106.

30 Forfeiture of wife and children's freedom on occasion of crimes committed by husband or father are discussed in Hoadley, 'Practice and Narrative', pp. 6-7. The fact that it is generally a sovereign prerogative makes its appropriation by the Dutch East India Company a clear indication of the commercial Company's sovereign ambitions at an early date.

in that manuscript, as well as a more complete, ostensibly younger, reference contained in the *Undhang Sénapati Jimbun* (LOr 2125). Common for them all is the combination of a short list of the 'Eight Thieves' (*astha corah*) – listed among others in the *Pepakem Tjerbon* (pp. 65-67) – with a variant of the *sad-atatayi* (Six Tyrants). More to the point, the titles specifically instruct the *jaksa* to use the *sloka* as the starting point (*miyos*) of their deliberations, apparently in both determining guilt and assigning an appropriate punishment.[31] While a one-to-one correspondence between *sloka* wording and textual explanation cannot be read from the *sloka*'s text, the title's context makes it clear that the ultimate punishment – *jarah-kukud* (seizure of goods) – stems from the *kusuma wicitra sloka*. As such the *sloka* upholds the characteristic feature of the genre by providing the basis of a legal resolution. This contrasts to the simile-like descriptions found in many of the *sinalokan* considered in Chapter 5.

As in the case of the *mustika brahmara* [...] *alun-alun* (Classic *Sloka*, no. 2), the logical conclusion of the *kusuma wicitra sloka* is that such *durjana/ duratmaka* should be punished. None of the other manuscripts specify judicial action. Only the *Pepakem Tjerbon* states that they should be subjected to forfeiture of goods and family. It stands to reason that this was grafted onto the Javanese rule at the behest of the Dutch officials responsible for the *pepakem*, namely team Hasselaer. What stands out in the statement is not the process of interpretation *per se*, which was part and parcel of Javanese law, but the act of tying a specific punishment, a harsh one at that, to a general description of the methods/guises of miscreants. In contrast, the nine *duratmaka* in the *Jugul Muda* were sentenced for a specific deed, namely the theft of the king's golden image one established via traditional instruments,[32] *saksi* (witness) by Dustha's wives.

Just how well established the *sloka* is in the legal literature is shown by examples from other texts. The *kusuma wicitra sloka* is found in two versions of the *Surya Alam* and even in a tangential version in the *Luwangan Undhang-Undhang*. For example, § 23 of the Kartasura *Surya Alam* (Berlin 402) and LOr 1832, reads in translation:

> A righteous king[dom] is brought to uproar by two causes, [namely] *kapir* and *durjana*. These destroy the nation and if the king does not right the

31 Explanation of versions of the respective *sloka* relationship to the *astha dustha* and *sad-atatayi* is found in Appendix IV. 'Diverse Components'.

32 Traditional instruments for establishing guilt, i.e., *tarka* (suspicion) followed by degrees of valid evidence – *patra, saksi, cina, satmata, nyawana, permana/ubaya,* and *parusa* – are discussed in Chapter 4. '*Aksara*', Table 4.4.

> evil doers' crimes, [he] shares in those evil deeds. And whenever any kind of *durjana* is apprehended (*angilawan*), his crime [must be considered by] the *pradata* court taking as it point of departure (*amiyosaken*) *sloka*, the *sloka*: *kinir diya*. Its meaning: to be in one's guard against *durjana*. Of the *durjana* there are those like water, those like the wind, or like *matiraga; durjana* as water or mists [or such] are the guises of *durjana*.[33]

Yasadipura, in his verse version of the *Surya Alma*, provides all the elements of flowers, wind, mist, etc., as well as a warning to be on guard against *durjana*, because, 'they are like the sky, aestheticism, and mists, such are the actions (*sasolah*) of *durjana*'.[34] Less understandable are the *sloka* from *Luwangan* § 43. The relevant *sloka* fell under the rubric '*ngemasi*', which usually means one dying in battle alternatively counterfeiting. Neither fits in the present context. Moreover, the *sloka*: *rat réka kusuma ngibri citra, tirta saji awéh tisna leheng giniman yang rawita, déwa candra sucana drama* contain only likeness to flowers, and holy water, although the wording is substantially the same as that listed above.

A second example of a *sloka* whose authority rests on judicial interpretation is the *srengéngé piné* Classic *Sloka,* no. 19 from the Add 12 303 *Jaya Lengkara* and the *Undhang Senapati Jimbun* of LOr 2125. Although not technically an original source, the most telling version, complete with explanation, is found in *Javaansche Zamenspraken*.

> *Srengéngé piné banyu kinum bumi penendhem geni pinanangan*
> **Translation**: This is the *sloka* for the *catur manggala* (four commanders) [namely] king, *patih, pengulu, jaksa*. Its intention is as follows. In justly carrying out an investigation into someone's crime [it must be as] the rays of the sun, nothing furtive or secret (*kasilib*) [i.e., *srengéngé piné* = the sun bakes]. Within the investigation as to the justness of the crime [it must be as] water in a damn (*wawadah*), transparent and direct as clear water [i.e., *banyu kinum* = water immerses]. The order (*tata*) [must be as] the earth, meaning its baseness avoids (*singkiri*) chaos (*tembung sari* = xylophone noise?) [i.e., *bumi penandhem* = earth buries]. The judgement with authority (*wisésa*) [must be as] fire (*latu*), if burned it must not be

33 Usually the van der Hout translation mirrors the contents of Berlin 402 and LOr 1832, but not in this instance. The last half of the *sloka* concerns types of thieves, including water thief, wind thief, anchorite thief, etc., which are difficult to place within textual explanations of the Berlin *Surya Alam* or other titles.

34 Canto X, verses 7-8.

> by parts [i.e. incomplete], its meaning even to embrace blood relatives or friends [i.e., *geni pinanengen* = fire burns], such is the true application of authority which is authorized.[35]

A modern interpretation is: 'the sun is for sun-drying, the water is for submerging [...] the judge or person in authority must make a decision that is as just and appropriate as possible (so that he or she can function like the sun or like water)'.[36] This is echoed by versions of the *Jaya Lengkara*, including the younger *Undhang Senapati Jimbun* found in LOr 2125 (ff. 81-82).

> The meaning of *banyu kinum* is litigation immersed so that the court utters neutral (*padhem* = cool, dead) judgments, which are pure (*weningé*); the meaning of *srengéngé piné* is litigation baked so that the court expresses a view clear and clean; the meaning of *geni pinanggan* is litigation burned so that the court expresses all that is warmed [i.e., actual], if there is a passionate expression of the gods [a prejudiced judgment] uttered in the court's sentence, the fine is *asta-wara*.

Final examples of a type of *sloka ratu* are those existing in partial quotations rather than whole phrases. Of these *tekék mati déning ulahné* or a gecko dies because of its voice, i.e., to suffer or fail because of one's own words is conspicuous (Classic *Sloka*, no. 24).[37] It again illustrates the self-fulfilling nature of Javanese law. What differentiates it from those considered so far is that it appears as a subordinate clause in several *sloka* phenomena. Despite this, it functions in conformity with the genre's role. In the Yasadipura and Berlin versions of the *Surya Alam* it provides the decisive evidence in a dispute. The Dora-Temen vignette (Chapter 7) illustrates how a defendant, here Dora (to tell a lie) by his own contradictory testimony is led to downfall, hence 'condemned by his own voice'. A similar function is seen in the Japlak vignette, also considered in Chapter 7. Here is a twist. The *sloka* is included as part of a *prakara* – *akarya watang* – referred to by the judge as providing the basis for the decision in Wiraguna's favour. In the Berlin *Surya Alam* it is coupled with another phrase '*lir sima* [*bangga andurkaka*] *amét mangsa* (a modern interpretation is 'a tiger that struggles to rebel and commits a crime in order to capture is prey or [...] a person who rebels and commits a crime, such as killing someone, in order to obtain what he

35 Winter, *Javaansche Zamenspraken*, vol. II, pt, 3, no. 274

36 Suwarno, *Dictionary*, no. 1485.

37 *Ibid.*, no. 1527.

wants'.[38] Noteworthy, the principle of the *tekèk mati déning ulahé ulané sloka* conveys a parallel meaning as part of the *mustika brahmara* [...] *alon-alon sloka*. More specifically this is the phrase '*mati déning alun-alun*' ([a *durjana*] dies as the result of his actions), again reinforcing the expression that it is not the judges who determine guilt, but the expression of the litigants themselves (*Luwangan* § 50).

Given its simile character it is not surprising that some observers classify it as a *bebasan* rather than *sloka*.[39] This in turn re-emphasizes the challenge in differentiating the *sloka* from *peribasa, bebasan, ucapan, ibarat*, etc. The problem is not new. Despite listing hundreds of such phrases in the subtitle to *Javaansche Zamenspraken* (*zamenspraken over salokas, paribasans, wangsalan en andere onderwerpen*), roughly three-quarters of the fifteen-hundred or so phrases are termed *sloka*. Without questioning Winter's undoubted mastery of the language and subject at hand, a more nuanced judgment can be given. They are undoubtedly *saloka* in the broader meaning of *sloka* phenomena, which can be divided into more specialised categories such as *sinalokan, aksara,* and *prakara*. The position taken here is that legal *sloka* constitute the basis of decisions, settlements, or opinions. This sets them uniquely apart from the remainder of such 'idiomatic expressions'. In any event, *sloka* used as parts of other *sloka* phenomena prepare us for their prominence in all types of legal phrases.

Another example of combined phrases is provided by a *sloka* most often cited as *angon-angon* (*alt. angus-angus*) *ngadu pucuk eri,* Classic *Sloka*, no. 23. Curiously, it is referred to as 'the six affairs' from the number of words comprising the *sloka* as those found in Berlin 402/van der Hout *Surya Alam* § 46a, *Raja Niscaya* § 2, and Add 12 323 *Surya Alam* § 8. One modern translation simplifies it as: 'a wild bull pitted against the tip of a thorn'. This is interpreted as 'two powerful men (usually judges or lawyers) match skills and intelligence to win a court case'.[40] Another modern interpretation emphasizes the dilemma of *jaksa* in attempting to determine between what is true and what is false in respective claims.[41] Standing closer in time to the original, Winter's interpretation also emphasizes the striving of *jaksa* to separate truths from untruths. He explains that it is a *sloka* of a person intending to free his intelligence by being on guard for 'lies and truth within the haziness of actions and words of those suiting and being suited'. To

38 *Ibid.*, no. 1460.

39 Ngafenan, *Paribasan*.

40 Suwarno, *Dictionary,* no.134.

41 Ngafenan, *Paribasan,* p. 18.

the query by Winter's straight man, Tuan Anu, concerning the meaning of *angun-angun*, his mentor Kawitana replies:

> The meaning of *angun-angun* is a wild buffalo, which is an allegory of a *jaksa*. Competing horn against a thorn, a sharp competition, is a simile (*ibarat*) for the actions and words, which must be weighed in an ordered process.[42]

Conclusion

One of the most notable features of the Independent Kingdom's *sloka* is that they existed in their final forms prior to their use in a legal setting. This was true even in the semi-mythical kingdom of Medhang Kamulan. Patih Jugul Muda and his colleagues provided counsel on how the sovereign should deal with legal-political affairs. This embraced both the issue of royal priority in claims to discovered treasures, especially gold, and its subsequent theft by nine miscreants bearing the names of the *astha corah*.[43] Characteristically, the ministers do not offer advice based upon law books or their own opinions. They quote *sloka*. The latter epitomised rules of accepted/required behaviour based upon custom, law in its broadest meaning. Because they were quoted verbatim, often followed by a textual explanation, the 'text' or wording, is reasonably consistent. However, for those unaccompanied by references to the original text, the authenticity of transmission can be problematic. The nature of the extant sources means that the challenge is only partially resolvable. Yet, judging from the longevity and consistency of the *sloka* dealt with here, reconstructions are modestly reliable.

Another feature of the *sloka* flows out of 'text' but goes far beyond it. Obviously, the wording of *sloka* transmitted through various chains of preservation and communication greatly influences interpretation of what is meant or intended. Deciphering what the *sloka* say is possible; less so their functional intention. This is of minor importance in those *sloka* describing the authority of an ideal king, as in Classic *Sloka* nos. 8 or 10c. Yet when cited as the basis for a legal action, i.e., punishment, capital or monetary, it becomes a challenge. This is no less so within the nuances of intention. Tumenggung Raja Sasana's citation of the much-quoted *mustika*

42 Winter, *Javaansche Zamenspraken*, vol. II, part 3, no. 96.

43 An alternative meaning of *corah* as 'discord, chaos' fits the circumstances better that the standard 'Eight Thieves'.

brahmara [...] *alun-alun sloka* illustrates the relative imprecise connection between the literal wording of *sloka* and punishment expected. As with all the *sloka* quoted in the *Jugul Muda,* it conforms to the basic fact that *durjana* should be killed. However, they leave the question of how and why open. In this instance the *tumenggung* hedges his bets by adding a non-*sloka,* causal explanation; a thief of the royal goods may be executed on the king's command. In other words, the perpetrator may be a *durjana,* with all the negative association this carries with it. Yet the punishment is the result of a specific act for which evidence is clear, here the testimony of Dustha's wives. Less specific are *sloka* nos. 3-6. In them *durjana* are demonized, which implies that they should be executed. No. 6, the '*sloka* of leeches', is especially dependent upon interpretation, as are nos. 15, 16, 21, 22. Common for them – the last four coming from other texts – *durjana* are identified in various, often figurative, terms which only implicitly can be linked with their execution. The judicial response in transforming a simile-like description into actionable law comes about through a process of interpretation. Textually most of such transformations come from Winter. Thus, it is reasonable to conclude that their meaning was inherent to the specific *sloka* pre-dating Winter's lifetime but was explicitly recorded towards the middle of the nineteenth century and followed ever since. As suggested earlier, the process must have been similar to those of *adat*-law judgments, in which interpretation of custom by learned and/or experienced practitioners was crucial. The process had the effect of applying behavioural norms to criteria of actions, deviation of which led to putative reprisal by governmental authority.

4 Aksara

An appropriate follow-up of Aji Saka's *sloka* expressed in *aksara* is *aksara* authorized by *sloka*. The characteristic function of *aksara*, unique to Independent Kingdoms' law, was to provide a block of applicable provisions, often expressed in *sloka,* to supplement general statements of 'what ought to be'. They thus fill an obvious shortcoming of *sloka*, whose contents are seldom sufficiently specific to be used for judicial settlements. Even within the texts consulted here *sloka* apply to only a small number of affairs. These mostly concern the sovereign and his personal property, as in the case the golden image of King Mahapunggung. In contrast, *aksara* provide rules that can be decided in court. As such they stand between *sloka* statements of legal/moral principles and *sinalokan ex post facto* comments (Chapter 5).

Origins

At the outset it must be acknowledged that there exists very little information regarding the origins of *aksara* as part of the legal tradition. Even terms such as 'immortal' 'unchangeable' (Skr. *a̲-ksara* = not-changeable) lack specific definition. There seems no demonstrable connection to what little is known of the traditions preceding the period of Independent Kingdoms. This stems primarily from lack of access to 'Old Javanese' legal texts with a defined date and provenance. By default, one is limited to the *Agama* – Jonker's *Kuntara Manawa* – whose shortcomings as a representative of that era have been pointed out by its most recent editors.[1] In any event, the *Agama*, as well as other Java-Bali titles, are to all intents and purposes free of *sloka* phenomena, including the *aksara* in the meaning used here.

A way out of the dilemma of *aksara* as something other than letters of the alphabet which seemed promising upon further scrutiny is undermined by a crippling difficulty. The promise comes from a generally overlooked paragraph in Zoetmulder's *Old Javanese-English Dictionary*. It provides an extended meaning of *aksara,* namely: '*aksarâji*' (*aksara* + *aji*), defined as 'the 'royal science, the code of kings (*ksatriya*)'. 'Prohibitions of the *aksara*' cited by the opening paragraphs of the *Jaya Lengkara* stating its intention, comes close to the meaning proposed by Zoetmulder. However, difficulties arise from the lack of specification of what was meant by royal science. Citations

1 Hoadley and Hooker, *The Agama*.

of the term within older literature are limited to two instances, both from the Middle Javanese historical novel *Rangga Lawé*. In it they caution against ignoring the teachings of the *aksarâji* '...precepts esteemed' (*sasana néng alewih*). Rangga Lawé posed one of the most dangerous threats to the rule of Hayam Wuruk (r 1350-1389) the then boy king of Majapahit. In principle the revolt challenged 'kingship', the object of *aksarâji*. With wisdom born of hindsight the following presentation advances what seems to be a more appropriate interpretation of the 'precepts esteemed', namely the exercise of royal authority without recourse to judicial procedure. Direct punishment at the will of the sovereign was a crucial ingredient. In a nutshell this was the advice communicated in *sloka* to Raja Mahapunggung by his ministers in the *Jugul Muda*. It was also based on the assumption of loyalty parallel to that demanded of Dora and Sembada by Aji Saka.

Aksara in the *Jaya Lengkara*

The opening paragraphs of the *Jaya Lengkara* imply that the period under discussion constituted a departure from its predecessors. The great durbar convened at Medhang Kamulan specifically concentrated on two points. These were 1) *drigama*, i.e., experience/custom stripped of the Hindu concepts so common in the Middle Javanese tradition of the *Rangga Lawé*, *Agama*, or other works prominent within a Balinese context, and 2) the rules laid down by the *aksara*. The text of Add 12 303 summarised in *The Archive of Yogyakarta* provides the point of departure.

> This narrative tells of His Majesty, crowned king at Medhang Kamulan, Sri Jaya Lengkara, sitting in audience before all the kings who had come to submit under Medhang Kamulan from the five regions, the king from above the winds *sang* Anggas Kerta with his *patih* Kerta Basa, the king of metaphors (*ibarat*) *sang* Kuthara Manawa with his *patih* Sunduk Prayoga, king of Panunggul Angin, *sang* Raja Niti, with his *patih* Titi Syara, king of Tunggul Ametung *sang* Lembu Jawa with his *patih* Anggas Kara, and king of Petung Manglaras Jaya Pralambang with his *patih* Niti Sastra.

The list of ministers is similar to those cited by the *Jugul Muda* in which the dignitaries bear the names of recognizable law books. Unlike it, however, the *Jaya Lengkara* text departs by naming delegates from the lands 'above the winds', a characteristic it shares with the younger *Surya Alam* tradition.

From the introductory paragraph the narrative passes directly to the title's aim cited earlier.

> Sitting in audience were all the kings along with their *mantri* of olden times in the great audience hall at Medhang Kamulan. That discussed by all the *mantri* were the prohibitions (*wewaler*) of *drigama* [and] prohibitions of the *aksara,* which become law.[2]

Despite minor divergences in some versions, the intention is clear. The *Jaya Lengkara* focuses on characteristics of the *aksara* within the framework of *drigama*. As noted in analysing *sloka* cited in the *Jugul Muda, drigama* stands for worldly law based upon indigenous custom and experience as opposed to 'fixed' law (*agama*) ultimately based upon religion with a growing tendency in this period toward Islam. In some versions, notably that of LOr 7410 (f. 28r), the emphasis falls even clearer on the *aksara* from the wording '*drigama* and the prohibitions of the *aksara*'.

All the titles follow this standard opening. Half a dozen paragraphs follow in which the group of ten-to-twelve *aksara* are presented in groups of two or three. These are explained in summary form to the assembled dignitaries by the respective *patih*. Common for Javanese handling of *drigama*, the law is presented for confirmation and agreement by the assembled kings and their *patih*. It is not dictated.

> Sang Patih Kerta Basa spoke before His Majesty the king of Medhang Kamulan. That uttered was the intention (*karep*) of the *aksara*, the meaning *aksara bandan, aksara angin*, and *aksara banyu*. The meaning of *aksara bandan*: the actions of the courts (*sapolah ing kerta*); the meaning of *aksara angin*: the intentions of the court (*karep ing kerta*), [and] the meaning of *aksara banyu*: the coolness/concentrated nature of the court (*adhem ing kerta*).
> Then sang Patih Sunduk Prayoga spoke before His Majesty the king of Medhang Kamulan. That uttered was the intention of the *aksara*, [that of] *aksara bumi* [and] *aksara lintang*. The meaning of *aksara bumi* is the place of the court (*enggon ing kerta*), the meaning of *aksara lintang* the excellence (*luwih ing kerta*) of the court.
> Sang Patih Titi Sraya spoke before His Majesty the king of Medhang Kamulan. That which was uttered was the intention of *aksara thathit, aksara wulan,* and *aksara lék*. The meaning of *aksara thathit*, 'the king speaks with his ministers who are loyal' the meaning of *aksara wulan*,

2 Carey & Hoadley, *Archive of Yogyakarta*, vol. II, pp. 89-91.

> 'the king orders his army', the meaning of *aksara lék*, 'the king desires to warn his servants'.
> Coming forward Patih Anggas Kara spoke before His Majesty. That uttered was the intention of *aksara segara*. The meaning of *aksara segara*, he who owns the universe completes the great war [?]. Sang Patih Niti Sastra spoke before His Majesty. That uttered was the intention of *aksara kilat,* its meaning, the king's will before it is uttered.
> Coming forward Patih Madana Sraya spoke before his royal master concerning *aksara srengéngé* [and] *aksara kukus*. That which was uttered: the jewels of the *aksara*, two points. Thereby all the kings were struck by the utterances concerning the intention of the *aksara*. That uttered by sang Patih Madana Sraya: the meaning of *aksara srengéngé,* the king who lights up the entire world's inhabitants who are in the dark [dishonourable], the meaning of *aksara kukus* 'help with death [?], the meaning, support is always near (*embanan kang ngapadhet*)'.

The final paragraph containing the text's aim was uttered by the host *patih*, Madana Sraya, successor of Patih Jugul Muda.

> With the utterances of Patih Madana Sraya it is directly revealed the understanding (*grahita*) and intention (*karep*) of the *aksara* which become law, to which belong the transgressions/sins one by one requiring death, and to make honest all the *sloka* and *sloka-[dir]gama* which causes to fall the punishments of *undhang-undhang* (man-made laws, regulations). Thus, everything was confirmed (*anduluri*) by the assembled kings and ministers. All was thoroughly investigated.

In a typical Javanese manner, the *aksara* are explained by the *patih* to their royal masters. Nevertheless, the context is thoroughly royal law. Their contents provide the authority for man-made, hence subordinated, regulations (*undhang-undhang = ubaya*) by the individual kings at a specific time and place. This was confirmed by the great durbar of kings hosted by King Jaya Lengkara, successor to the sage kings Aji Saka and Mahapunggung of Medhang Kamulan.

Aksara modes

The contents of the *Jaya Lengkara* are supplemented by information provided by other texts from the Independent Kingdoms textual tradition. Discussion can be profitably divided into themes or modes. The first focuses on the names and attributes of the ten-to-twelve *aksara* (Table 4.1). These are couched in terms of natural elements with their suggestive properties, for convenience sake termed a 'descriptive mode'. Drawing upon particularly the *Cacad* and *Surya Alam*, the second theme, the 'functional mode' (Table 4.2 and 4.3), analyses the textual check-list of invalid suits and those deemed to fail as invalid suits before considering implications of a hierarchy of relative weight given pleas based on the type of evidence supporting them. They reveal how *aksara* are used in the legal tradition. The third theme considers the special, if limited, sovereign authority for punishing certain classes of cases without recourse to judicial process, a true 'science of kings' (*rajâji*) mode.

Descriptive mode

Study of the relevant texts provides a more or less inclusive list of *aksara* and their attributes.

Table 4.1 ***Aksara***

badan (body)	action of the *kerta*
angin (wind)	intention of the *kerta*
banyu (water)	coolness/purity [impartiality] of the *kerta*
geni (fire)	ardour/radiance (*panuoring* = streaming out as fire) of the *kerta*
bumi (earth)	place of the *kerta*
lintang (star)	excellence of the *kerta*
kilat (lightening)	know king's wishes before they are uttered
thathit (thunder)	king addressing his servants (*bala*)
kukus (smoke/cloud)	~
srengéngé (sun)	vision of the *kerta*
lék [?]	king warning loyal people/ministers
sengara/sengkara	[either destruction of the world or intentional lies] *sangkara* of the *Jugul Muda's* first vignette

As with most of the *sloka* phenomena, the terms are far from self-explanatory. The question of origins seems the logical point of departure.

One possible explanation of the origin of the *aksara* is that they come from the same cultural environment as the *'Astha Brata'*. These are the eight lessons of leadership found in the Old Javanese *Ramayana*. They were taught by Rama either to Bhatara, who was to substitute for him as king of Ayodhya in his absence, or to Wibasana, who was to be crowned king of [Sri] Langka after the death of his brother, the evil Ravana, at Rama's hands. Even a superficial review of the terms and attributes reveals a close resemblance to the *aksara* of the *Jaya Lengkara*. For example, characteristics for an ideal leader in the broadest sense include the sun (*srengéngé*), which shines on every person and thereby gives life to all. A secondary virtue connected with *srengéngé* is the ability to differentiate between essentials and non-essentials. Additional exemplary features are conceptualized by parallels with the stars (*lintang*), which stand out above all others; wind (*angin*), which reaches to even the most difficult places; water (*banyu*), which erodes and cleans everything; fire (*geni*), which is undeviating without flickering; and the earth (*bumi*), which has a receiving nature able to accept all manner of human behaviour with sincerity.[3]

Under the circumstances it is not surprising that many of the *aksara* in the descriptive mode reflect both general ideals of leadership expressed by the *Astha Brata* and specific legal virtues contained in the '*giri jaladri* [...] *tanu' sloka* cited in the *Jugul Muda* (Classical *Sloka*, no. 8). These include impartiality (*banyu*), ardour (*geni* = punishments, fire), outstanding excellence (*lintang*), prescience (*kilat*) as the often-cited qualification of *mantri*, and vision (*srengéngé* = *surya*). In other words, *aksara* in this mode are in tune with the criteria of exemplary *abdi-Dalem* (servant at court).

Functional mode

So far discussion has attempted to account for the definition and composition of the *aksara* by reverence to the contents of the dedicated text, the *Jaya Lengkara*. A transition from abstract principles to concrete action is found in the *Cadad* (§ 12).

> This is what is created, the *aksara bener* (*aksara* of right/truth) and *aksara salah* (*aksara* of wrong) which decide *padu* and *pradata* (quarrels and

3 Mertono, *State and Statecraft in Old Java*, Appendix III. '*Astha Brata*', pp. 152-155, citing Yasadipura's *Serat Rama*, p. 432ff. Another possibility is that they derive from the 'thirteen witnesses' named in the Sarwadharma Charter of 1269. As a means of ensuring that no one interfered with the provisions of the freehold established by that charter, all possible miscreants 'were watched (over) by the Thirteen Witnesses'. Several of them parallel the eighteenth-century *aksara*. The charter continues: '[The] Sun, Moon, Wind, Fire, Sky, Earth, Water, the Heart, Yama, Day, Night, Twilight and Dharma (*aditya, candrâ pânilonalaçcâ dyoh bhûmirâpohrdayam yamâçca, âhaçca ratraçca tathâçcasanmyâ dharmmaçca*) know man's doings', Pigeaud, *Java in the 14th Century*, vol. III. 'Translations', p. 150. The possibility is strengthened by citation of the 'thirteen witnesses' in Yasadipura's verse version of the *Surya Alam*, Canto I, verses 17-18.

> civil cases respectively). One who relies upon *aksara salah* loses because the origin of these *aksara* is from the glowing coals of the fires of Hell; one who relies upon *aksara bener* wins because true *aksara* have their origins from the smoke of the fire [sacrificial fire or incense used by a priest or *pangulu*?] which become the radiance of the king.

The *Arya Dilah* confirms the paragraph's contents. Although *aksara* are not specifically cited, the context of § 3 makes it clear that the reference is to the *aksara* phenomena. It also adds that a king who is noble 'raises up (*adheg*) the *aksara*'. More important is the last sentence stating that he who is obscure (*petang* = lit. dark) will not be protected by Yang Sukma (the highest god).

Aksara of the right/truth

Abstract rightness and wrongness are important. Yet on a practical level the whole process is dependent on the existence of a recognized legal contest between two or more parties. Hence litigants are exhorted to build on *aksara bener* and avoid *aksara salah*. This is good advice under any circumstances, but without more specifics it does not take us very far. Reflecting a general attitude toward legal process, the cited instruction is relative: one must choose the best, or the least negative, basis for one's case. To the relative good or true belong the *andhih-andhihan*, also termed *ékral/ikral* (guiding principles). As one of the more often cited instruments of litigation, they constitute a set of some ten types of evidence, almost invariable arranged in order of precedent in deciding a legal affair.

The term *andhih-andhihan* derives from *endhih*, (1 to beat, overcome; 2 to take over, pre-empt; 3 to take s.o.'s seat by pushing them off). In the form used in the texts, i.e., *kandhih/kendhih*, it becomes 'to lose, get overpowered; pushed off the seat'. Paragraph 4 of the *Adilulah* classifies them as 'expressions of the *aksara*' (*ujaring aksara*).[4] The *andhih-andhihan* are positive models for winning a case in the sense that a one based on a concept lower in the validity scale will defeat a case based on a higher one. In short, the schema is a progression of types of evidence in which each is overruled by its successor. The universality of their acceptance is seen from the fact that they are repeated with little variation in most of our key manuscripts. A

4 Listed in the Combi *Surya Alam*, § 16, Add 12 329, § 6; IOL 99; Raffles, Appendix C; Berlin 402, § 48; Yasadipura, *Surya Alam*, Canto V, verse 5; as well as in LOr 7440 and 7442.

standard list of the hierarchy (X is overruled by Y as *tarka kandhih kéning patra* and so on) has been distilled from the relevant titles.

Table 4.2 Andhih-andhihan

	Literal translation	Interpretation
tarka tegesé ujar ing angrah	words of the plaint	accusation
kening déning (is overruled by):		
patra tegesé tutulisan	written documents	documentation
kening déning (is overruled by):		
saksi tegesé anangendi weruh	one who truly knows	witness
kening déning (is overruled by):		
bukti tegesé metu saking k. den-arah	that coming from the defendant	proof
kening déning (is overruled by):		
cina tegesé metu saking k. nganarah	that coming from the plaintiff	sign, mark
kening déning (is overruled by):		
satmata tegesé akéh kang weruh	many who know	generally known
kening déning (is overruled by):		
nyumana tegesé wangakuné	acknowledgment	confession
kening déning (is overruled by):		
parmana/ubaya tegesé layang sarta ing kartané	letter from the court	agreement
kening déning (is overruled by):		
parusa layang pangandika ing ratu	words of the king	sovereign power

Except for confession (*nyumana* or *anumana*), all terms formally derive from Sanskrit, although their meanings in the Javanese texts depart from Sanskrit usage. The hierarchical arrangement means that all things being equal, a suit based upon one higher on the scale would automatically be defeated by one lower down. A *tarka* affair is defeated by one based on *patra*, a *patra* one by a *saksi*, and so on down the scale. The lower on the list, the greater authority, with the sovereign's words (*parusa*) seen as the ultimate authority. But what happens if things were not equal? Is a strong *tarka* automatically defeated by a weak *patra* or even a very weak *saksi*? This loophole seems to have allowed ambiguous cases to be submitted to the court, subject to among other things the negative pre-judgments of the *uger-uger* discussed below. In other words, the lack of fixed or set principles (*agama*) brought such an affair to *drigama*, whose specialty was necessary judicial discretion based upon custom or experience.

The proclivity to use common Javanese words in an unusual manner tends to work against coming to any precise judicial definitions. Yet the general function of the paragraphs can be reconstructed with some confidence. In the first place the *aksara* are neutral. There are *aksara salah* and *aksara bener,* which derive from Hell or holy smoke. Whatever the exact reference of the latter, it is unreservedly positive. Reliance upon (*lungguh*) it leads to victory in quarrels (*padu*) and affairs of civil law (*pradata*); reliance on the other leads to defeat. In either case this is a simple statement of a causal relationship without recourse to moral judgment.

Aksara of the wrong

In the textual tradition *aksara salah* are more generally known as the *uger-uger* (pillar, post (to which s.th. is tied)). As a prop, support, or buttress it applied literally in the case of a door jamb or door post in the context of holding something up. It is the second meaning that draws our attention because it brings us back to the context of the tradition as instruments for settling cases/suits.

These are the reliance on the *aksara salah,* those which are termed *unger-ager* [*sic uger-uger*] of which there are eight affairs, that which is first ...

Table 4.3 Uger-Uger (aksara salah)

1	*Anyawadi*: differences between complaint and plea
2	*Akarya dési*: a person claiming to know, but in fact does not know
3	*Anir paksa*: a person who admits that he does not know
4	*Anir yukti karah*: unclearness of accusations or plaint[5]
5	*Panca-balah*: differences between plaint and defence and its support
6	*Atoyamarta*: untruthfulness in the testimony
7	*Maha-pralaya*: relying on a dead person[6]
8	*Akari wesi*: after submitting the *pisaid* continuing to suit, i.e. changing testimony[7]

Several points are of immediate interest. First, each of the *uger-uger* is introduced by the phrase 'the first (second, and so on) as made into a *sloka*'. As instruments of law their contents were turned into phrases. Fully half of them can be matched with phrases contained in the titles drawn upon here. Two of them – *anir yukti* and *maha-pralaya* – have come down to the present as proverbs or idiomatic expressions. Discussion of their linage and often radical changes in meaning during the interim is postponed to that

5 Coincides with the contents of no. 143, Suwarno, *Dictionary*.

6 *Ibid.*, no. 808.

7 LOr 7440, f. 192ff, supplemented by those of the *Senapati Jimbun* text (*Ibid.*, f. 125 ff), *Undhang-Undhang Luwangan* (*Ibid.*, f. 314ff), as well as those of the *Surya Alam* of Berlin 402 and the *Pepakem Tjerbon* of 1768.

of the much larger number of the Thirty *Prakara* in Chapter 6. While some of the terms stem from high Javanese (*krama*) with a possible Old Javanese derivation, more often they are *ngoko* words of everyday usage. None have a discernible Sanskrit origin. A more significant point is their function. As to be expected from precepts originating in the coals of Hell, they bring about defeat. At first glance they seem to describe formal defects or inconsistencies. In fact, the *uger-uger* do not so much weaken a case or suit as invalidate it. Key here is the fact that such deviations from the law require the plaintiff to compensate the defendant (nos. 1, 4-7) and are fined in addition.

As found in the legal traditions the message of the *uger-uger* seems clear. Those bringing a suit before the formal authority, the *sosoca ing negara* (the jewel of the land, i.e., the sovereign or his surrogate the *patih*), must conform to a set of standards known in advance through the requirements of the *uger-uger* and similar prerequisites. These include congruence between written documents recording the plaint and the plea – later texts specifically rule out making the one from the other – between documents, and between documents and witnesses. Witnesses must not only measure up in their actions, that is, they experienced or saw what they testify to, but also fulfil basic moral and physical standards in order to qualify as acceptable (cf. *Surya Alam*). If these standards were not met, the suit could not be accepted by the authorized legal body. In such cases this often carried an additional punishment of levying a fine (*dhendha*) on the initiator of an unsupported, and by implication false, case.

Rajâji mode

The third stage of the *aksara* presented by the *Jaya Lengkara* is marked by the transition to '... the meaning [of the terms]' (*tegesé/artinipun*) followed by an abbreviated epitome of the individual *aksara*, several of which cite the relevant *sloka*. Derived implicitly from the text's contents, Table 4.4 lists the functions of the *aksara* as legal instruments.

On the simplest level the *aksara* of this mode signify a division of labour between king and *kerta* with a single provision for the *pangulu/pengulu*. The first five (*badan*, *angin*, *banyu*, *bumi*, and *lintang*) expounded by *patihs* Kerta Basa and Sunduk Prayoga apply to courts of justice (*kerta*), the next six (*thathit*, *lék*, *bulan/segara*, *kilat*, and *srengéngé*) expounded by Anggas Kara, Niti Sastra, and Madana Sraya are coupled to sovereign authority; while *kukus* (smoke), also mentioned by Madana Sraya, is surrendered to the *pangulu*. Regardless of whether they were delegated, and thus handled by the *kerta* or *pangulu*, all ultimately fell under the responsibility and authority of the sovereign. If this was the only information available, then we would have little more than a nominal explanation. Fortunately, the title's following paragraphs repeat this information and, more important, add specific measures to be taken. Nearly half of them are backed by an appropriate *sloka*.

Table 4.4 ***Aksara*: punishment and *sloka***

Aksara	Punishment	*Sloka*
badan:	*dhendha paréntah* (*ing ratu*) punishment of the (king's) government	~
[*angin*:	~	~]
banyu:	*dhendha maduka sirat* (?): fine 40,000	*triyaksa dasa-gurem rahmé naksa, akarinayem padu wangsaranem, antamunih cawayahé*
geni:	*dhendha* of a *patih* on the king's orders	~
bumi:	*dhendha ginotama* (ultimate) punishment of a high minister; breaking the king's prohibitions	*ataneman ayag orem bona istri watem maling urap kanayaka kapala darma, kang sinatriya*[8]
kilat:	*dhendha lalayon* (death); fine 40,000	*anglima…*
thathit	*dhendha wisuna* (sowing discord): fine 80,000, meaning one attacking the government	*gawon lumepating papalang, tebuh tuwuh tumen ing sikilé tumenam ng kutané,*[9]
lintang	*dhendha sinembrana*: fine 40,000: enslavement of a patih (*paradhah*)	~
kukus	~	*dhendha upata* (oath); fine for lying to the *pengulu*
srengéngé	*dhendha jineraken* (confiscation): fine 80,000	*denta-denti, kusumah wersa, sari cakra* (Classic *Sloka*, no. 15),
[*lek* (?)	~	~]

In keeping with the *rajâji* mode, the *Jugul Muda*'s second vignette focuses on one of the most important functions of the 'science of kings', namely the duty to punish (*dhendha*). As experienced by King Mahapunggung this is a double-edged sword (or rod as the original meaning of *dhendha*). In order to preserve the *tata tantrem,* miscreants must be punished to prevent them preying on the kingdom's subjects (*bala*). On the other hand, the rod must be wielded justly and righteously on pain of retribution of the gods. In either case does concentration on *dhendha* constitute a departure from the traditions of Javanese law. Naked provisions for punishment – fines,

8 A variant of Classic *Sloka*, no. 10.

9 The first part is usually opened with *kebo*, see Suwarno, *Dictionary*, no. 673, which in turn is a paraphrase of Classic *Sloka*, no. 16.

enslavement, and death – imply a mandatory duty. As such they depart from the usual contents of the legal literature in which meting out of punishment is quite limited. They may be assigned (*wenang*), but rarely must be imposed and then only under well-defined conditions. The *rajâji* mode arms *aksara* with additional authorization through citation of a demanding *sloka*. They are, by definition, causal.

But here research runs against a logical constraint. If, as is implied, carrying out *dhendha* is done solely on sovereign authority, which is not documented, how do we know if or how it is applied? The answer comes from a couple of references found in the legal literature supplemented by indications of their workings within their application to cases involving Dutch East India Company officials. The two sources can be considered in turn.

Textual conformation that the *aksara* of Table 4.4 are, in fact, provisions for punishment, 'those that provide punishment' (*kang dados dhendha*), come from the *Cacad* § 2. The paragraph, adding some details by way of clarifying the crime/sin entailed, in principle duplicates the contents of Table 4.4. Exceptions are seen in the first and last, i.e., *badan* and *segara*, plus the possibly superfluous *angin* and *lék*, which are not mentioned by the *Cacad*. In any event, the clarification of these four are merely statements, without directives for legal action. Moreover, they concern respectively the 'conditions of the world', 'actions of the *kerta*', or 'punishment of the government'. Other provisions for punishment so far remain unclear. These include those authorized by *banyu: 'dhendha maduka sirat* (?)*', kilat: 'dhendha lalayonh* (death?)', and *lintang: 'dhendha sinembrana'* (punishment for frivolity?)'. All levy the same a fine of *catur wara* (40,000).

Case confirmation comes from attempts by Dutch officials to utilize the contents of Javanese law, at least as far as they understood it, to achieve East India Company ends. Several transcribed '*surat salaran*' (certificate of loss) are found in Company records pertaining to cases against local *mantri* occupying high positions in the Javo-Dutch administration. Only one deals directly with the *aksara*. '*Aksara geni'* was referred to in a 1717 case involving a Priangan Regent punished on the orders of the sovereign, at that time the Dutch East India Company. In fact, the punishment fit better with *aksara bumi* 'punishment of a high minister for breaking the king's prohibitions' or even *aksara lintang* entailing 'enslavement of a *patih'* brought on by his own actions. It seems likely that the *kerta* combined the meaning/intensions of three *aksara* in order to satisfy Dutch demands to hand down a ruling in a case where there was no claimant and the evidence was weak.[10]

10 State v. Puspa Nagara case of 1716-17, Hoadley, *Selective Judicial Procedure*, p. 37 ff.

Unfortunately, the few references do not allow fuller understanding the sovereign prerogative to punishment, one that stands in contrast to the usual conservatism in setting punishments. An, albeit vague, clue lies in the motivation for punishment or *aksara thathit*, namely *dhendha wisuna*, the crime/sin of 'attacking the government'. *Raja wisuna* is, in fact, one of the 'Six Tyrants' (*sad-atatayi*) mentioned frequently in legal tracts. The provision was employed by a Cirebon court in 1696 to convict a high-ranking minister, the *peranakan* Ki Aria Marta Ngingrat.[11] Again the punishment of death, commuted for political reasons to exile, fits better with *bumi* as the ultimate punishment, *kilat* (= death?), or even *srengéngé* with forfeiture of goods and freedom. In keeping with the prior example, the solution seems to have been forced by Dutch pressure to remove the minister. Ki Aria was not only of Chinese origin but also had been involved in the 'smuggling' of pepper, obviously not a punishable act under Javanese law. Hence there was recourse to punishments of acts seen as threatening the ruling authority, which fits the spirit rather than the letter of the law.

The implication is that the area of sovereign punishments somehow derived from a 'modernized' version of the *sad-atatayi*. From this it would follow that during the Independent Kingdoms period space was being created for a kingly power generally lacking in Javanese governmental traditions of the period. According to the texts, the ultimate punishments prescribed by the *astha dustha, astha corah*, and *sad-atatayi* could be applied in the period under consideration. Yet this begs the question of instruments for establishing that those actions had, in fact, taken place and the degree of culpability entailed. This is, of course, baring confession from the doer. Hence the *aksara*, and particularly the three 'sovereign *aksara*' singled out by the *Arya Dilah* § 1 – *bumi, srengéngé*, and *kilat* – resolved the problem by giving the sovereign a monopoly of rights to pre-empt judicial process. Given the fact that the period overlapped with expanding European control, including introduction of European-influenced rules and regulations, it seems likely that local potentates were attempting to imitate the type of unchecked sovereign power enjoyed by the newcomers.

Sloka support for *aksara*

To return to Table 4.4, it can be noted that the right-hand column turns to *sloka* proper. Punishments prescribed by five of the *aksara* are followed by

11 State v. Ki Aria of 1696, *Ibid.*, pp. 25-26.

citations of *sloka*. Regrettably they are without the type of internal clarification provided by the core vignette of the *Jugul Muda* and other titles. Three of them, *bumi*, *srengéngé*, and *kilat* are also singled out by the *Arya Dilah* and *Cacad* as descendants of the Medhang Kamulan legal tradition starting with King Angkarabasa, a predecessor of King Mahapunggung. For *aksara bumi* is repeated the 'sloka of kings', namely *giri jaladri* [...] *tanu* cited by Rangga Panjang Sora. It was one of the more important pieces of advice on how to live up to the demands of an ideal ruler. The definition of *aksara bumi* also reflects the contents of the *aksara* as a body. [*badan* = body of *aksara*?]. *Srengéngé* is linked with the well-known *sloka*: *denta-denti kusuma warsa sari cakra* (Classic *Sloka,* no. 15). The *Arya Dilah* provides a shortened version of this *sloka* as an attribute of a king who guards the realm (§ 4). Explanation of its meaning is not without poetic qualities. According to Winter, it draws a parallel between an elephant's tusk (*denta-denti*), which once fallen out cannot be re-grown, a flower (*kusuma*) once bloomed cannot be closed up again, and rain once fallen cannot be returned. They underline the finality of a legal decision; once made it cannot be altered. Less literary is a modern translation stating that it has the character of judgment.

> [T]hat which is true is to be condoned; that which is false, forgotten. Do not accept that which is false as true or the truth as false.[12]

Another states that it stands for:

> [T]rue justice that cannot be negotiated, modified, or changed: a just decision, situation, or action described as being like ivory or teeth growing naturally, a flower withering in the rain, or a weapon striking and killing a person.[13]

Much in the context of creating a moral philosophy, it adds that

> This was a piece of ideal Javanese morality that good leaders should apply in their efforts to create and maintaining justice in the society.

Another relatively easily understood *sloka* is that cited after the specification of *bumi*'s 'ultimate punishment'. This concerns a high minister violating the king's prohibitions. The actual *sloka* is none other than *tataneman* of Classic

12 Ngafenan, *Paribasan*, p. 34.
13 Suwarno, *Dictionary* no. 328.

Sloka, no. 10, a *sloka drigama* cited by Patih Jugul Muda to King Mahapunggung. In reaction to the king's inquiry about appropriate punishments in the case of Dustha and the eight *duratmaka*, Patih Jugul Muda interpreted the *sloka* as allowing the execution of a miscreant's wife along with her husband if she was actively engaged in the crime, i.e., theft of the golden image. For present purposes the phenomenon is important in showing the application of a pre-existing *sloka* to clarify and/or defend the ostensibly younger and more specific provisions of the *aksara*.

Somewhat more complicated is the case with *thathit* and *kilat*. There is some question if the two are separable. The dictionary definition of *thathit* 'lightening followed by thunder', renders *kilat* (flash of lightening) superficial. Yet several of the relevant manuscripts list them separately. *Thathit's* 'the king addressing his servants' is descriptive, although the *dhendha wisuna* for attacking the government is followed by an interesting *sloka*, namely *sragala* [*sic kebo*] *lumupat ing papalang* and *tebu-tuwuh ing socané* (*tumanem sikilé*). The first is 'a buffalo jumps over a wooden barrier at the entrance of its stall', which means 'a judge who defends his family members or who decides in favour of his family members despite knowing that they are guilty'.[14] According to Winter, who in principle agrees with the first, the second means roughly the same. Pooling the information leads to the conclusion that *kilat/thathit* concern high officials whose sheltering of relatives undermines the government.

The *sloka* quoted for *kilat* has defied interpretation. At most '*dhendha lalayon*' has association with death in some form. Lack of formal and nominal clarification of *aksara kilat* is, however, belied by its contents. 'Knowing the king's wishes before they are uttered' is not only a crucial piece of Javanese administration, i.e., foresighted loyalty, but also one repeated in other forms by the titles drawn upon in this work. While use of the specific term of '*kilat*' or lightening is limited to the *Jaya Lengkara* supplemented by the minor texts, its contents are repeated in most of the texts consulted in this work. For example, the Yogyakarta *Surya Alam* states that:

> He who is called [i.e., qualified] to be a *jaksa* knows before it is uttered that which is clear [either the law or the king's will] (§ 1).

The paragraph goes on to state that that which is known comprises the 'three *aksara*' (*aksara kang tigang/tri*). This is undoubtedly a reference to the three 'kingly *aksara*' – *bumi, srengéngé* and *kilat* – named in the

14 *Ibid.*, no. 673.

Arya Dilah and *Cacad* quoted above. The seriousness of the demand is emphasized by the following lines specifying draconian punishments for a *jaksa* '*Wira paksa*', that is a *jaksa* who does not carry out his duty justly. If so, his tongue shall be cut off and he will be banished from the realm, his return depending on his observing the *pepakem* consisting of the principles of the *aksara*.[15]

Aksara of a *Surya Alam*

Although the *Jaya Lengkara* and related texts provide the bulk of information on *aksara*, they are not completely absent from the *Surya Alam* legal tradition. One of the manuscripts from the Yogyakarta *kraton*, Add 12 329, provides a list of *aksara* not too different from that of the 'standard' *Jaya Lengkara* discussed earlier. Table 4.5 is based on folios 31v-32v of that title.

Table 4.5 *Surya Alam aksara* and punishments

These are the assigned punishments (*patrapené dhendha*) strengthening (*manggala-manggala*) the *aksara* which are assign the responsibility (*bubukan*).	
aksara brenggit (?)	*dhendha yèn menggala*, punishment of the leader: a person lying to his lord, falling under (*anggadoni*?) *raja wisuna*
aksara gadén (?)	*dhendha paréntah*, punishment of the government: a person nonchalant/disrespectful [to the government]
aksara banyu	*dhendha made*: a person denying the government (*anikakaken paréntah*) in suiting employs neither *jaksa* nor *patih*
aksara geni	*dhendha pepathi sa-aji ing pepatih*, a fine of 1 *laksa*: punishment of a *patih* praising himself
aksara bumi	[*dhendha*] *amemade ing ratu*, a fine *tumpesan sak rowangé*: secrecy from the king
aksara linthu	*dhendha sakarasané*, a person who takes suitable *tatrapa dadi* (?) measures for the country (*rekakaké negara*)
aksara gara	*dhendha wuwa*, punishment of 8 *laksa*
aksara lintang	*dhendha paradah-pinaradah*, bondage punishment *ameradah amaratakaken sabatré*
aksara kukus	*denda supata*, a fine of oath/promise
aksara grah [garah?] rata amot kang amis kawadhahan bacén (?)	

15 *Jaksa Wira Paksa* is named in the Combi *Surya Alam* § 2, Raffles IX, and Yasadipura Canto VI, verses 1-5.

Comparison with Table 4.2 reveals a rough correspondence in names, meanings, and punishments of those listed by the *Jaya Lengkara*. This applies mostly to *aksara banyu*, *geni*, *bumi*, and *kukus*, with *aksara brenggit* [*brenggéh* = false, perfidious] standing as an alternative to *aksara thathit*. However, for *aksara gadén*, *linthu*, *gara*, and *grah* there is no recognisable equivalent. *Aksara gadén* seems to touch on *aksara lintang* in relation to nonchalant or disrespectful (*sembrana*) behaviour, which may or may not be related to Add 12 329's *lintang* as the 'punishment of bondage'. *Aksara linthu* is likely the equivalent of *aksara kilat* of the *Jaya Lengkara*, while *aksara gara* (confusion, uproar) and *grah* (*garah* = to chat irresponsibly) remain unexplained.

Even so, some observations can contribute to understanding the *aksara* concept. First, the introductory sentence shows that the Add 12 329 *Surya Alam* follows the standard *aksara* of the *Jaya Lengkara* tradition. Second, there is an apparent ease of mixing elements from different traditions. That such was the case for *sloka* has been demonstrated earlier and will be so subsequently for *sinalokan* in Chapter 5 and vignettes in Chapter 7. That it was also the case for *aksara* tends to confirm the impression that traditional Javanese written law is based upon a collection of free-standing elements or paragraphs rather than on texts of fixed or even moderately consistent contents. This fits the basic character of *drigama*. Set texts with fixed contents, which were consulted by way of precedent, comes only with *agama*, more particularly *agama Islam*, and Dutch rule.

Although of a lesser dignity, no less revealing are indications in both the 'standard' *Surya Alam* and the verse rendition of Yasadipura. The introduction to the Yogyakarta title proclaims that it 'tells by means of a *pepakem* of *aksara* [contributing] to the *tirta* (water of life = prosperity) of the country (f. 72r)'. The grammatical form '-é' indicates that the *aksara* as related to the well-being of the land are the centre of focus. Only with a great deal of difficulty could this be interpreted as a 'compendium composed of letters'. Such would be a statement of the obvious. How else could it be written? A more likely interpretation is that the phrase indicates a compendium built up of legal precepts or principles. Indeed, § 1 following the introduction alludes to the qualifications of a *jaksa*. This must be a person in possession of 'the three *aksara* from 'the' *aksara* (*aksarané*)'. The same form is used for the definite article. This impression tends to be confirmed by reference to what could only be *aksara kilat*, namely 'knowing before it is uttered', one of the three *aksara* (with *bumi* and *srengéngé*) singled out as the most important by the *Arya Dilah* (§ 1) and repeated in a number of *Surya Alam* versions, including that of Yasadipura (Canto II, verses 8, 11).

Discussion

Because the function of the *aksara* within legal texts is limited to the Independent Kingdoms period, some reflection seems in order. The first point of note is that the *aksara* comprise neither a new nor an oral tradition. Gobius' observation of 1717 can only have been a repetition of information provided by the *jaksa*, Pangéran Arya Cirebon, or some other well-informed contemporaneous source. Following too blindly European observations can easily lead to misjudging the situation. From the above it seems clear that Gobius got it wrong, regardless of from whom he received it. More appropriate punishments for Puspa Nagara's shortcomings fell under *aksara bumi* 'punishment of a high minister for breaking the king's prohibitions' or *aksara lintang* 'enslavement of a *patih*' which was, in fact, declared by the Company. In any event by the early eighteenth century *aksara* were an established feature of the island's judicial tradition. Just how far back in time they go is impossible to determine. However, given legal texts' inherent conservatism – one of their functions is a senatorial effect – it seems likely that they had their origins in the post-Demak era. That they were part of a written tradition, as opposed to the oral *adat* first recorded by Van Vollenhoven and his disciples in the early twentieth century, again rests on Gobius' testimony of 1717.

If *aksara* were so much a part of Javanese written law, then why has their importance been overlooked? The answer lies partially with misdirected scholarly emphasis exacerbated by flexibilities in Javanese grammar. In consideration the sources at our disposal in Chapter 2 it was noted that the only translated and published law texts from the period were two versions of the *Surya Alam*, namely that found in Raffles' *History of Java* and the van der Hout translation. The fact that *aksara* are only mentioned in passing in the *Surya Alam* textual tradition makes it is easy to underestimate their importance, a factor supported by the structure of Javanese. Within the *Surya Alam* tradition *aksara* are often used as, or associated with, *prakara*, a point to which we shall return. In contrast, the text *par excellence* for *aksara*, i.e., the *Jaya Lengkara* and the minor texts emphasising the *aksara bener/salah*, a*ndhih-andhihan*, and the *uger-uger*, have neither been translated nor have attracted scholarly interest, much less become the object of research. One reason for neglecting the role of *aksara* in traditional written law is scholarly preference for texts lacking them.

Even so, the oversight by those responsible for the 1768 *Pepakem Tjerbon* is remarkable. The relative early date and the accepted view that it constituted the 'standard' of Javanese law conflicts with the partial absence of *sloka* and total absence of *aksara* in the meaning used here. The original compilers/translators of the mid-eighteenth century can be excused because of being a *jamur tuwuh ing sela* 'a mushroom growing on a stone',[16] an impossible task. They were expected to fulfil an unrealistic task of uniting the contents of authentic Javanese titles with Dutch Company demands. In practice the principles of local law had to give way to practical exigencies of foreign rule. The archives leave no doubt that the intention was to create a text for handling the legal affairs of the 'natives' by indigenous law, an ambition seemingly forgotten within a couple of decades. Apparently for the new rulers *aksara* and *sloka* did not offer immediately recognisable functions. Hence, they were omitted in the finished product. As a result, later researchers were confronted with an emasculated standard text.

Even more difficult to explain is how this lack could have been ignored in the textual edition of 1905. This was a half-century after the publication of Winter's *Javaansche Zamenspraken* and Keyser's comments as to the importance of the *sloka* phrases. More notable were the investigations of Brandes and Keyser leading to the transcription of several of the British Library manuscripts, in which *aksara* and *sloka* played an obvious role, as for instance LOr 6203. Even the Javanese text wed to the original Dutch of the *Pepakem* in the publication of 1905, i.e., the de Nooy text, must have contained many references to *aksara* and *sloka* which were simply left out in trying to match Javanese with the original Dutch text, ostensibly itself a translation of even earlier Javanese texts.

16 Suwarno, *Dictionary*, no. 529.

5 Sinalokan

While *sloka* tend to be over-rated, especially in the Berlin *Surya Alam,* and *aksara* locked into a dictionary meaning, *sinalokan* are almost invisible in the scholarly literature. This contrasts to their documented presence within most legal texts of the Independent Kingdoms era supplemented by a modest number of cases contained in the Dutch East India Company records. Equally perplexing, the titles containing *sinalokan* provide no textual clarification of the type seen in instances of explanations for *sloka* or clarifying context for *aksara*. This is with the partial exception of those found in the *Jaya Lengkara* created by a process of *kinawi,* i.e., being formulated in literary Javanese considered below.

The number of *sinalokan,* in fact, greatly surpasses the limited number of Classic *Sloka* or *aksara*. The *Jugul Muda* contains a dozen or so *sinalokan* in the title's second half. The *Jaya Lengkara* cites roughly the same number, albeit in a special form, and a smaller number are contained in the minor works as the *Adilulah, Arya Dilah,* and *Cacad*. These are, however, outnumbered by those cited in the *Luwangan Undhang-Undhang*. Each of that title's fifty paragraphs contains between one and three *sinalokan*. To these come the *sinalokan* expressed in two published didactic cases, as well as half a dozen or so resulting from judgments of the Cirebon-Priangan *jaksa* court of the early eighteenth century recorded by the Dutch East India Company archives. This makes their absence in the *Pepakem Tjerbon* text even more puzzling. The *Jimbun Slokantara II* contains mostly, but not exclusively, *sloka*. Less clear is why the Kartasura *Surya Alam* of ca 1737 terms the dozen or so cited phrases as '*sloka*', even though they are clearly *sinalokan*. Other versions of that title are exceedingly sparing of *sloka* and *sinalokan*.

A contributing factor must be the concept's grammatical ambiguity. *Sinalokan* are formed by the addition of the passive infix '*-in-*' plus a general suffix '*-an*'. Among other things, the latter specifies the 'means or instrument of the action'.[1] In the titles under consideration it can be read as 'made into *sloka* as an instrument', or 'as contained in the *sloka* [which follows]'.[2] An idea of how they functioned in relation to *sloka* is illustrated by the *Jugul*

1 Prijohoetomo *Javaansche spraakkunst,* pp. 76, 124.

2 An alternative explanation is that the text consists of the passive infix '*-in-*', plus the causative suffix '*-aken*' to make the passive causative, 'made from a *sloka*'. The tendency to read '*-aken*' as '*akan*' as written comes from the fact that the vignettes in fact do create a *sloka/sinalokan,* but via the verb of *kinawi,* 'to set into *kawi* (literary Javanese)'. This, however, holds true only for the autonomous *Jaya Lengkara* titles (Add 12 303, LOr 7440 and LOr 7410, etc.) and the Javanese text

Muda's opening vignette considered earlier. When asked by the king for his opinion on the transgressions of Dora and Sangkara, the *patih* quoted the *sloka*: '*sima* [...] *taru*'. The *sloka* implies that their death at each other's hands was an act of divine retribution, at the same time warning of the inevitable punishment for such 'disobedience' and/or 'defiance'. How this applied to more mundane human frailties is shown by the *Luwangan*'s § 18. It explains that one suiting over an alleged theft without having submitted a written complaint (*pisaid*) to the proper authorities was punished by a heavy fine. The description follows the legal decision, which has been expressed as a *sloka* to become a *sinalokan*. That is, the original phrase from the *Jugul Muda* has been modified. From the parable of a 'disobedient lion' (*singa bangga*) it has become a 'defiant/disobedient suit' (*padu bangga*), one which consciously defied legal praxis, thereby bringing about harsh practical consequences.

Sinalokan in the *Jugul Muda*

As noted earlier, the *Jugul Muda*'s primary commitment is to *sloka*. Yet the second half of the title as reported by the two Leiden manuscripts, supplemented by the *Serat anger: Jugul Muda* published in 1929, introduces the *sinalokan* genre. This takes the form of short vignettes dealing with the culpable acts committed by persons bearing the names of significant crimes. All the vignettes are closed by *sinalokan*, one for the perpetrator, often followed by another for accomplice(s). Concrete examples come from misdeeds as *corah* (theft), *walat* (violence), *sidhem-pramanem* (evasion), *sanggraha* (*sic sanggama* or illicit sexual relations), as well as some less easily identifiable. The first affair in this part of the *Jugul Muda* concerns *corah* (thief, bandit, evil person).

> Corah was well known for stealing water buffalo, horses, *kris*, and even cash. On being opposed by someone named Bégal (dacoit), Corah stabbed him, taking his *kris* and *dodot* (*sarong*) in the process. All this took place on the main thoroughfare. He even raided the market place and took the goods of several traders, caching them with his accomplices Karahita and Saeka. The victims, Ni Kuntil and Ni Sayak suited before the *pradata* (civil) court. As a result, the king ordered his body-guard, at that time

appended to the Dutch of the *Pepakem Tjerbon* paragraphs. By ignoring the Javanese equivalents, the compilation's editor, G.A.J. Hazeu, avoided the *sloka-sinalokan* conundrum.

> under the former *duratmaka*, Dustha, to arrest Corah. Expectably the king asked for advice from his *patih* concerning suitable punishments. Patih Jugul Muda declared that the crimes fell under *raja-dhendha* which prescribed monetary fines, in all amounting to 24,000.[3]

After the fines were levied, Corah and his mates were tagged by *sinalokan*. Corah was described as a *singa* (*sic sima*) *bangga andurkara amet mangsa* a tiger with a bad character seeking prey. As noted earlier, the *sinalokan* was originally a *sloka* with a modern interpretation as 'a person who rebels and commits a crime, such as killing someone, in order to obtain what he wants'.[4] According to the continuation of the sentence in LOr 7410 (f. 84r), Corah's accomplices Karahita and Saeka (names of two of the Eight Thieves) fell under the *sinalokan*: *asragalem* (*sic srenggala*) *atri dusthem amri boga jodanem*. According to Winter, 'This is the *sloka* of a person in contact with or being used by a *durjana*'. A modern interpretation is 'a dog stealing in order to feed an enemy [or warrior]'.[5] As with the first *sloka* of the *Jugul Muda*, the two *sinalokan* quote *sloka* verbatim. However, their identification as '*sloka*' ostensibly seems to have come from Winter, who identifies indiscriminately nearly all such phrase as such.[6] The originals have either not turned up or are contained in the *sloka*.

That both *sinalokan* fit the culprits' deed is not surprising. In keeping with the genre's character, the phrase is cited after guilt had been determined and punishment set. Thus, there was no need of interpretation to motivate punishment or resolution. *Sinalokan* describe guilt and set the sentence; they do not constitute its basis as do *sloka*. The simile nature of *sinalokan* is confirmed by the fact that the literal wording is readily translatable. Characteristic for the closing paragraphs of the *Jugul Muda*'s last section, the special nature of the infractions is explained. They had already been identified as offences punishable directly by the sovereign through anthropomorphic identification of actor with the nature of the crime – theft, violence, illicit sexual relations, etc. For example, Corah was punished for thievery to which a *sloka* is added, with or without modifications. In such

3 The vignette is found in LOr 7440, ff. 343-345 and LOr 7410, ff. 83v-84r.

4 Suwarno, *Dictionary*, no. 1460.

5 Winter, *Javaansche Zamenspraken*, vol. III, p. 183 and Ngafenan, *Paribasan*, p. 126.

6 The predominance of *sloka* identifications is probably due to the contents of the Kartasura *Surya Alam* (Berlin 402 and LOr 1832), which likewise names only *sloka*. Similar considerations may also account for the fact that Winter does not mention *aksara* or *sinalokan* at all and *prakara* only once and then in vol. 1, p. 418. Despite this, the *Jugul Muda* and *Slokantara* contain enough *sinalokan* to merit attention.

cases *sloka* phenomena function much as a simile by drawing parables to circumstances after the fact.

Similar conditions apply to the remainder of cases dealt with by the second half of the Leiden manuscript versions of the *Jugul Muda*. An almost predictable, second example of *sinalokan* is the affair of Tatayi. Not only does his name derive from an abbreviation of the *sad-atatayi* (Six Tyrants), thus anthropomorphically a *durjana*, but also he manages to carry out most of the misdeeds comprising that concept. More specifically, Tatayi had:

> set fire to Pun Prenah's house then poisoned Ki Sadah, kidnapped Ki Garadah, compounding his sins with the practice of sorcery, and stabbing Pun Astra.[7]

In contrast to the direct punishment by the sovereign prescribed by the *Agama* and similar texts of Java/Bali, in the Independent Kingdoms era the victims or next of kin had to file a suit before the king in order to have the case handled. As a result of the suit Corah – then head of the royal bodyguard – was sent to bind Tatayi and bring him before the court. On the advice of Patih Jugul Muda he was sentenced to a monetary fine (*yatra dhendha*), plus compensation. The case is capped by the *sinalokan*:

> *gajah* [*sic kenanga*] *andaka adurakara*
> 'A bull elephant disturbing' or 'a person taking pleasure in making disturbances'.[8]

The vignette provides another instance of a phrase used as a *sinalokan*, which has been reinterpreted by modern compilers as a *sloka* being used as a *sinalokan*. The end of the paragraph states that Tatayi was to replace Corah as head of the king's royal bodyguard. He was subsequently ordered to arrest Walat (violence) in the following vignette.

A third example of *sinalokan* in the latter half of the *Jugul Muda*, that of *sanggraha*/*sanggama* (sexual intercourse), is also mentioned in the *Luwangan* §§ 11, 31, & 35.

> There was a villager called Sanggraha who was owed a debt of 1000 by a fellow villager, Malecca (the unfortunate). When Sanggraha came to collect the debt Malecca's wife informed him that Malecca was not at

7 *Jugul Muda*, LOr 7440, ff. 349-351.
8 Respectively Ngafenan, *Paribasan*, p. 45 and Suwarno, *Dictionary*, no. 422.

> home. Subsequently Sanggraha behaved arrogantly, going so far as to lay hands on her. On his return, Malecca suited (*pradata*) Sanggraha before the king of Purwa Carita and was found guilty.

Sanggraha was singled out as an *andaka angunga(ng)s sari (baud) tan weruh ing baya,*

> Its meaning, as a wild buffalo sniffing flowers but not listening to the feeling of unease [caused by engaging in immoral behaviour]. The *sloka* concerns a man seizing another's wife.[9]

A modern version is explained as

> A [macho] man (*andaka* = bull) who flirts with someone or treats someone else's wife as his own (without realising the danger).[10]

The case also appears in the *Luwangan,* although with some unclear points. Paragraph 31 applies it to a man slipping into a woman's private quarters or *jamban* (bathroom (and toilet combined)), 'it is allowed that all his weapons be confiscated (*kapulungan* by a higher power)'. Given the texts' prohibitions against men having close contact with women who are not related, it is possible that it provided a sanction to be killed by the woman's next of kin.[11]

A final example of the use of *sinalokan* in the latter half of the *Jugul Muda* comes from the *Sidhem-Pramanem* vignette. Not one, but several *sinalokan* resulted from this vignette. It is built around the story of a dwarf and a hunchback. In the process of collecting taxes for the king they fell out over the division of the spoils and ended up killing one another. The incident was covered up by the villagers, who apparently hoped to profit from the collected booty. One of the main actors, Pun Sidhem (soundless, with nothing to be heard, i.e., guilt accruing from not reporting a crime), was tagged by what was apparently the original phrase, namely *camra (sic tambra) ambrik mangsa* or a speckled/albino carp and evil-smelling (*ambrik*) prey. The similarity in *sinalokan* shows the case to be parallel to one cited in the *Luwangan* (§ 3), which deals with a person who is accused of murder

9 Winter, *Javaansche Zamenspraken,* vol. III, p. 22.

10 Suwarno, *Dictionary,* no. 78.

11 Provisions which allow the injured party – husband or next of kin – to kill one guilty of improper sexual acts are found in, among others, Berlin 402, § 40 and the *Luwangan* discussed in Appendix IV, under '*Cendhala-Sanggraha*'.

three times but fails to respond. He is subsequently fined heavily. If clear guilt is established, he could be executed (*kisas*) and wife and children forfeited to the crown. This was confirmed by the same *sinalokan.*

To this was added another phrase, namely *anyet-anyulawéti singa wirodha pati krama yo(w)ana* (roughly): holding on to a secret, an infuriated tiger dies [*krama yowana*?]. A shortened variant of the last phrase makes better sense. This is *anyepa-anyulawéti baud tan weruh ing baya* or 'holding on to a secret not recognising the dangers', which was used to single out several of the village leaders who conspired to keep the murder hidden. In addition, several other leaders were tagged with parts of known *sloka*, as *tekèk mati déning ngulahé,* Classic *Sloka,* no 24, and a popular phrase *gana-léna rebut mangsa nista.*[12] The latter was followed by a modern vignette relating a cover-up at the village level. These are not repeated in *Luwangan* § 3, which also cites a *sinalokan* (after levying a fine) for the accused's master. It draws a parallel between him and a jackal (*sardula*) searching for prey or an ogre taking the form of a virtuous person (*buta mangrupa sadhu*).

The introduction to the somewhat ambivalent genre of *sinalokan* could have easily extended to the dozen or so vignettes from the second part of the *Jugul Muda*. However, a more useful approach is to delve into the distinguishing characteristics of their least complicated features. As *ex post facto* clarifications in the manner of a simile, their text is straightforward. It can be read literally, which greatly eases translation by dispensing with textual exegesis. This is reinforced by the fact that *sinalokan* tend to be one-off affairs, a feature congenital to their incorporating parts or, not infrequently, whole *sloka* as explanatory phrases. The last point underlies the near impossibility of attempting to gather the *sloka* phenomena into watertight compartments purely of the basis of form. Function seems to be a better indicator.

Other sources of *sinalokan*

Consistent with text-genre relationships, specialized aspects of *sinalokan* are associated primarily, but not exclusively, with individual sources. Closest to the *sinalokan* of the *Jugul Muda* is the much younger *Luwangan* title. An additional source of information on *sinalokan* is, surprisingly enough, found in the records of the Dutch East India Company. As a by-product of

12 The first part of no. 430 meaning '[careless] men that die fighting with each other over their prey [are gone without a sound]', Suwarno, *Dictionary.*

monitoring Javanese affairs, the Dutch archives contain relatively detailed data on a half-dozen cases in which *sinalokan* were used to complete actual legal affairs handled by the Javo-Dutch courts of the early eighteenth century. Another source, which will be considered under vignettes in Chapter 7, consists of two didactic cases from the era's titles. Last and by no means least, a third class of *sinalokan* consists of those produced as a result of a process of *kinawi,* that is made into literary Javanese. According to the textual tradition, it documents one way in which *sinalokan* were created, at the same time suggesting a parallel means of creating *sloka.*

Luwangan sloka

In contrast to the *Jugul Muda*'s dedication to pre-existing *sloka* with *sinalokan* derivations appended to vignettes, the *Luwangan* contains only *sinalokan.* These conclude short paragraphs focusing on commonly arising affairs. In the LOr 7410 version the subjects are further indicated by key words written in the left-hand margin of the manuscript. Their completeness extends to multiple *sloka.* One is for winners, corresponding to a *jayapatra,*[13] in the Independent Kingdoms period called a *surat kukudung;* one for losers, an almost identical *surat salaran;* and often a third for the master involved. Concern for the loser(s), as well as the winner, was part of the self-fulfilling character of traditional Javanese law. Whereas victors seldom need incentive to carry out the terms of the ruling, it was crucial that it be accepted by the losers in order to avoid the necessity of evoking instruments of enforcement, which in any event were not normally part of the island's governmental instruments.

On first reading, the *Luwangan* gives the impression of a random listing of misdemeanours and crimes. This includes prescribed resolutions and/or punishments sealed by the appropriate *sinalokan.* Two have been discussed earlier. These include the *sima bangga* [...] *taru* and *mustika brahmara* [...] *ngalun-alun* phrases found in the first part of the *Jugul Muda* and repeated in *Cacad* § 4. Confusingly they are referred to as *sloka,* which shows the ease with which *sloka* could be appropriated in part or wholly by *sinalokan.* According to the marginal notations in LOr 7410, the *Luwangan* contents touch on such elements as murder (*mamateni* § 3), robbery (*bégal* § 4), stabbing (*suduk* § 6), sorcery (*neluh* § 7), as well as 'the crime of silence' (*sidhem papatih* § 16), ending with cases not allowed to be tried due to

13 Hoadley, 'Continuity and change'.

prohibitions on *riba* (usury) (§ 46). Somewhat more numerous are instances of parts of *sloka* incorporated into *sinalokan*. A telling example comes from the *sloka*: *lurung buntu*, which means 'a court case that cannot proceed because of insufficient evidence and [or] lack of witness.[14] It is found in the *Luwangan* (§ 48) with reference to a case of theft in which the homeowner is passive. The text adds that 'the miscreant's crime is caused to be lost (*dustha mangilangkan*)'. According to a judgment of a Javo-Dutch court in 1717 discussed below, it suggests that the whole process shows the danger [uncertainty] of accusations (*kelebet tarka baya*). Again, the modified phrase is purely descriptive and has been tailored to fit the specific occasion.[15]

Closer inspection of the *Luwangan*'s fifty or so paragraphs reveals a more ambitious plan of integrating older judicial concepts into the context of the *sloka* phenomena. This is seen most clearly in the *sad-atatayi*. As documented in Appendix IV, these seem to derive from Old Javanese legal precepts, which in the Independent Kingdoms era were transformed into *sloka*.[16] On the basis of similar wording – the actual rubrics as *sad-atatayi, sanggraha/sanggama, astha corah,* etc. are not cited directly – and related end phrases, it becomes clear that the *Luwangan* was attempting to '*sinalokan*-ize' such concepts. Paragraphs 2-12 list the *sad-atatayi*, albeit in more numerous variant forms and overlapping definitions, in order to turn them into recognizable *sinalokan*. The *sloka* of three *aksara* – *kilat/thathit, bumi*, and *srengéngé* seen as key terms by the *Arya Dilah* (§ 1) – are likewise co-opted as implicit *sinalokan* in the additional paragraphs listing the *aksara bener* (*andhih-andhihan*, §§ 51-52) and *aksara salah* (*uger-uger*, § 54), both from LOr 7440. The *astha corah* are given block *sinalokan*, one for the first seven as named in the *Luwangan* and one for the last three. And finally, the *sanggraha* (illicit sexual intercourse) provisions, consistently 'named' (*arané*) in other texts are transformed to *sinalokan*, whose meaning reinforce the nature of the transgressions. Because '*sinalokan*-ification' of the *sad-atatayi* is the most comprehensive, it is worth pursuing further. Table 5.1 sketches the contrast. The left-hand column gives the *Luwangan* paragraph number, the Javanese term, and the relevant *sinalokan*; the right-hand one lists the equivalents drawn from the legal literature of the period.

14 Suwarno, *Dictionary*, no. 796. See also Winter, *Javaansche Zamenspraken*, vol. II, pt. 3, no. 356.

15 *Jimbun Slokantara* III: § 41, *slokaning karta: lurung buntu dustha mangilangkan*.

16 See *Kuntarakara* § 16 and Berlin 402/van der Hout § 42. Old Javanese evidence comes from citations of specific parts of the six elements in tenth- and fourteenth-century inscriptions, as seen in discussion of *amok* (blind attack) and *mumpang* (molester of women) from the Kaladi inscription and all three categories by implication in the 'Ferry Charter'.

Table 5.1 Luwangan sinalokan

Luwangan sinalokan	*Pepakem Tjerbon*, p. 54-55 Berlin/van der Hout, § 42
§ 2 *krida: dana rasa sari baya,*	– [adultery]
§ 3 *maténi: tambra belang ambri mangsa anyet*	– [murder]
anyulawéti singa wirodha pati krama yojana (master): *sradhula ngamét mangsa, ambina pati buta mangrupa sadhu*	
§ 4 *bégal: ambima krama kredita amangsa kala*	– [robbery]
§ 5 *maling: mustika brahmara corah, titir pinajarakan* *surak ing ngampuhan mati déning angalun-alun*	– [theft]
§ 6 *suduk: dana prana…*	– [stabbing]
§ 7 *neluh: sima wirodha…*	[*ekawarna* or sorcery]
§ 8 *maliya: …?*	[*raja wisuna?* = slander of betters]
§ 9 *amok: ambima krama…*	[*awad akara* or amok]
§ 10 *upasi: angumbar wisa…*	[*awesade* or poisoner]
§ 11 *murugul: anggora-ga(n)da krama…*	– [sexual assault]
§ 12 *telik: sata angem muli wis…*	– [accomplice of a spy]
obong: angumbar pawaka…	– [arson]

Two paragraphs whose *sinalokan* have already been introduced (§§ 3 and 5) provide specific examples.

3.

When a person is suspected (*tarka*) of killing [or ordering to kill], if the accusation [has been raised] two or three times, [he is] not allowed to pursue (*idhep*, obedience to) a defence, but is fined 80,000; if it is certain (*nyata*) that he killed, he receives a capital sentence, a sentence of death (*kisas*). His wife and children are forfeited to the crown.

The *sinalokan*:

Tambra belang ambri mangsa, anyet-anyulawéti singa wirodha pati krama yowana

A speckled carp and evil-smelling prey hide the truth, an angry lion dies[?].

His master is fined 80,000. The *sinalokan*:

Sradula ngamet mangsa, ambima pati, buta mangrupa sadhu

A jackal seeking prey dies violently, an ogre appearing virtuous.

5.

When a person is suspected of violent theft, if it [the accusation] has been brought a second time before the court, let alone a third time, [he is] not allowed to pursue [the defence] and is fined 80,000 by the sovereign.

If it is brought before the *patih* (*kang dadi sosoca ing nagara*) and the court includes it with *lokika* (indications of guilt), double restitution is demanded. The meaning of *lokika*, there is someone who knows of the evil deed. If the person falls under the authority of *tidarsa* [a form of double indemnity], the entire sum of that taken must be restored. If it is certain that he has stolen, he is fined 80,000.
The *sinalokan*:

> *mustika brahmara corah titir pinajaraken surak ing nga(m)puhan mati déning alun-alun*
> [The presence of] mice and bees as discordant [elements] (*corah*) [should] trigger the alarm, [even with] supernatural powers (?) [such miscreants] die because of their own actions (cf. Classic *Sloka*, no. 2).

That the *sad-atatayi* were not the only concept '*sinalokan*-ized' is attested to by parallel developments in that of *sanggraha/sanggama* (adultery), as well as with the *aksara* and *astha corah*. As named in Berlin 402 (§ 20) under the rubric '*sanggraha*' a half-dozen seemingly common culpable acts are singled out. As discussed in Appendix IV, they include speaking in private with a woman who is not a relative without purchasing anything, termed *kamarga baya*, picking up a flower dropped from a woman's hairdo, *kembang baya*, relieving oneself at the same place as a woman, *katahi baya*, and washing a man's *dodot* (*sarong*) or offering a change of clothes. All were considered connected with illicit sexual intercourse. They are punished according to the wishes of the woman's executor (*wakil*). What the *Luwangan* has added to these acts, loosely identified as *sloka* in the Berlin text, is a *sinalokan*, often with the nature of the sin woven into the phrase. In a few cases *Luwangan sinalokan* continue in the line opened by the *Jugul Muda sinalokan* vignettes, as for example the former's § 31.

31.

If there is a man slipping into a woman's bathroom, it is allowed to confiscate his weapons [*kris* as a symbol of nobility],
the *sinalokan*:

> *andaka angungang sari baud tan wruh ing baya*
> Its meaning, as a wild buffalo sniffing flowers.

The *sinalokan* is the same as used in the vignette concerning Pun Sanggraha, although with a somewhat different narrative content. A similar replication is seen in *Luwangan* § 16 concerning *sidhem papatih*, which quotes the same *sinalokan* as the *Jugul Muda*'s vignette concerning Pun Tidhem. An interesting difference is that the longer version for *sidhem papatih* is split into two parts in the *Jugul Muda*. The first part, the speckled carp with evil-smelling prey (the tax thereby collected from the villagers) applies to the two tax collectors, the second one conspiring to keep a secret without knowing the danger fits with the actions of the villagers.

A slightly different fate befell the *astha corah*, illogically increased to ten in the *Luwangan*. The first seven are provided with a joint *sinalokan*, another one to the last three (§ 44). And finally, *sinalokan* are added, with a bit of clarification to the '*sloka*' cited in the *Jaya Lengkara* description of *aksara kilat/thathit, bumi*, and *srengéngé*.[17] The possibility of a '*sinalokan*-ization' of *sloka* is as near a nonsense phrase as one can find.

But why it was felt necessary to transform existing concepts to *sinalokan?* At this point all one can say is that it follows a similar [earlier?] tendency to re-phrase such concepts in *sloka* terms. The authenticity of the process is strengthened in the case of the *sad-atatayi* by the fact that the concept is documentable from Old Java. Hence its new form must mean that it is an innovation of the Independent Kingdoms era. With the remainder it seems likely that such was also the case.

Although inconclusive, discussion of *Luwangan sinalokan* adds to our understanding the phrases. Important here is that they conform to the basic principles of the genre. Even when co-opting pre-existing *sloka* or parts thereof, they function as after-the-fact simile. They also illustrate the facility with which parts of the *sloka* DNA could be re-assembled to make *sinalokan* to fit a specific affair. Perhaps most significant, *sinalokan* are not only spread throughout the era's legal textual tradition but also were employed in the course of practical litigation where *sloka* would have been expected. Examples are found in the extant sources, here those of the Dutch East India Company considered in Chapter 7. 'Practice'.

Kinawi

From the above the question becomes how phrases were pasted together from *sloka* parts. A partial answer comes from the special type of *sinalokan* documented by the *Jaya Lengkara*. The Ki Awas v. Ki Samar case introduces this class of *sinalokan*. Information on the affair comes from two independent sources. The first is the middle part of the *Jaya Lengkara*, more

17 Parenthetically §§ 51-52 and 54 of the LOr 7410 version repeat the list of *aksara bener* or *andhih-andhihan* and *aksara salah* or *uger-uger*.

specifically nos. 13 and 18 of the case summaries cited by most versions of that title, primarily Add 12 303, f. 29r. It is also found in the *Pepakem Tjerbon* section entitled,

> Diverse rendering of procedure, together with various laws drawn from the *Jaya Lengkara pepakem.*[18]

A second and somewhat more complete source is an autonomous *salaran* found in LOr 7440 (ff. 201-207). In describing legal procedure used, including the *sinalokan* at its end, the 'didactic' *salaran* is indistinguishable from authentic documents found in the Dutch East India Company archives. In addition to being included in a manuscript containing primarily legal titles, among others the *Jaya Lengkara*, what ensures that the affair is a didactic one is that it was handled by a *jaksa* court headed by Wiranata, a well-known figure in the kingdom of Medhang Kamulan. It will be recalled that the kingdom was seized by Aji Saka, who is credited with introducing the Javanese alphabet with which he composed the first ever *sloka.* Jugul Muda was its most famous *patih* and King Jaya Lengkara presided over the great durbar there leading to the acceptance of *aksara* and *drigama.*

Both sources relate that the case turned on a controversy over a pair of water-buffalo. They were claimed by Ki Samar (vague, obscure [...]; 2 worried, apprehensive) after borrowing them from Ki Awas (able to see, sighted [...]; 3 alert, on the lookout). Despite claiming ownership of the *kebo,* when asked Samar could not describe the animals. According to the manuscript version, the plea thus fell under two of the *aksara salah* or *aksara* of the wrong, namely *anir yukti karah* (unclearness of plaint) and *toyamarta* (untruthfulness in testimony), named in Table 4.3, nos. 4 and 6 respectively. As a result, Ki Samar was felled with a losing *salaran* and further degraded by being identified with the *sinalokan*: *kinajeng tumémpél ing bom, anyangking lacak ing kuntul asembada alayang.* Even though it is repeated at greater length by the *Luwangan* in § 26, its meaning and significance is not entirely clear. A rough paraphrase is that its intention is stuck to the sky (alternatively, dry grass) following the trail of a will-o'-the wisp (*kuntul alayang*). *Kuntul alayang* (a white heron flies), is an expression for something that is impossible. For Ki Awas, the winner, the *sinalokan* was *catur sadarana amarti.* It is repeated in both the *Luwangan* §§ 20, 39, which involve false claims, and the *Cacad* § 10, used as a *sloka* for the

18 *Pepakem Tjerbon*, pp. 71, 78-79.

winners of suits. It can be understood as: the four steadfast expressions, which are true to the plaint.

The much shorter version of the Ki Awas case from the *Jaya Lengkara,* no. 13 of Add 12 303, and the *Pepakem Tjerbon,* also no. 13, seems to be a summary of the manuscript version provided by LOr 7440 with a few differing details. Neither version is included in the Dutch narrative. The *sinalokan* closing them reads *dadamar tanggal pisan awas yén kasamaran mantri désa sadaya,* that from the *Pepakem*: *andamar lintang asulu tahun awas wutuh cacad sambat ing nyala yén kasamaran.*[19] In both cases the *sinalokan* are woven around the names of the actors, as well as the two *kebo* named Damar Wulan and Salu Lingtang. What is recognisable and must have been for the users of the manuscripts, is the apparently older *sloka: adedamar tanggal sapisan kapurnaman* 'while using the dim light of the moon on the first day of the Javanese year, suddenly the full moon shines brightly'. The first part refers to Samar's (false) claims, which in the clearer light (the recognition of the distinguishing characteristics of the *kebo*) 'suddenly find(s) a way out of trouble [i.e., the case is solved]'.[20]

A recurring issue is the role played by the *sloka* phenomena, here *sinalokan,* in legal affairs, textual, didactic, or actual. Their most obvious contribution was to clarify the affair through context. In the present instance the *sinalokan* draws a parallel between the darkness before the judicial handling and the light afterwards as a revelation of true justice (*kaadilan*). The impact of the message is strengthened by its literary flavour. This seems to be a common characteristic for *sinalokan,* thereby raising them above the level of prosaic similes or proverbs. A complication in this context comes from the *kinawi* phrases. In them the apparent aim was to integrate within the phrase the names of the actors, thus leaving less room for words conveying the meaning. While the literary tone increases impact, it simultaneously makes it more difficult to unravel the *sloka* origins of the resulting phrases' respective parts.

According to the LOr 7440 *Jaya Lengkara,* the practice of weaving the names of the actors into *sinalokan,* themselves often composed of recognisable phrases, was done by the court (*kerta*) handling the case. The prime example is the first vignette, quoted in *The Archive of Yogyakarta*. It concerns

19 If it could be established that the LOr 7440 version was the eldest, then we would have a good example of the procession from vignette, most likely ultimately deriving from an actual case, to incorporation into compilations of legal writings as the *Jaya Lengkara* and to a lesser extent the *Surya Alam*. Here we can only note the possibility.

20 Suwarno, *Dictionary,* no. 6.

the suspected misbehaviour of the painter Sungging Panuksma and the wife of Anggas Kara, Ni Prana, who was sitting for a portrait.

> This is the situation of one who paints (another's wife). In the land of Me(n)dhang Kamulan lived a man called Ki Anggas and his wife Ni Prana. Due to her exceeding beauty Ki Sungging Panuksma wished to make a painting of her. During the work a drop of paint accidentally made a black spot on the breast of Ni Prana. When the painting of his wife with a black spot on her breast was seen by Ki Anggas he was shaken by jealous anger. Subsequently Ki Sungging Panuksma was found stabbed to death at Ki Anggas' house. After conferring with the court and all the ministers of Me(n)dhang Kamulan, Patih Ma(n)dana Sraya declared Ki Anggas to have lost his case [i.e., he was responsible for the death of Ki Sungging Panuksma]. As such he fell under the penalty of *raja-dhendha* [crown punishment] and a fine of *asta-wara*.[21]

The core of the vignette is a recognisable folk motive with examples from the Independent Kingdoms era. It is repeated in the story of Ki Jaka Prabangkara from the *Babad Jaka Tingkir* and more recently in Sindhunata's Indonesian novel *Putri Cina* from 2007.[22] The difference between them and that found in the *Jaya Lengkara* is that at the vignette's close the names of the persons involved have been intertwined to create a rubric. The result is 'this is called, *anggas prana anuksma*'. It alludes to the fact that interference in the relation between the couple Ki Anggas-Ni Prana and Ki [Sungging] Panuksma resulted in the latter's death.

However, the *Arya Dilah,* of LOr 7440 (ff. 157-158), contains another interpretation. It suggests that Ki Anggas' regret was false. The full reading of the *sinalokan* in § 6 is: '*ang(g)as prana sandhi upaya krama yojana*'. The addition of *sandhi upaya*, 'a hidden trick or scheme' and *krama joyana* 'healthy marriage' changes the vignette's intention. *Angas* (one who seems brave but is afraid), that is, a bluff; *prana* (heart, innermost feelings; 2. *lit* breath, breathing) and *suksma* (soul, life) are the literal meanings. On this basis the conclusion can be drawn that Ki Sungging Panuksma's life was taken by a fearful Ki Anggas from the cravings of his innermost feelings of vengeance.[23] In any event, the phrase *anggas prana* underlines our depend-

21 Carey & Hoadley, *Archive of Yogyakarta*, vol. II, p. 90.

22 Florida, '*Babad Jaka Tingkir*', Canto III, verses 26-30, cited in *Writing the Past*, p. 108ff. and Sindhunata, *Putri Cina,* respectively.

23 A puzzling detail is that in the *Pepakem Tjerbon,* p. 71, the roles were somehow reversed, which makes little sense. The de Nooy manuscript adds the *sinalokan* and attributes it to the *Jaya Lengkara*.

ence upon vignettes for arriving at the intended meaning/message. While *sloka* appended to cases are common in the era's texts as the *Adilulah, Arya Dilah, Cacad,* and *Luwangan*, there seems little overlap with those of the *Jaya Lengkara*.

But how did such a phrase come into being? A clue is provided by reconsideration of the *Jaya Lengkara*'s handling of the Sungging Panuksma-Anggas Prana affair. The Add 12 303 version (ff. 20v-21r) states that the *sinalokan anggas prana anuksma* was formulated by the court (*kerta*) at the conclusion of its deliberations. The Javanese reads: *kinawi* (lit. 'made into *kawi*' via the infix -in-), namely rendered into a (high-sounding) Old Javanese verse (*kawi*) collectively by the assembled officials' (*déning para nayaka sadaya*). Many of the text's two dozen vignettes end in this manner. If they were only rubrics, in that their meaning was (*tegesé*) so-and-so or they were named (*arané*) such-and-such, they are of only passing interest. However, in several of the vignettes as the present one the court not only coined a phrase/verse on occasion of the decision (*kinawi déning kerta*) but also formulated an appropriate *sinalokan*. For example, in the second vignette of the *Pepakem Tjerbon* the case turns around the '*panca sadarana*' or five *force majeure* outside one's control – fire, flood, seizure by the king, taken by an enemy, and loss by theft – which by accident destroys something held in pawn. This freed the pawn taker from legal responsibility (§ 4). Again, a *sinalokan* was created through weaving together the names of the participants *sembada binabaraken ing tidhem pramanem,* or that which had been kept hidden by Sembada was made public.[24] Moreover, of the *Jaya Lengkara* (Add 12303)'s twenty odd vignettes the process of *sinalokan* is mentioned in some fourteen. Several of the sub-texts likewise contain *sinalokan*.[25]

24 The moral seems to be a condemnation of secret or double dealings by the main figure in the vignette, Sembada. If this is the same Sembada referred to in the Aji Saka vignette which opened the chapter, there seems to be a conflict in meaning. More likely, the Sembada is that of the Dora-Sembada expression of 'a cover-up lie', Robson and Wibisono, *Javanese-English Dictionary*, also mentioned in connection with the § 22 of the *Cacad*. The last part of the *sloka*, from *s(t)idhem pramanem*, is not only a *sloka* proper but also one of the few phrases originating from the older Javanese legal literature as one of the most serious of offences.

25 In the *Cacad*, which to some extent combines the contents of the *Jaya Lengkara* and *Surya Alam*, virtually all the paragraphs end with in *sinalokan*. These are rarely identifiable from other titles.

6 Prakara

The fourth component of traditional Javanese law consists of *prakara*. While *sloka, aksara,* and *sinalokan*, are specialised, each having their own consistent core, *prakara* (*perkara* ng *prakara* kr 1 matter [...] 3 lawsuit case) are derivatives. Albeit in abbreviated or random form, they repeat, quote, or embroider on phrases identified as belonging to other *sloka* phenomena. For example, *sloka* are not uncommonly included under both the standard 144 *prakara* items as, for example, in the Combi *Surya Alam* § 11 nos. 19, 20; § 14 no. 6; and § 15 no. 1; as well as in those standing outside the standard 144 as §§ 24, 29, 34 no. 3, and 36. If the Berlin *Surya Alam* is included with its mixing of *sinalokan* and *sloka,* several dozen full-fledged *sinalokan* are recognisably listed as *prakara*. Equally common is the inclusion of *aksara,* both *aksara bener* (*andhih-andhihan*) and *aksara salah* (*uger-uger*) within *prakara*. In the latter case they are listed under the Twenty *Prakara* in the Yogyakarta *Surya Alam* § 11 as a block mixed with other concepts such as *corah, tatayi,* enumeration of the scourges (*gegetheng*) in Classic *Sloka,* no. 6, and vignettes such as Ni Indun, etc. Because they are copies or representations, a great number of them have come down to the present. *Sloka* are thereby transformed from pithy phrases into idiomatic expressions and proverbs. Of the Thirty *Prakara* (Table 6.1) nearly half of them have found their way into modern Javanese proverbs. This argues that *prakara* were both shorthand for *sloka* phenomena of traditional Javanese texts and the source of future proverbs.

By way of documenting the first point, namely *prakara* borrowing from other *sloka* phenomena, a small, but revealing number of examples can be considered. The Twenty *Prakara* (§ 11) from the Yogyakarta *Surya Alam* provides an appropriate starting point. It includes as the next to last item the common *sloka/sinalokan*: *adedamar tanggal sapisan kapurnam*. The phrase's original emphasis is the figurative shift from the dim light of a new moon to the brightness of a full one. The message is illustrated in the Ki Samar v. Ki Awas vignette presented in Chapter 2 under didactic *sinalokan*. The narrative of the *Pepakem Tjerbon* (nos. 18, 13) illustrates how the darkness surrounding the claim of Ki Samar (vague, obscure) was dispelled by the veracity of Ki Awas (able to see, sight, proof). Modern compilers explain this as a *bebasan* (saying, set expression): when the lamp becomes brighter, then the victory finishes the suit, alternatively: using the illumination of the rising moon, suddenly comes the light of the full moon [which clarifies things]. From the natural parallels to practical jurisprudence comes another interpretation, 'to suddenly drop charges that have been brought against another in a court case (because of feelings of sorrow/pity).[1] Functionally the *sloka/sinalokan* has been transformed into a *prakara* simile. At least one modern commentator has re-interpreted it in even more general terms as '...to suddenly find a way out of trouble',[2] thus giving it broader application.

Another common *sinalokan*, which has been drafted into defining a *prakara* apophthegm, is found in the 'Seventeen *Prakara'* (§ 14 no. 6) of the Combi *Surya Alam*. The original *sloka* describing one being hoisted on one's own petard, so to speak, is re-cycled as a partial explanation of the otherwise incomprehensible *akarya walang* (the work of a locust[?]). As in the case of *sanggraha*, the narrative surrounding *akarya walang* seems divorced from reality. In fact, the paragraph's contents follow that of a didactic legal vignette from the *Serat Arok*. In it the main actor, Ki Japlak, literally got away with murder by drawing upon the rules originating from the formulation of the *akarya walang prakara* from the *Surya Alam*. The vignette, to be discussed in Chapter 7, has been considered elsewhere.[3]

A similar process is observable with known *sinalokan*. A particularly telling example is found in the Fifteen *Prakara* (§ 15 no. 13), also from the Combi *Surya Alam*. There is found the *prakara*-like *sinalokan: sima bangga abima-paksa angrusak sdana* or disobeying/arrogant tigers [*sic* lions], using force (like Bima) destroys property. The paragraph adds the explanation ('*artiné*, its meaning) *wong anguculaken babadan déréng pedhot celatuné* or a person freed from bonds [from being arrested] before the case is broken off. It makes little sense without supplementary information. Typically, this comes from a vignette. In the present instance clarification is found in the *sinalokan* concluding the case of Ki Walat (retribution) in the second half of the *Jugul Muda*. In the LOr 7440 version (f. 356) the arrogant tiger/lion destroys the *pradata* or civil case. The explanation is found in that vignette in which Ki Tatayi confesses to being responsible for the destruction, thus freeing Ki Walat by destroying the case against him. This fits better with the *Surya Alam's* explanation.

Change in wording reflects a shift in the legal instrument's function. In the *Jugul Muda* it was cited by the *patih* at the conclusion of his investigation and the sovereign's response; in the *Surya Alam* it had become a defence, which resulted in the suit's defeat. Even § 15's cryptic reference to freeing

1 Suwarno, *Dictionary*, no. 6. See also Darmasoetjipta, *Kamus Peribahasa Jawa*, no. 3; Ngafenan, *Paribasan*, p. 9; and Hariwijaya, *Kamus Idiom Jawa*, p. 2.

2 Suwarno, *Dictionary*, no. 6.

3 Hoadley, 'Literature as Law'.

the suspect, Ki Walat, before breaking off the suit fits into the *Jugul Muda*'s vignette. Walat was ordered to be freed by the *patih* prior to sentencing, at which time no plea/suit (*pradata*) by the injured parties was allowed. This contrasts to the preceding vignettes of Pun Corah and Pun Tatayi and the succeeding ones of Tidhem, Pramanem, Sanggraha, etc. in the second half of the *Jugul Muda* text. The procedure is not unique. As we shall see in the following chapter on vignettes, several versions of the standard *Surya Alam* build upon the *sinalokan* concerning the question of seizing lands and end up by repeating the *sloka* and even strengthening *pramana* (II clear and evident) as the goal of the *aksara bener.*

Along with *sinalokan*, *aksara* are also regularly repeated in the *prakara* of the Yogyakarta *Surya Alam*. The first paragraph (§ 1) concerning *jaksa* behaviour contains a phrase which can only refer to *aksara kilat.* It opens with 'He who is [worthy of being] *jaksa* is one who knows [the king's will] before it is uttered.' This is followed by a reference to the three *aksara* by naming *aksara bumi* and *aksara srengéngé* in addition to *aksara kilat* cited in the opening paragraph of the *Arya Dilah*. In other words, the *Surya Alam* follows the *Arya Dilah* in singling out for emphasis just these three *aksara*, dealing with the place of the king/court, its radiance, and anticipation of its wishes. This is expressed somewhat more poetically but no less explicitly in the *Kuntarakara/Adilulah* (f. 33) as 'knowing the truth from of old, a fire before it flames, a flower before blooming', a key determinant of the worth of a *mantri*.

More substantial information on the borrowing of *aksara*, particularly *aksara salah* and *aksara bener*, comes from the presence of elements in the 144 *prakara* – '*prakara* apophthegms' (Table 6.1). The Thirty *Prakara* discussed in more detail below include as no. 18 *pralaya/kapralaya*, 'one suiting with support from a dead man',[4] which is one of the *uger-uger* (no. 7) cited by, among others, the *Cacad's* § 13 (Table 5.6 above). Just as the single reference to one of the *aksara salah* provides one of the Thirty *Prakara*, so too in § 11 all the *uger-uger* are included among the twenty items of that paragraph. The explanations match those given by the ostensibly earlier titles as the *Arya Dilah* (§ 1). For the equivalent of *aksara bener* or *andhih-andhihan* one must go outside the core 144 items to § 16, as well as to the obvious references contained in § 6 and 7. In § 16 the *andhih-andhihan* are listed as the Ten *Prakara*, complete with the scale of relative weight before the *karta*.

Some of the diverse components discussed in Appendix III can be cited by way of rounding out discussion of *prakara* summarising *sloka* phenomena.

4 See Suwarno, *Dictionary,* no. 808.

The *sad-atatayi* are cited in five of the paragraphs constituting the Fifteen *Prakara* (§ 15); *corah* are named in § 30, one short of the ideal number of eight to make up the *astha corah*. Witnesses debarred due to lack of credibility, tellingly termed Dora-Sembada, are specified in § 29 and the scourges of land, water, and the realm (*gegetheng*) – instrumental in Classic *Sloka*, no. 6 – are named in § 26. Curiously neither the *astha cendhala* nor *sanggraha* or even the *sidhem* concepts are found within the standard *Surya Alam*'s *prakara*. This is more than made up for in the Berlin/van der Hout versions where they take a prominent place in among others §§ 4, 20, 24a, 29, 34-35 respectively. They also appear in the Yasadipura verse version (Cantos XI, X, verses 32, 15).

Carry-overs

The other feature revealing the catholic nature of the *prakara* concerns carry-overs into the present. As in the case of the *sanggraha*, they are usually linked with modest changes in form and/or contents. These in turn provide the opportunity for seeing the modifications for what they are. Among the most numerous proverbs and idiomatic expressions are the Thirty *Prakara*. Roughly half of them can be identified as present-day *sloka*, *paribasan*, *bebasan*, and the like.[5] With greater understanding the percentage of identified Javanese proverbial expressions could be even higher. Why otherwise formulate apophthegms requiring explanation if they are not to be used as gems of inherited wisdom in the future? A second reason for singling out the Thirty *Prakara* for further consideration is that they form the first and longest of the *prakara* lists found in the *Surya Alam*'s half-dozen paragraphs (§§ 9-15) comprising the standard 144 items. The exception here is again the Berlin 402/van der Hout text. A special version of a full list is given by the Raffles translation (1817). They all open with the characteristic, if somewhat unclear, *prakara*: *jamur amét kadang* or 'mushrooms cling to the ceiling [of thatched palm leaves]'. The closest documented phrase is *jamur tuwuh ing sela/wato*, 'mushrooms growing on a stone', i.e., 'a strange happening'.[6] This would seem to be particularly applicable to the study of *sloka* phenomena.

For reasons at present unclear *jamur amét kadang* and the twenty-nine following items took on a corporate identity recognisable by reference to that near-unique phrase. While *prakara* composed of *jamur amét kadang* are

5 Ngafenan, *Paribasan*, p. 8.
6 Suwarno, *Dictionary*, no. 356.

limited to the *Surya Alam* tradition, the Thirty *Prakara* concept is quoted, albeit in an attenuated form of some ten items, by the *Adilulah*, as one of the titles specifically cited as providing the basis of the *Pepakem Tjerbon*. The paragraph in question (§ 5, p. 24) opens with:

> This is the saying of the *Adilulah* included in the expressions of the *aksara* (*kalebet ing wedhar ing aksara*), thirty instances (*prakara*) which bring about defeat in *padu* cases. The first is a person falling under [the category of] *jamur amét kacang*.

Table 6.1 ***Prakara* evolution**

***Prakara* apophthegm**	**meaning *(artiné)***	**Winter *(tegesipun)***	**Modern interpretation**
1. *jamur amét kadang* (Raf. *amra kadang*)	accused accuses an innocent person	~	~
2. *akundhang ciri* 'well-known defect'	add to a document outside given time	person who is a well known evil (III:161)	known as a bad character; wickedness & crimes are known
3. *amuk punggung* 'pointless amok'	attacking one's own plantings	destroy property; slash w/o reason (III:560)	rampage blindly causing damage and hurting persons
4. *putung pamatang* 'break the lance'	during a suit leaving one master for another	(sl) setting himself to peace & harmony with the suited (III:439)	accord between suited and plaintiff (##952)
5.[*sarudenta*] *ngarudenta* (*Adilulah*: *santa pralaya)*	plea lessened or supplemented	~	~
6. *anréka patra*	a letter which is not a [true] document	dishonestly making up a letter or seal (I:397)	falsifying a letter or seal i.e. manipulate document
7. *nidra pramana* 'destroying life'	wishing to kill by deceiving an enemy	illicit love; plan to kill s.o. by pretending to be on close terms (III:106)	betray awareness: try to hurt or kill by becoming his good friend (##1122)

***Prakara* apophthegm**	**meaning *(artiné)***	**Winter *(tegesipun)***	**Modern interpretation**
8. *amasang damar ing ngatariksa,* (Raf.) *dámar kitudah* 'a glowing lantern'	witness supports the plea where a person on first making a complaint, of his own accord brings evidence in support of it	~ person not accused feels or imagines accusation by others (III:234)	~ a person feels as though he has been accused although not charged (##325)
9. *angréka warna* [*parusa*] 'manipulate power'	plea comes not from own master but from a person of note	being 'covered' by one's master or powerful person (III:526)	invoke name of powerful person (##1084)
10. *sirna ing jaya* 'vanquishing victory'	suspicion of witnesses without documentation	disputing the words of a witness (I:214)	for a victorious person to be felled: to lose power and suffer defeat because one disagrees with testimony of a witness (##1474)
11. *ina pralena* [*kulina*] 'debasing custom'	not reporting a found object or sounding the alarm	(sl) one unwilling to report [an object found] (III:11)	(describes) a person finds a lost valuable, but does return it to the owner or the police (##509)
12. *anganti watang* 'change a spear handle'	a witness cordially visiting before the *jaksa*	(sl) a single witness for both parties (III:470)	lack conviction, consistency; when a conflict is witnessed by only one person, he/she has to testify in court for both parties (##436)
13. *satosa nukma pramana* [same as in Raf. 13, but different apothegm]		poor person behaving as if rich (III:294)	a poor person claims to be or acts as if rich (##1493)
sudésit kemú 'dull witted'	[makes little sense]		
14. *saksi rumembé* 'multiplying witnesses'	one witness, but four persons who know	witness of family or those contradicting one another (I:218)	another witness, a relative or one related to a previous witness, is added (##1390)

***Prakara* apophthegm**	**meaning *(artiné)***	**Winter *(tegesipun)***	**Modern interpretation**
15. *patra pralaya* (Raf.) *sastra pralaya*]	decision based on date 'a written statement of *anirna patra* (III:298)	~ (sl) evasive plea, = 'dead letter'	~ to deny one's own writing grievances w/o a date' (##1420)
16. *angréka raja* [*parusa*] 'manipulate king/ power'	polish by citing [the name of] a powerful person	a high-ranking witness (I:394)	claim to be backed by king (e.g. as a witness) (##1086)
17. *candra pati* [?] (Raf.) *Chini ropati* [?]	(*angukuwé utang-utangé uwong*) ~ where a person acts in a compulsory manner towards the people or relations of another		~
18. *maha pralaya* [*kapralayan*] 'destruction'	a case resting on [the testimony] of a dead man	(sl) leaning on a dead person (III:410)	a court case that depends on s.o. who has already died (##610)
19. *ina perdana surya* [?] (Raf.) *Abíndu páya* [?] 'poison deceit'	~ or the case of breach of promise	~ (sl) jaksa who frightens the accused of losing so that he brings out a gift/bribe (III:498)	~ trick a person w/ poison; judge scaring the accused so that, fearing to lose case he will give the judge a large bribe (## 216)
20. *anilatkara* [?] (Raf.) *Nileb lura* [?]	~ (recovery of duties…)	~	~
21. *amutung rakit* 'breaking the team'	action of witnesses who have agreed to come but do not dare nor give news of his departure	~	~
22. *anambung watang ing bubuken* 'connecting with a worm-eaten spear' (III:347)	replacing an old spear	(sl) stop in the process due to sick-ness or un-fulfilled promises	to sue an-other person only to find that – due to sickness, lack of evidence, or lack of witnesses – the case can not proceed (##870)

***Prakara* apophthegm**	**meaning *(artiné)***	**Winter *(tegesipun)***	**Modern interpretation**
23. *atinggal* [*pu*] *geran* 'departing from the rules'	having already paid for the tutur, he does not appear in court	~	~
24. *panca prakopa*	anger and cunning in word and deed at court	~	~
25. *anukma wacana*	often being received by the *jaksa*	~	~
26. *panca resi*	(same as #25)	–	–
27. *andiyu wreksa* 'ogre uprooting trees'	oppose the orders of the *jaksa*	(sl) person willing to go against jaksa and government (III:26)	for a person to fight against authority (he must be strong and powerful) (##90)
28. *surya candra niroda wacana* 'sun & moon avoided'	expressions that both diminish and increase the evidence	one who has already fixed a plea later changes the plea	(oj) after giving complicated information, accused person finally reveals truth ##635); (III:191) (sl) not accepting a *jaksa* decision (Ng. 63, Raf.)
29. *tri reksa upaya* (Raf.) *Katóya rasa* (#27) *upaya*	~ changing a document already before the *jaksa*	~ (sl) person with a pending suit makes gifts to *jaksa* (III:266)	~ gifts to the *jaksa* (##1490; Ng 127.
30. *sabda maléca* 'outcast's answer'	person's plea obscure	~	~
			III & I: Winter, vol. 3, 1; ##: Suwarno 1999; Adi.: *Adilulah* Ng.: Ngafenan 1995; oj: Old Javanese Raf.: Raffles 1817. sl: *sloka*

Table 6.1 seems the most convenient way of bringing a body of disparate materials into some sort of order. The Table concentrates on the Thirty *Prakara* of the 'standard' Combi *Surya Alam*. The contents of this combination of RAS 6 and Add 12 303 (see Chapter 2) are supplemented by several other manuscripts taken from the Yogyakarta *kraton* by the British in 1812. This apparently includes the text used as the basis for the translation published by Raffles. To these can be added § 5 of the *Adilulah* from the early eighteenth century. As pointed out earlier, the Berlin/van der Hout manuscripts in their narrative form do not include *prakara per se*. Despite its origins, the Yasadipura rendition is closer to the contents of the Yogyakarta tradition than the Kartasura/Surakarta versions.

The left-hand column is numbered following the contents of the manuscripts listing the terms/phrases in Javanese, i.e., '*prakara* apophthegm'. Differences in terminology come mainly from the Raffles version, nos. 1, 8, 15, 17, 20, 29. An alternative from the *Adilulah* (Adi.) is noted for no. 5. Directly under the term is an English translation within inverted commas. As there is no definitive equivalent for the terms/phrases the translation is based on a literal reading of the Javanese tempered by their intention expressed in columns two to four.

Clarification of the terms is provided in the second column. These consist of the manuscripts' own explanations (*artiné*) immediately following the phrases in translation. By way of anticipating later discussion, it should be noted that there is no unique connection between the apophthegm and the explanations in *ngoko*, themselves concise to the point of obscurity. Other versions of the *Surya Alam*, particularly the English translation published by Raffles, are helpful in unravelling their meaning, but not always so. For example, no. 3 'pointless *amok*' is explained by the titles as a person damaging his own plantings during a pending suit. There seems little connection. However, the authority of the phrase, even though it seems to have evolved into a broader concept without a corresponding change over time, is well documented.[7] Others have seemingly even less connection with the explanation, as nos. 25 and 26, or have broader intentions, as no. 28 in embracing both sun and moon.

The third and fourth columns 'Winter (*tegesipun*)' and 'Modern Interpretations' are summaries or quotations of later collections from respectively the mid-nineteenth and late twentieth centuries. In this respect Winter's *Javaansche Zamenspraken* from 1858 constitutes a half-way house between the original titles and their modern interpretations. It was written in *krama*

7 *Pepakem Tjerbon/Adilulah*, pp. 24, 46, 64 (*Jaya Lengkara*), 90.

or high Javanese and published in the ha-na-ca-ra-ka alphabet. Thus, due to differences between *ngoko* and *krama* vocabulary the wording is not always consistent. Yasadipura's text is also written in *krama*. Of the sources used for 'Modern interpretations' only Suwarno (1999) is published in English, the *Paribasan* booklet by Darmasoetjipta (1985), as well as the *Kamus Idiom Jawa* by Hariwijaya are written in Bahasa Indonesia, while Ngafenan's booklet (1995) is written in *ngoko* Javanese. Hence the summaries derive mostly from Suwarno with due concern for the contents of the other compilations of proverbial phrases communicated in my translation from Indonesian and Javanese.

A couple of points are noteworthy in the analysis of Table 6.1. First and foremost is the fact that the majority of the Thirty *Prakara* are cited in both *Javaansche Zamenspraken* and modern proverb collections. Slightly less than one-third, nos. 1, 5, 17, 20-21, 23, 24-26, 30, have no discernible younger equivalents. Yet, the fact that they are absent from both the nineteenth and twentieth century list suggests that the gap has as much to do with the state of our information as their lack of modern usage. Even within the works consulted here alternative forms and varieties of spelling, exacerbated by differences between *ngoko* and *krama* forms, constitute challenges for composing Table 6.1. These and others might well conceal eighteenth-century *prakara* which have otherwise lived on to present. Totally different apophthegms for the same meaning, as in nos. 8, 19, and 29, in which the English transliteration proved to be more productive than the Javanese texts, provides a measure of the amount of work that still needs to be done in this field.

As there is little more to be said on the quantitative side, closing observations in this section must rest on qualitative impressions gained from reading across the columns. We can start with the problematic *jamur amét kadang*, which signals the opening of the Thirty *Prakara*. In a quirk of fate, modern day realities seem, at first glance, to fill the gap left by its absence in collections of proverbial expressions. More specifically, a contemporary corruption case against a village chief took an unexpected turn when the defendant was accused by the chief of his own misdeeds![8] Due the special character of rules governing corruption-related misdeeds the case became derailed and the chief went free, a modern equivalent of those allowing Japlak to get away with murder in Majapahit times (Chapter 7). Hence the parallelism with the apophthegm: *jamur amét kadang* breaks down as the latter specified that such a situation invalidated the plaint, i.e., *tan dadi*. Leaving aside the possibly spurious example, a thorough search in modern

8 The very likely apocryphal, but widely believed, example is sketched by Hoadley and Hatti, 'Notes on Corruption and Morality', pp. 6-7.

proverb collections turns up only one 'mushroom' affair, namely *'jamur tuwuh ing sela/waton'*, a mushroom growing on a stone. This is explained as 'a strange happening', in short 'an impossible dream'.[9] Noteworthy is that the original apophthegm does not have the same natural connection with its explanation as the modern one. Thus, we are dependent upon the explanation (*artiné*) found in the manuscript with, of course, hints provided by the Raffles translation dating from roughly the same period. The point is of some importance in accounting from the differences between the eighteenth-century versions and their modern derivations. To the extent we can trust the philological reconstruction, such deviation can be interpreted as altering the contents of the *prakara* while keeping the core wording.

The apophthegms in eighteenth and twentieth century versions can be profitably separated into those that show continuities and those that do not. In the first group, nos. 6, 7, 9, 10, 11, 16, 18, 22, 27, there is little to analyse [possible cases of 'proverbial-ization'?]. Some of them almost literally follow the terms of their respective phrase. For example, nos. 6 and 16 mark the unacceptability of manipulation of documents and power, while no. 9 seems to be a repetition of the latter that has undergone minor changes. Others, as 'destroying life' (no. 7), 'vanquished victory' (no. 10), 'destruction' (no. 18), 'connecting with a worm-eaten spear' (no. 22), and 'an ogre uprooting trees' (no. 27), clearly follow the *prakara*, or at least are easily recognisable once the meaning is revealed. The poetic qualities of particularly the last two, as well as no. 10, render them aesthetically appealing. At the same time, their lack of specificity strengthens dependence on the titles for understanding their meaning and thereby their function as legal instruments. This is particularly so when, as in nos. 15 and 18, a well-known Sanskrit term has been borrowed. In the former case *'pralaya'* is the term used to describe the destruction of the universe at the end of the unending cycle of cosmic decline. Tellingly it is expressed in a unique Javanese form as the *tirta* [...] *sangkara sloka*, which opens the *Wadigun Wangkara* text and this work's beginning.

Excluding the nearly a dozen for which there seems no apparent modern equivalent, the majority of the *prakara* show considerable change over time. This is marked by the differences between columns 1 and 2 and those of 3 and 4. Some of these seem to stem from variant readings within titles. For example, the *'asuradenta'* is found in no. 5 of the standard *Surya Alam* titles, as well as in the *Kuntarakara* (Add 12 303). Even the Raffles translation gives its equivalent as *sana-denta* and all agree on its meaning. The *Kuntarakara*

9 Winter, *Javaansche Zamenspraken*, vol. I, p. 284, Suwarno, *Dictionary*, no. 356 and nos. 529, 530, or '... hopes which are difficult to satisfy', Hariwijaya, *Kamus Idiom Jawa*, p. 107.

further specifies that the evidence is not self-evident (*ora tetéla*). Yet the key words of 'lessening or adding (to a plea)' are identical with that of no. 28 discussed below. Just to make things more complicated, the Javanese text of the *Pepakem Tjerbon/Adilulah* gives a different term, namely *santa pralaya*, defined as 'evading the plea', which echoes no. 10. Here one must note the problem of apparent textual errors in the extant manuscripts. Thus Add 12 333 and 12 329 list several longer phrases, which on further examination are revealed to be parts of the following paragraph (§ 10). For unknown reasons the copyist has skipped part of the text before continuing roughly in conformity with the standard *Surya Alam* found in most of the manuscripts examined in this study. Possibly explained by such a textual misplacement is no. 29, *tri reksa upaya*. The phrase appears in § 3 of several *Surya Alam* titles and is directly related to the duties of a *jaksa*. Hence the reading of the Raffles translation of no. 5 – 'where a person destroys his property while he has a law suit pending', § XVI, no. 3, p. xlii – would seem to be more likely.

This in turn brings up what should be more significant aspects of Table 6.1, namely the apparent shift of meaning over time. Here again we must be cautious in interpreting the contents of titles/manuscripts which are sorely in need of in-depth philological analysis. Even so, the examples provide strong indications of the type and direction of such changes. A couple of must them suffice here. The explanation for *akundhung ciri* 'a well-known defect' (no. 2) fits better with the younger interpretation than that found in the titles. One can say it has been 'proverbial-ised' to a descriptive term. From providing specific motivation for invalidating a case it has become merely an after-the-fact observation. A similar process seems to hold true for many others. *Amuk punggung* apparently developed from attacking one's own plantings,[10] undoubtedly a ruse during a legal conflict, to a general description of running *amok*. In the case of no. 4, *pulung pamalang*, the original meaning has not only undergone a similar process but also has become the common modern expression of *sambung watang putung* (assembling a broken lance or reconciling people who are fighting). Similarly, '*angganti watang*' (no. 12) has derived from an eighteenth-century version of the Republic's famous KKN – *korupsi, kolusi*, dan *nepotisme* (corruption, collusion, and nepotism) – namely suborning a judge. Somehow it has come down to the present with the meaning of a single witness for both parties, an impossible situation leading to automatic defeat in such a case. Number 13 seems to be another example of mixing term with meaning. The *Surya Alam* gives *satosa mukma pramana*. This is not found in the other titles or

10 See explanation in Chapter 7, p. 159 and Chapter 8, p. 177, and cited sources.

in any modern reference but agrees with the Javanese *artiné* of them all. In contrast, the Raffles translation reads *sudésit kemú* (dull-witted), which has been 'proverbial-ised' into 'a poor person behaving as if rich'.[11] And finally, if we return to number 29, the Raffles translation provides a more productive alternative to the problematic *tri raksa upaya*, namely *katoya rasa upaya* or changing a document submitted before the *jaksa*. This meaning, however, is at odds with the literal translation of the phrase which fits in well with the youngest interpretation of a person with a pending suit making gifts to the *jaksa*'.[12] A not implausible explanation for the continuation or expansion of *prakara* terms during the late Independent Kingdoms period is suggested by earlier discussion of their appearance in modern dress. *Prakara* as non-specific, even nonsensical, terms provided flexibility for altering their intention to fit the perceived needs of the time. It should be remembered that *sloka* phenomena have legally binding aspects. This differentiates them from mere observations associated with proverbs. Such flexibility is lacking in other *sloka*-like phenomena. Although *sloka* can be difficult to interpret, once unravelled their meaning, intension, and function is difficult to alter. A disobedient tiger seizing prey dying by a falling object, alternatively felled by fate (Classic *Sloka*, no. 1), cannot become an ideal king, firm and just, caring and forgiving, etc., as reported by the *giri jaladri* [...] *tanu* phrase of Classic *Sloka*, no. 8 or no. 24 as a gecko dying from its own admission and so on. In principle the same applies to *sinalokan*. While the major actor – a tiger, jackal, lion, or even *kebo* – can be changed to suit circumstances, the basic meaning remains the same. Both *sloka* and *sinalokan* genres are expressed in a mini-narrative form with resultant demands on internal logic and external consistency.

Conclusion

Coming to the end of the *sloka* phenomena in the literal meaning, a summary of their respective place within the phenomena seems in order. An overview is provided in Table 6.2.

11 Suwarno, *Dictionary*, no. 1493.

12 Winter, *Javaansche Zamenspraken*, vol. III, p. 266; Suwarno, *Dictionary*, no. 1490; and Ngafenan, *Paribasan*, p. 127.

Table 6.2 Place within the textual tradition

Sloka	Aksara	Sinalokan	Prakara
Definition of sovereign duties and obligations opened by the contents of the *Jugul Muda*	1. Sovereign preroga-tives plus delegation to *kerta* and *pangulu* 2. determination of civil cases: -positive = *andhih-andhihan* -negative = *uger-uger* aspects	Wisdom after the fact, i.e., used as proverbs or similes; part *sloka* part simile	144 negative criteria, the presence of any one resulting in the case's loss

Sloka in the legal tradition are concerned mostly with issues of sovereign authority. The earliest source by tradition, namely the *Jugul Muda,* shows them to have centred on sovereign rights and obligations to punish miscreants, with an additional one proclaiming kingly virtues (Classic *Sloka,* no. 8, *giri jaladri* [...] *tanu*). In the *Jaya Lengkara sloka* are more closely connected to the practice of justice. This takes two forms. The first comprises the ten-to-twelve statements of sovereign authority concerning *pradata* affairs, with some delegation to court officials. These are the *aksarâji.* The title also cites *sloka* emphasizing the importance of officials (*jaksa, kerta*) (Classic *Sloka,* nos. 17-19), ending with the ideal qualities of kingship no. 22. As developed by subsequent titles, another level of authority set the criteria for determining the results of civil affairs in both positive and negative terms. The latter or *uger-uger* turn up frequently in the greatly expanded list of 144 phrases constituting the *prakara* guaranteeing defeat in a case. As such *aksara* represent a development from *sloka* proper with greater applicability as interpreted and applied by Patih Jugul Muda and his colleagues. This transitional character is further emphasized by the fact that the '*aksara* of the wrong' (*uger-uger*) lead directly to the *prakara,* most of which are contained in § 11 of the Yogyakarta *Surya Alam.* Their closeness in terminology and numbers makes the *sinalokan* an ambiguous part of the phenomena. They are used both as *sloka* proper, often with literal working or paraphrases thereof, and as *ex post facto* less common proverbial expressions. These leave the *prakara* as the least active of and most descriptive of the *sloka* phenomena. At the same time, they are the most numerous, being reduced to a core list of 144 by King Surya Alam. Prakara are also the ones most likely to continue into modern Javanese usage, albeit as simile-type shorthand reminders of the functional *sloka.*

7 Vignettes and Practice

Vignettes may seem to be figurative narratives employed to illustrate bookish constructs with tentative connections to law. Yet, when supplemented by a limited number of related 'diverse components' they provide context for the ***sloka*** phenomena within traditional Javanese law. From the view point of external scholarship, the concept of vignettes in the meaning of 'a short descriptive essay or character sketch'[1] applies equally well to the narratives of cases resolved by Javanese courts vetted by Dutch East India Company officials. Information on the course of such cases is not something European officials of the time could have known through participating in institutions foreign to their own administrative praxis, let alone those conducted in a language rarely mastered by administrative personnel. Consequently, the information concerning the workings of the legal system and its law found in the Company archives constitutes second-hand sources. It was not gained from experiences of the reporters; it was received from local personnel, passed on to their superiors, and preserved in official reports. Under the circumstances can such material be considered more real than those found in Javanese textual traditions? By stating the obvious the intention is not to underrate the potential contribution of Dutch reports to the understanding Javanese law, but to point out that what is reported by European sources must be subjected to the same standards of logic and veracity as those of indigenous writings considered in this work.

This variant of 'many ways to the prayer house' sets the chapter's agenda. The first half focuses on textual vignettes. It should be noted that there is a possibility, at present unsubstantiated, that they are based on actual cases that over time have become textual illustrations of legal principles. In contrast 'practice', those few cases found in the Dutch Company archives dealt with in the second half of this chapter, are contextually alien contributions. However, when checked by the contents of information found in Javanese legal literature, they can provide valuable information.

Vignettes

Taken by themselves *aksara, sinalokan,* and *prakara* are difficult to understand without the insights provided by the vignettes in which they are

1 *The Concise Oxford Dictionary.*

embedded. Although *sloka* consist of self-contained phrases, their broader implications are grasped fully only within the proper context, that is, in a vignette as those of the *Jugul Muda*.

Almost all the *sloka* phenomena considered in the preceding pages are connected to vignettes. Most of the Classic *Sloka* originated from the first two vignettes of the *Jugul Muda*, namely the Dora-Sangkara affair and the Dustha band. Their contents and significance are confirmed by parallel references in other titles. More common are the mini-vignettes ending in a dozen or so *sinalokan* concerning *Corah*, *Tatayi*, *Walat*, etc. found in the second half of most *Jugul Muda* versions. Specialised vignettes, many ending in *sinalokan* bearing the names of the actors, provide the material of the middle section of the *Jaya Lengkara*. Even the generally tabular *Surya Alam* titles are the source of vignettes related to the components under discussion. While bringing in additional vignettes is indeed akin to 'hauling coals to New Castle', the following discussion confines itself to a half dozen. They have special significance for embedded *sloka* phenomena because their contents touch on nearly all the key components dealt with in this work. In short, they illustrate how the individual components functioned within the broader context of written law. Lacking obvious organizational principles, they are presented in order of increasing complexity, when possible, gathered about a common theme.

Jugul Muda and *Jaya Lengkara* vignettes

Given that change is one of the few constants of human existence, a revealing insight is provided by the contrast between the *Jaya Lengkara*'s *sinalokan*: '*boga andrawinah...*' as found in the *Pepakem Tjerbon* and that of the *Jugul Muda's* '*tidhem* [...] *pramanem*'. A summary of the former follows.

> Two hunchbacks, Boga and Andrawinah, sent out to collect taxes fell out over the division of the spoils. A fight ensued, ending in their deaths. Since they were royal favourites, out of fear of the king's wrath, supplemented by general greed, the villagers chose not to report the matter. A middle-ranking official subsequently informed the court of the situation. This resulted in the *patih* of Medhang Kamulan summoning the villagers and their chiefs. All were fined for neglect of duty. The informer was rewarded.[2]

2 *Pepakem Tjerbon*, no. 16, pp. 82-83.

The vignette is closed by a *sinalokan* supplied by the de Nooy manuscript that the editor, G.A.J. Hazeu, has matched with the original Dutch of the *Pepakem*,

> *boga andrawinah kalebet sira ing kasaru ditan ing ngalaras lokikaning bogandrawihan*

Very approximately it can be paraphrased as follows. Boga and Andrawinah got into an indecent [exchange] of words (*kasaru,* alt. 'to address or interrupt with indecent remarks')[3], [which] were not in harmony with the world [= intransient or preventing] enjoyment [of the loot]. The first phrase, *boga andrap(w)inah* repeats the names of the tax collectors. However, the repetition at the end of the vignette stands for enjoyment, which may have an implicit connection to tax collectors. More likely the 'enjoyment prevented' refers to the royal messengers, who missed out on the funds due to their death. It could also be interpreted as emphasizing the villagers not being able to enjoy the loot due to being sabotaged by the informer.[4]

Although basically similar, the *Jugul Muda* version provides more detail and slightly different perspectives.[5] The crucial difference lies in the names of the principle actors. In it the two messengers are named T(s)idhem and Pramanem. Taken together they constitute a well-known legal instrument of some antiquity. Literally *sidhem pramanem* means 'remaining silent.' As a legal function it more accurately translates as 'the crime of silence' (Appendix IV, 'Fail to witness'). It was stringently applied on occasion certain situations, mainly instances of death by an unknown assailant. A variant is the finding of a 'bedewed corpse' in which those living within a fixed radius of the discovery of a person killed by an unknown assailant are responsible for the *wergeld*.[6] In such cases the discoverer is responsible for reporting the event immediately to the sovereign on pain of punishment. Moreover, the *Jugul Muda*'s use of different names of the actors misses the opportunity to anticipate the final *sinalokan* suggesting the missing out on illicit gain by the messengers or villagers. On the other hand, use of the *tidhem pramanem* phrase focuses more directly on the lack of fulfilling

3 Suwarno, Dictionary, no. 1173).

4 Hazeu gives another explanation of the transcription in the notes to the *Pepakem Tjerbon*, p. 165.

5 LOr 7440, ff. 356-361; LOr 7410, ff. 86v-88r; and *Serat angger: Jugul Muda*, pp. 28-31.

6 Finding a 'bedewed corpse' see Hoadley 1994, p. 122, n.23.

expectable obligations to the crown. Hence, the death of Tidhem fell under the *sinalokan*: *tambra belang ambrik mangsa* (*sic cambra* [alt. *sona*] *belang mati rebut mangsa*) or fighting for prey, spotted carp/dogs die together. This is explained as 'a misfortune resulting from greed; to suffer or to die because of fighting for an object or person'.[7] The *sinalokan* for the villagers is: *anyupa-anyula weti baud tan weruh ing baya.* Although not immediately decipherable, it is most likely a fragment of a *sinalokan* from the *Luwangan* § 16, which reads *tambra bela[ng] sidhu prana wéti daratikrama yojana*. The paragraph to which it is belongs concerns punishment of officials guilty of *sidhem papatih* or the silence of ministers, which is roughly equivalent to *sidhem pramana* for commoners (see also § 3).

Those who reported the villagers' crime to the king – Atur and Wisuna – were marked by Classic *Sloka,* no. 16, as a gecko that dies because of its voice. As we have seen, this is explained as to suffer or to fail because of one's own words. Despite that fact that in this case they were rewarded, 'whistle blowers' were not universally respected. This is indicated by the fact that the name of one of them, Wisuna, constitutes one of the *sad-atatayi*, namely 'causing unrest among kings (through evil gossip)' (Appendix IV. Diverse Components). And finally, the village chiefs received the *sloka/sinalokan*:

> *gana-léna rebut mangsa nista sobawa* [(*sic*) *gana-léna regut mangsa nir tan sabawa*]
> A person who remains silent concerning the event of a killing (*raja pati*) because of seizing treasures.[8]

Alternatively, it has been interpreted as

> Two persons arguing over the seizure of property, to the point that one of them dies, but the affair subsequently disappears and is not reported.[9]

Except for not reporting the affair, the phrase fits the Dora-Sangkara vignette which opened the *Jugul Muda*.

A final point concerns what seems to be a follow up to the vignette. Dating from a century or more after the titles considered here, Winter's *Javaansche Zamenspraken* includes a *sloka* that is too close to the present

7 Suwarno, *Dictionary*, no. 1479.
8 Ngafenan, *Paribasan*, p. 46.
9 Darmasoetjipta, *Kamus Paribahasa Jawa*, no. 300.

vignette's to have come into existence purely by chance. Usual for such *sloka*, a lion provides the dark foreboding.

> *Singa papa ngulati mangsa*, its meaning, a lion of misfortune seeking prey. It is a *saloka* of person(s) ordered to produce money from villagers for the purposes of the king's messengers [or tax collectors as Boga and Andrawinah].[10]

If the *sloka* was current when the original vignette was shaped, then one could speculate that the emphasis fell on the breaking of the rules contained in *sidhem pramanem* rather than anything to do with the collection of the king's revenues. Whatever the case, its existence again illustrates the interconnections existing between the *sloka* phenomena.

A triangle drama

Another example from the vignettes constituting the middle section of the *Jaya Lengkara* is the affair of Ki Anggas, Ni Prana, and Ki Sungging Panuksma. It is included as the opening vignette in virtually all versions of that title. In this capacity it is representative of these special *sinalokan* into which the names of the actors were woven, much like the Boga-Andrawinah vignette. The story, summarised in Chapter 5 (p. 79), revolved about Ki Anggas' responsibility for the death of the painter Ki Sungging Panuksma. The motive was apparently Ki Anggas' jealousy over a drop of paint spilled on Ni Prana's breast while her portrait was being painted.

Yet the *Arya Dilah* (§ 3) suggests a deeper connection on the part of Ki Anggas. The paragraph in question reads:

> This is the case of persons engaged in adultery (*jinah*), who are caught in the act by the family, it is permitted to take the life [of the man] without fear of punishment. [However] if one [the adulterer or the protector of the woman] dies, the alarm must be sounded, and a plea submitted to the authorities. After the death has been established it is allowed to levy a fine (*raja dhendha*) of eight *laksa*, with the *sinalokan: anggas prana, sandhi upaya krama yojana, ing pati* or in the Anggas-Prana affair a hidden stratagem [has been used to destroy] a healthy marriage [resulting in] a death.

10 Winter, *Javaansche Zamenspraken*, vol. II, pt. 3, no. 338.

The death of Sungging Panuksma was justified by the (suspected) act of adultery. Therefore, the king levied a fine instead of the more expectable compensation to the injured party in the form of a *wergeld*. This would seem to clarify the otherwise ambiguous point in the *Jaya Lengkara* vignette. It also confirms recycling with modification of *sinalokan* in different titles.

Bok Ening/Ni Indun

A relatively uncommon Islamic theme within the *sloka* phenomena comes in the Bok Ening/Ni Indun vignette. It occurs in two versions of the *Surya Alam*, namely the Combi Yogyakarta version (§ 23) and the Raffles translation (§ XIV). They provide the bare outlines to illustrate the workings of *tarka* (suspicion). A third version by Yasadipura I turns the dry exposition into a true vignette by setting the narrative in the period of the prophet Daud (David) with his son Nabi Suleiman as chief actor and originator of a Solomonic judgment.[11] A widow, Bok Ening (Ni Indun in the Yogyakarta version) was accused not only of illicit sex, but of fornication with a dog! Only the first is mentioned in the Raffles version. The accusers were four men as required by the *shari'a*. Bok Ening was brought before the tribunal, understandably in tears. Very likely suspecting that all was not as it should be, Nabi Suleiman was persuaded by his father to investigate the case. Apparently, a departure from the usual, it was decided to hear the accusers separately one by one. From this it appeared that for one the dog in question was black, white for another, spotted for a third, and so on.

The incompatible differences in the accounts of the accusers, who were also the witnesses, fell under the *panca bakah* (Table 4.3, no. 5) of the *aksara salah* or *uger-uger,* 'differences in the supporting evidence'. Although not stated in the titles, subsequent action by court officials shows that the accusations against Bok Ening were discredited, thus freeing her from the authority of the law. The four accusations were reversed; the accusers stood accused and convicted. The Raffles translation adds that:

> With regard to the *Páncha báka*, which is the case of a woman accused by four men of fornication; if on examination these four men do not agree in their testimony, they ought to be put to death, or else fined agreeably

11 Yasadipura, *Surya Alam*, Canto VII, verses 10-34.

> to the *Jána trésna* [?], which leaves it to those who have charge of the woman to determine the extent of the fine, § XIV.[12]

In broader perspectives the vignette provides a rare example of differences between *shari'a* and the traditional law of Java. More specifically, the verdict did not refer to a *hadd* punishment, i.e., *kadhf*, false accusation of unchastity' (unlawful intercourse). Such could be based upon *Sura* XXIV, verses 4-20.

> And those who accuse honourable women but bring not four [acceptable] witnesses, scourge them (with) eighty stripes and never (afterward) accept their testimony – They indeed are evildoers.[13]

In contrast, the Javanese *Surya Alam* prescribed the alternatives of death or fines, both deferred to the wishes of the woman's guardian, although fines are not generally recognized under Islamic law.

Indelibly Dora

It will be recalled that the contest between Dora and Sangkara over a cache of gold precipitated the beginning of the present *Sengara* Epoch (*Kali-yuga*), bringing with it all the miseries of human kind. Although not so spectacular, vignettes surrounding Dora and Sangkara in various guises are common in the titles consulted in this work. Limitations of time and space allow consideration of only a couple. The first, Ki Dora v. Ki Sembada (aka Sangkara), brings the vignette's context from the van der Hout translation into what would become standard modern Javanese usage of *dora-sembada* as a cover-up lie. The following summary is based upon the Berlin 402/van der Hout version (§ 24) and that of Yasadipura (Canto XI, verse 24).

> *Ki Dora and Ki Sembada*
> Under the leadership of Ki Bawa, five messengers were sent by the king to seize an evildoer (*durjana*). They included Ki Laksana, Ki Prayoga, etc. making four with Ki Sembada and five with Ki Dora. Before departing

12 The present vignette does not seem to have been taken up in West Javanese manuscripts (LOr 7410, 7440, or 7442). This might be explained by the fact that they contain the *Adilulah*, a likely predecessor of the much longer *Surya Alam*, in which the vignette is lacking. Its significance comes from illustrating the workings of the *aksara salah*.

13 Quoted by Schacht, *Islamic Law*, p. 179ff.

> they agreed to stick together. Deviation would be interpreted as being in collusion with the *durjana,* such an individual must be seized by the others. On the journey Dora – according to Yasadipura a *jaksa* – asked leave to go to the river [in order to relieve himself]. Once there he fell ill with incapacitating diarrhoea and was cared for by his *panakawan* (follower, servant), Ki Sembada. Becoming even more ill, Dora ordered Sembada to catch up with the others in order to complete their assigned task. Taking a route which proved to be faster, Sembada arrived before the others at the *durjana*'s house. With the unexpected appearance of a court official (a bad sign under any circumstances) the *durjana* fled. When Ki Bawa and the others arrived, they found only Ki Sembada and an empty house. Despite Sembada's explanation, he was seized and bound by the others. The delegation then returned to report their failure to the *patih.* Sembada was seen/considered (*ulat*) as an *anirna dustha,* 'a shelter of thieves', a *kalinga baya,* 'one protecting by promise', as well as *apiduluran* 'posing as a relative [?]'. Furthermore, he fell under the obligation to catch the original *durjana* as an alternative to being declared one in his place. The goods, cloths, and *kris* of all five messengers were confiscated by the crown motivated by *saeka prayaning durjana,* 'having the same intensions as an evil one', *kamarga baya* 'dangers of the journey [?]', and *sikuning sadu* 'deviating from virtue'.

At this point the Van der Hout translation breaks off. Both the Berlin and Yasadipura versions continue at some length to show how various degrees of assisting, conspiring, or consorting with known evil doers relegates one to the same category. It also brings with it the same punishments. If there is any indication of cooperation with evildoers, 'even if a *pangulu, kitab, modin,* or *mantri* are included (*kalebet baya*)' the prohibition takes effect. Indications include, among others, having traces of stolen goods, hiding the evidence (*anamur tilas*), implication of a guest, and even not himself seizing a *durjana* for which the punishment is *maling raja peni* (a thief of beautiful objects), as well as a number of instances of theft/miscreants.[14] The essence of the vignette, which casts Dora and Sembada in a very different light than in the Aji Saka story, is contained in the final *sloka,* namely, *aleboer andhoer* which apparently led to seizure (of property and person) by the sovereign. This in turn contains the functional message as to the undesirable results of being considered as falling

14 *Maling marga, raja pening, raras, kenya arep temmon anamdodoken*, Berlin 402, §§ 25-26. Without going into the details, one can only note the close parallelism with the various categories of aiding and abetting *durjana* found in the *Jaya Lengkara/Pepakem Tjerbon* tradition.

into the various categories, with possibilities of attendant punishments. Again, the legal literature as interpreted by well-informed officials provides the legal sanction for punishment; carrying it out was in the hands of the sovereign.

Ki Temen v. Ki Dora

The other Dora-Sembada vignette reflects more closely the original Aji Saka story. Dora has become a more an out-and-out deceiver called Dupara (impossible, absurd). Sembada has become Temen (true, honest).

> Ki Temen from Kejekten (validity) had loaned Dora/Dupara from Pangoran (lies) a sum of money. This the latter denied, resulting in a suit before the *kerta*. Ki Dupara disclaimed even the possibility of being indebted to Ki Temen because he had been deep in the forest, calling on a banyan stump as witness. The *jaksa* felt this [the banyan stump as witness] to be impossible (*dupara*) and asked if Ki Dupara really meant it. The latter not only asserted that this was indeed so, but also proposed that the court visit the banyan stump, which he claimed was not far away. The *jaksa* then prepared to go home. Seeing this, Ki Temen asked for the decision, to which the *jaksa* replied that Temen had won and Dupara had lost and had to pay compensation on top of repaying the loan. The case fell under the *sloka* of *tekèk mati ing ulahé* 'a gecko dies from its own words.'

From reading the versions contained in Berlin 402/van der Hout version (§ 47) and Add 12 323 (ff. 25-26) it is not immediately clear why Dupara lost the case. As it turns out it had nothing to do with calling a banyan stump as witness. The riddle is cleared up by a supplementary document apparently appended to the case much in the same manner as the Ki Awas case was written up in a mock *surat kukudung*. The immediately following paragraph in the Add 12 323 version of the *Surya Alam* opens with the phrase 'These are the words of a *piagem* (royal decree) at the conclusion of the legal case'. It then goes on to briefly describe the affair. Crucial was the statement 'That which bore fruit was the shifting (*gingsir*) [of testimony] in the case'. This was a variant of the *aksara salah* (Table 4.3, no. 4) '*toyamarta*', which also explains the decision. Dupara had shifted the basis of the suit by first claiming that it was impossible to have contracted a loan because he was deep in the forest, but subsequently stated that the place was not far away. This is confirmed by the *sloka*: *tekèk mati ing ulahé* (Classic *Sloka*, no. 24). The first part of the *sloka* merely states that he lost the cases from his own utterances. The second part filled in by the Berlin manuscript – *lir sima* [*bangga andurkaka*] *amét mangsa kanuken pejah tan weru* [*ing baya*] – is double bottomed. It also contains the moral. The literal meaning is 'a disobedient tiger looking for prey means trouble'. This seems clear enough, although one wonders what it has to do with Dupara's debt. The real meaning of the *sloka* is that someone who habitually steals and is finally caught 'kills the goose that lays the golden eggs'. Yasadipura then draws an extended moral from the case, one which leads to what the Javanese apparently perceived as the essence of law,

> a simile or lesson of caution (*wiwéka*); do not shift [the claim], look to the essence of *tirta*, [*kerta*], *yoga*, (ka)*dupara, sengara*, coupled with the truth in words.

Kartiguna/Japlak

When all is said and done the strongest argument for the utility of the vignettes comes from the Japlak case.[15] Like the Ki Awas case mentioned in Chapter 4, it is a fictive judgment producing a *kukudung* and a *salaran*, each with its own *sinalokan*. The affair derives from a manuscript calling itself the *Serat Arok* (LOr 10.554). The episode is introduced in an offhand manner roughly in the middle of the *serat*. The plot line, such that it is, is broken by the inebriated discussion of two high officials at the *Kedemangan*. There it is revealed that Malandang Japlak has almost come to a fight with someone named Citrawangsa. Things had gone so far that they had drawn their *kris* before being separated by onlookers, which seems to have been a common occurrence to judge from the texts. The reason for the incident was that the Citrawangsa's fighting cock had beaten Japlak's. Earlier Japlak's cock had defeated that of Kartiguna. More important, it appears that the wagers at this last match were so high that the loss of the cock fight resulted in Kartiguna wife and children becoming debt-slaves (*paradah*) of Japlak.

Later that night Kartiguna planned his revenge. First, he stabbed his pet dog and spread its blood on the alley outside the house. Then he warned his niece, who was living with him, of the plot and departed for Malandang Japlak's house south of the river. Just then Japlak was bragging to his wife about the cock fight incident. His high spirits were somewhat dampened when she related a dream prophesying impending death. Later that same night an intruder entered their house and stabbed Japlak without waking his wife. Robson's summary of subsequent events follows. Stanza numbers are given in parenthesis.

15 A detailed consideration of the affair is found in Hoadley, 'Literature as Law'.

Kartiguna had reached home and raised a cry that he had stabbed a thief, while Ken Rarakenya [his niece] sounded the alarm (*titir*) (135). The neighbours came out and he asked them for help, but they were not able to catch any fugitive.

Japlak's wife had been roused by the sound of the alarm (*gentangan*) and tried to wake her husband; she touched blood and saw that he was dead. She in turn raised the alarm and the neighbours rushed in (139-140). They examined everything, and a police officer (*paliwara*) called Ngabehi Panca-Wirati arrived (141), sent by the magistrate (*mantri jaksa*) Ki Arya Rajaniti (142). Panca-Wirati questioned Japlak's wife on all that had happened (143). She said that her husband was innocent of any crime – his only fault was that he betted and often won, so people persecuted him and he was killed (144). When asked why they had failed to cut the thief off, the servants said that they had thought the uproar nothing unusual (?) (145-147).

Meanwhile, north of the river the alarm was still sounding and many had come out to help (Japlak's house was south and Kartiguna's north of the river) (149). Police-officer Ngabèhi Warastuti arrived, sent by Arya Rajaniti (150). While he was questioning Kartiguna, 40 messengers from the Kapatihan arrived to find out why two alarms had been sounded (151). They were led by Lurah Jala-Sutra and Lurah Kembu-Kawat, who joined in the investigation (152). Kartiguna said he had detected the thief breaking in; he got only his heirloom kris worth 100, etc. (153-155). Wirasastuti left and then morning came. Kartiguna proceeded to the Jaksa to give his testimony (*naid*) (157).

[Temporary return to the mainstream of the narrative]

Arya Rajaniti was in court at the Balé Watangan, with the assembled *paliwara* and *pañarikan* (164). Kartiguna came to give his evidence; his complaint (*gugat*) was written down and signed. Before long Japlak's wife came to do the same (166). Then they both withdrew, and Arya Rajaniti asked Ngabèhi Wirasastuti for his opinion and the experts quoted *salokas* (172). Compensation was awarded, and the clerk ordered to make a record (181). The two complainants were recalled (185), and Japlak's wife was awarded [assessed a fine of ?]133 *réyal,* 9 *uwang* and 30 *kèteng picis,* enough to free Kartiguna's wife and children, so he got them back and was given a *surat kukudung* (190).[16]

16 Robson, 'The *Serat Arok*', pp. 287-289.

The literary summary does not do justice to the legal aspects of the case. Comprising some two dozen verses, the trial scene is particularly informative. It provides a unique witness to legal process before a traditional Javanese court. Whatever the inaccuracies arising from poetic license, they are more than compensated for by its indigenous character, one apparently not influenced by European concepts. Because the narrative is self-explanatory, only a few points need emphasizing here. As to be expected, *jaksa* supplied the textual expertise. This included several *sloka* and *sinalokan*, as well as references to legal instruments in which *aksara* and *prakara* played an important role. Moreover, the ending graphically emphasizes the major concern of traditional Javanese law, namely a return to relative *tata tantrem* over abstract concepts of justice.

Yet there appears to be an anomaly in the affair. This is because the ending seems to indicate that crime pays. By skilfully using principles of Javanese law – the evidence of the (dog's) blood (*bukti*) and the order of the alarm – Kartiguna literally got away with murder. One cannot dismiss the possibility that the episode addresses a higher order of morality. In long term perspectives the settlement may have been aimed at providing a counter to the type of arrogance characterizing Japlak's actions. This had gone so far as bragging about taking Kartiguna's wife and children as debt-slaves resulting from a wager. Had it been a question of only legal tricks, then stanzas 187-191 would be superficial. Yet their message is clear: the case is resolved by litigants accepting the equity contained in the *salaran* and *kukudung*. Both explicitly accepted them: 'Finished is this case, not to be heard of again (190)'.

The concluding *sloka/sinalokan*: *yukti bukti* [...] *taru* brings us the full circle back to the *sloka* of *Jugul Muda*. To Classic *Sloka*, no. 1: *sima* [...] *taru* has been added '*yukti bukti*' to create a *sinalokan* through which the affair was summarized. While the *sloka/sinalokan* was contained in the *kukudung* intended for Japlak, the message of its contents was that his arrogant behaviour expressed as *sato bangga amet mangsa* or an arrogant dog seeking prey resulted in the unlikely/accidental results of the affair.

Jimbun Era texts

Another set of cases revealing *sloka* function in litigation comes from post-*Pepakem Tjerbon* texts retrospectively associated with Senapati Jimbun (aka Radèn Patah). As mentioned in an article under construction,[17] the

17 Hoadley, 'Javanese Case Law'. The Jimbun Era texts come from RAS 33, with the *Gajah Mada*, ff. 1-84 and *Raja Niti*, ff. 86-175; LOr2125, with *Jaya Lengkara*, ff. 1-40, *Kuntara Manawa*, ff.

summaries concern secondary claims on the results of the primary cases dealt with only obliquely. Thus, they are neither literal transcriptions nor narratives of the cases' unfolding. They are synopses of textual civil contests, that is, matters of *padu/paben* (to quarrel [...] to have a dispute or difference of opinion), concerning payments awarded the winners or dunned from losers, with or without related complaints concerning the respective court's action or non-action. They provided grounds for claims on the judicial results of the cases in the form of monetary compensation, restitution, or criticism of the legal process, which form their *raison d'être*. Of the nineteen case summaries identified in the Jimbun Era texts[18] only four contain data relevant to present discussion. The four include examples of *prakara,* a couple of identifiable *sloka,* a *sinalokan,* and one phrase yet to be identified.

Pun Dalu

> Accused of theft (*colong*) by an unknown party, Pun Dalu counter sued the authorities. He had paid the fees (*prabéya*) necessary to file a complaint and engaged witnesses. This resulted in issuing a *layang ubaya* (here an agreement to appear at a later date) in order to contest the accusation. Subsequently, the *layang ubaya* was withdrawn. The summary states that this was due to his not having paid in full the court fees listed in the *layang*. Somewhat unclear this fell under (*kalebu*) *ananggul pralaya* (holding back disaster).[19]

Dated Sunday 9 *Jumadilakir,* the summary does not specify the results. Clarification comes from the following paragraph, where it is stated that all fees had to be paid 'by Wednesday, 12 *Jumadilakir,* at the court's audience-hall (*paséban pakertan*)'. Noteworthy is the threatened forfeiture to the crown of wife and children in cases of non-payment. The phrase used for this is *amujangaken ing anak-semahipun* (to become a bachelor through his children and family being taken from him), which seems to be a paraphrase of the *Luwangan* (§ 1):

> If a person does not pay the tax (*pajeg*), let alone the court payment (*prabéyan*) due to lack of resources, if he continues [with the suit] for four

41-171, and *Undhang Senapati Jimbun,* ff. 172-289; plus NBS 56, with the *Jaya Lengkara, Kuntara Manawa, Senapati Jimbun,* and *Gajah Mada,* see Pigeaud, *Literature of Java,* for references.

18 The manuscripts containing the Jimbun Era texts are discussed in Appendix IV.

19 Summary of RAS 33's *Raja Niti,* ff. 94-95 and *Kuntara Manawa,* § 9:6.

> *weton* (sittings) his children and wife become the tax/*prabéya* obtained as loot, who cannot be redeemed living or dead,
> *sinalokan*:
> *Papahu pataning jiwa-patanén ing krama yojana.*

The *jiwa-panenén* (living or dying) of the un-deciphered *sinalokan* must refer to confiscation of wife and children without possibility of redemption. The defendant's action is described as *ananggul* [*sabda*] *pralaya*, (holding back disaster). More than just a description, the phrase, either a *sinalokan* or *prakara*, shows that the threatened forfeiture of wife and children was avoided by his action.

Ni Guna v. Pun Tarka

A similar threat of a more stringent punishment was cited in the Ni Guna v. Pun Tarka affair.[20] In the affair *sloka* phenomena are expressed in *prakara* phrases, which clarify the intention of the case and establish their connections to legal traditions.

> Pun Tarka, who had fallen out (*ganggang*) with Ni Guna, accosted her with language both foul and disrespectful (*mimisuh, awah-awah,*). The first of the two paragraphs dealing with the affair refers to Tarka's unacceptable conduct. For this he was summoned (*undhang*) to appear before the court, which issued a homily on appropriate behaviour. A following paragraph relates that Pun Tarka's actions had been investigated, but apparently found to be minor enough to be categorised as *sumingga katutuah* (evading reprimand). Consequently, he escaped the harsher penalty for *sabda parusa* (violent speech).[21] According to the *Gajah Mada* law text (ff. 80-81), this would have entailed fines payable both to the victim and to the crown. Tarka claimed that he had been trying to bring about reconciliation with Ni Guna and thus used only proper language. This was partially accepted by the court. He was felled on the lesser charge of inappropriate language as found in a *layang kéwala* (ordinary document), not the punishable *sabda parusa or wak parusa* (violent or harsh speech).[22] Ni Guna was to be compensated with eight real and

20 Summary of RAS 33's *Raja Niti*, ff. 99-100 and LOr2125's *Jaya Lengkara*, ff. 7-8 and *Kuntara Manawa*, ff. 129-130.

21 The *sabda parusa* is named as one the *prakara* by the *Jimbun Slokantara I*, § 7, and the *Arya Dilah* § 5 and is the equivalent to the *wak parusa* of the *Agama*, discussed below, p. 176ff.

22 Specific references are contained in, among others, the (non-vintage) Javanese *Agama* § 219 and that of Bali §§ 295-296, cited in Hoadley and Hooker, 'The Law Texts of Java and Bali'.

Tarka fined ten *suku* (one half *rupiah*) by the crown for middling verbal violence. The *layang* is dated Saturday, 2 Jumadilakir, Alip.

Pun Bama v. Pun Diwal

A final example of the use of *sloka* phenomena in litigation comes from two land disputes.[23] The first revolves about *amuk punggung* (senseless violence) with reference to land disputes. Belonging to the Thirty *Prakara* (no. 3 of Table 6.1), the *prakara* was one of the few clarified by a text of Java/Bali.[24] In contrast to the two prior summaries, land disputes drew directly upon recognizable legal *sloka*.

As reported in the *Raja Niti* the two affairs turned about a claim to a dry field (*tegal*) and destruction of *sawah* lands. In both Pun Bama expressed (*matur*) his dissatisfaction (*tan rena*) with a Pun Diwal. In the first case a *layang leleresan* ('letter of truth') recorded that Diwal's claims to Tegal Siba Karang had been rejected. His claim was found wanting in three respects; 1) *aprangwa* ('*a*' = negation; *prangwa* = to contest), namely that it did not disprove his opponent's defence, 2) *masang damar tan murub* (lighting a lamp that does not burn), an often cited *sloka* pointing out the inconsistency of witnesses, and 3) *kawiyat,* advancing a claim that was too old. The *layang* is dated 9 Jumadilakir, Alip, with the *sangkala* standing for the *saka* date of 4251 = 1524 or 1602.

The second case dealt with Diwal's alleged destruction of Bama's *sawah* lands, namely *amuk punggung*. As a form of *awasa-wasa* (*lit* to use force), it concerned up-rooting Bama's mature plantings (*kerti tuwuh*). This part of the affair is dated *saka* 1281 or 1358. A third paragraph of the summary is more specific. Pun Bama's two *ancing* (a measure of wet-rice land) in Palantengen village were destroyed. Determined by an *in situ* investigation, Diwal's evil deeds (*ala-ala*) included 1) *ambima paksa marusak tan wring baya,* namely, acting as a Bima, forcing destruction without knowing the danger/consequences, thereby stealing [by destroying] *sawah,* 2) being a *durga awasa-wasa tan wring baya or* a Durga in unchecked violence, without knowing the danger/consequences, and 3) carrying out *amuk punggung* (stupid, i.e., ill-considered, violence) named in the preceding

23 Summary of RAS 33's *Raja Niti*, ff. 148-155 and *Undhang Sénapati Jimbun*, f. 59, plus LOr 2125's *Raja Niti* ff. 157-158, 162-164, and 168-167, respectively.

24 The *prakara* is explained in the Bali *Agama*, Art. 83 and further discussed under the following rubric.

paragraph. This part of the case contains several dates falling between 1648 and 1656.[25]

More interesting in terms of legal issues are the reasons for the court to reject the defendant's claims. Along with relatively self-explanatory reasons, motivation for the negative settlement was expressed as the *sloka*:

masang damar tan murub
placing [lighting] a lamp that does not burn

Masang damar is a recognized *sloka* clarified by the *Pepakem Tjerbon* citing the *Adilulah* as its source as 'one's support or witness are found to be not credible before the law'.[26]

The other land dispute, one concerning the destruction of wet rice fields by the defendant himself, also drew upon the repertoire of *sloka*. Motivation for rejecting the plaintiff's claim is cited as *ambima paksa marusak tan wiring baya* (acting as a Bima forcing destruction without attention to the consequences), which is similar, but not identical, to the *Luwangan* § 1.[27] A subsequent paragraph in the affair cites the *sloka* phrase '*Durga amas-amas*', referring to Durga, the goddess of destruction. To date no counterpart in *sloka* literature has been found. The phrases cited by the last-named land dispute resemble the function of *sloka* phenomena within the textual tradition as summarised by Table 6.2. They are more in the line of defining duties and obligations to punish miscreants than of providing specifics. In contrast the first phase of the case cites a well-known *prakara*, one of the 144 negative criteria leading automatically to defeat in a law suit according to the textual tradition.

25 In addition to that of 1358, another date is given for the destruction of *sawah* (wet rice fields) and the resultant falling (*tiba*) of the accord as Monday, 6 Jumadilakir, Èhè, plus the numbers //o// 751. This could be read as 0751 or A.J. 1570 = 1648 or, if the 'o' was 0-9, between 1570 and 1579, thus between 1648 and 1656. The final paragraph states that Diwal had appeared before the court *paséban* on Sunday, at the sounding of the mosque drum on 10 Sapar in the year Wau.
26 The Dutch text on p. 26 reads *diens Sasandan off getuigen bevonden werd niet gelofwardig te sijn na de Wet*. Another more complete version is *adedamar tanggal sapisan kapurnaman*, although with a slightly different meaning than that provided by Suwarno, *Dictionary*, no. 6. Here the translation emphasizes the lighting a lamp, which in the Suwarno version – while using the dim light of the moon on the first day of the Javanese month, suddenly the full moon shines brightly – is intensified by contrasting the need for a lamp, i.e., darkness, with the brightness of a night with a full moon. In short, something that is dark (obscure) comes into light, in this instance the legal settlement.
27 The *Luwangan sinalokan* reads: *ambima paksa, angrusak praja, daratikrama yojana* (acting as Bima forcing destruction upon the realm as a violation of the land). It also is close to the modern proverb *ambima paksarsa dana* 'to force someone to do something in the way Bima would have done', Suwarno, *Dictionary*, no. 51.

Practice

The preceding discussion of Javanese law as defined by the *sloka* phenomena are utilized as the standard for accessing the veracity, and thus usefulness, of information recorded by intruding European officials. This approach reverses that of the author's earlier work on the subject which of necessity was built information supplied by foreigners supplemented by choice bits of local lore, when available. More than an exercise in Asian-centric history by harmonizing the data contained in foreign and local sources, the approach leads to a more realistic view of traditional Javanese legal practice. Four legal cases resolved by joint Javanese-Dutch courts during the first quarter of the eighteenth century are analysed with reference to the contribution of the *sloka* phenomena. Because the cases have been analysed in detail within the context of Company Dutch v. Javanese legal system,[28] their contents are summarised below.

Karta Nagara v. Karta Dinata *et.al.* 1722

As close as possible to an autonomous case record from the Independent Kingdoms period is the Karta Nagara theft case of 1722.[29] What prevents it from being acceptable as an authentic Javanese judgment are two points. The first is its acknowledgment of submission to both the Dutch Resident of Cirebon, Willem Tersmitten (1720-1726) and Pangéran Aria Cirebon, the Company's overseer of the Priangan region and co-reigning regent of Cirebon.

> The case agrees in the first instance with the wishes of the honourable Resident who governs at Cirebon and secondly with those of His Majesty Pangéran Aria Cirebon. The time of writing this certificate of victory is on Thursday in the month of Rabingulakir the 23rd of the year Jé.[30]

28 Hoadley, *Selective Judicial Competence*.

29 The case has been presented within the context of tracing developments in the legal system of the Cirebon-Priangan legal administration during the eighteenth century, *Ibid.*, pp. 78-79. That it is not entirely unique, at least from what is known of Javanese case law, is attested to by the existence of a case handled by the Yogyakarta *Pradata* court in 1790, Carey and Hoadley, *Archive of Yogyakarta*, p.104. Despite its potential, the case as recorded in Add 12303 provides few details.

30 Pangéran Aria Cirebon (1697-1723) was appointed 'Overseer of the Priangan' through the Resolution of 2 March 1706, an office he held until his death in 1723 (*Ibid.*, pp. 40-42, 68-69). During Pangéran Aria's tenure in office the Javanese year *Jé* fell on 1707, 1714, and 1721. From the correspondence of the name of the day of the week, i.e., Thursday, and the Javanese year of *Jé*, it appears that 1721 is correct. However, because Javanese and Christian years do not always correspond, a calculation arrives at Thursday, 12 February 1722. The date is of some importance

The second point undermining its veracity as reflecting purely Javanese legal tradition is the implication, reinforced by Dutch citations, that *jaksa* were judges in the European sense. The titles considered here lack data on *jaksa* duties and responsibilities. One assumes that this was because were well known by the practitioners and reference works. From a reading of those texts it seems clear that contrary to accepted wisdom, they were not judges in the European sense, but keepers of the law, so to speak. As Gobius pointed out in 1717, it was the jaksa who kept the *pepakem* or handbooks, each with his own variation.[31] In the present case the letter of victory (*surat kukudung*) was issued by the four *jaksa,* in their capacity as assessors-at-law. 'Assessor' seems particularly appropriate given a dictionary definition of '[...] a person called upon to advise a judge, committee of inquiry'.[32] Elsewhere it has been argued that theirs was the responsibility for providing the deciding executive authority – *patih*, *tumenggung*, etc. in their capacity as surrogates of Sultan or Susuhunan – with the contents of traditional law. As seen in the texts this was usually multiple in that the court could choose between various recognized options that best fit the circumstances and, more important, were most likely to restore the *tata tantrem* (order and tranquillity) so honoured by Javanese society. The point has been belaboured here because the *kukudung* is the only extant document written in Javanese, the remaining three are translations into eighteenth century Dutch preserved by being incorporated into the Company records.

A summary of the case follows. Subsequent discussion attests to its compatibility with what has been learned of the *sloka* phenomena through study of the textual tradition.

> The *kukudung* [letter of victory] relates the course of a case between Kyai Karta Nagara, son of Tumenggung Tanu Baya, Regent of Parakanmuncang, and Karta Dinata of Bandung with several accomplices. According to its contents, Karta Dinata and three helpers, one of which was never apprehended, had stolen a variety of objects, among them two ancestral *kris*, named Megah and Petyatoek, the property of Kyai Karta Nagara. The stolen goods were found with Karta Dinata of Bandung and Praja Dita of

not only for the present document but also because one of the *jaksa* signing it was Candra Yuda of Sumedang, to whom the key manuscript LOr 7440 is attributed, see Chapter 2.

31 'Gobius on the Priangan jaksa', 26 March 1715, Appendix IV, Hoadley, *Selective Judicial Competence.*

32 *The Concise Oxford Dictionary.*

> Ciamis. Constituting unambiguous proof (*bukti*) for the court, the find implicated two others. The four were judged guilty of theft and fined according to the legal principle of *raja dhendha*, amounting to some eight *laksa* (80,000 pici?) each, for which an appropriate *sloka* or *sinalokan* was cited. Sentences were also handed down to almost a dozen individuals who were in some manner associated with the theft and their sentences likewise followed by *sinalokan.*

The two major culprits, Karta Dinata and Praja Dita were ordered to return the *kris* and pay double compensation, the remaining miscreants were punished under the auspices of *sloka* phenomena. This drew upon several of the *astha corah* (Appendix IV). The four culprits '[knew] the actions of an evildoer'. This led to their being named as 'helpers of *durjana*' for which they were fined eight *laksa*, in addition to being saddled with the *sinalokan:*

> *Mustika brahmara corah, culika-culikem, daratikrama yojana* (sic *yuwana*).
> Thieving mice/rats and bees known to be criminal, who destroy the welfare of others, not taking into consideration the danger.[33]

Two more individuals were guilty of 'shelter[ing] an evildoer', another of the *astha corah.* Their property was forfeited to the crown and they were fined 8 *laksa*. They fell under the *sinalokan*:

> *Dustha manganjut amangrupa sadhu, nyaud, tan weru ing baya.*
> Evildoers expert at maintaining the face of respectability, not taking into consideration the danger.[34]

And finally, Prajadita, who resisted arrest and wounded two of those sent out from Parakanmuncang to apprehend Karta Dinata, was fined and saddled with a *sinalokan* that has defied direct translation.

33 *Mustika brahmara* [...] *alun-alun*, Classic *Sloka*, no. 2, denotes the presence of miscreants seen as all-present mice and bees whose character is *culika-culikem* (untrustworthy, dishonest). *Daratikrama* is literally (violent assault, rape), one of the *sad-atatayi* (Appendix IV). It is used here in a more general sense as 'rapacious, predatory'. *Yojana/yujana* must be an equivalent of *yuwana* (*lit* healthy, well, safe and sound), which describes the situation prior to the presence of miscreants in the anthropomorphic form of mice and bees. *Yojana* (*lit* a league (measure of distance)) does not make sense within this context.

34 *Dustha* is clearly a criminal miscreant who was (*manganjut*?) expert (*baud*) at *rupa sadhu*, maintaining the 'appearances of virtue'. 'Not knowing' or 'ignoring the danger' [of punishment] is a common ending for such *sinalokan*.

Sing kardita tatas prana braja mispeka.[35]

Given *sloka* phenomena's dominance in textual law, their presence in recorded cases is expectable, if only sporadically documented. In the present case *sinalokan* clarify the type and by implication the seriousness of the behaviour in question. The opening phrase in the first *sinalokan*, i.e., *mustika brahmara corah,* is part of Classic *Sloka*, no. 2 cited by Tumenggung Raja Sasana in the *Jugul Muda* as part of the *dustha pandung* (evil of thieves). It not only allowed but required punishment by the sovereign. While the main actors in the Karta Nagara case were sons of the Regents, and thus would be punished only under exceptional circumstances, their accomplices were felled by clearly criminal charges under the *astha corah* as indicated in the original *sloka*. Here they were cobbled together to make a one-off *sinalokan* completed by the addition of commonly used phrases designating the harmful result of such action and of ignoring possible consequences.

In contrast, the nature of the second *sinalokan*, i.e., *dustha manganju,* is more in line with a description or an exposé of the doers' nefarious activities. It is a variant of the *sinalokan* cited in the *Luwangan* § 45. The latter explains that this type of *dustha* is of a special nature in that he/she is a close neighbour sharing a house, bathroom, cooking facilities, etc. This sort of betrayal of mutual exchanges (*wéwéhan*) with an evildoer makes him/her the equivalent of one liable to the same penalties, all the while outwardly maintaining an air of respectability. *Sinalokan* not only classified the terms of the deviant behaviour but also motivated, if not set, the resultant punishments. Noteworthy here is that these are free of punishments introduced by the Dutch as branding, flogging, terms on the chain-gang, etc.

During the early eighteenth century *sloka* phenomena were sporadically drawn upon by tribunals operating in the Cirebon-Priangan region. In them the *jaksa* sat with representatives of the executive bodies as princes, Regents, and Company officials. At least on paper a division of labour was recognized. The *jaksa* supplied the alternatives recognized by traditional

35 '*Singa Kardhita*' seems to be a play on Praja Dita's name. Another possibility is 'a lion (*singa*) going to work, i.e., attack, which depends upon *kardhita* = *karya*? The remainder of the *sinalokan* is constructed of another *sinalokan* from *Cadad* §§ 2, 19 and *Luwangan* § 6, no 2. The former explains the terms as: *Tatas* = wound; *Prana* = within; *Braja* = he who orders the wounds; and *Mispeka* = the darkness in the middle of the *alun-alun*. Put together this can be interpreted as someone who wounds others, here those sent to detain Karta Dinata and Praja Dita, experiences the darkness of the execution place, (cf. Classic *Sloka*, no. 2). In fact, Praja Dita was fined four *laksa* (literary for *real*?), or eight according to the *Luwangan* plus compensation to those he attacked.

Javanese law; decisions were made by Regents, Princes, and other rulers. Both were monitored by the Dutch Resident of Cirebon sitting on the court and subject to further vetting by the High Government at Batavia. Company preoccupation with documentation guaranteed the preservation of information concerning the handling of legal affairs. As we have seen, this commonly took the form of pronouncements, translated *surat kukudung* (letter of victory) or *surat salaran* (letter of defeat), and occasionally edicts issued in the name of the Cirebon-Priangan rulers in Dutch. While this sometimes is the source of ambiguity, preservation of the Javanese *sloka*-type phrases, even in eighteenth-century Dutch transcription, is an asset. Three cases are particularly instructive.

State v. Wira Wadana and Tanu Patra, 1715

The case is reported in a translated *surat salaran* dated 13 April 1715.[36] It revolved about local officials' lack of diligence in carrying out governmental orders, i.e., those of Javanese Regents and the Dutch East India Company, to report and/or arrest troublesome 'foreigners' who had come into their districts. For this oversight the district chief, Wira Wadana, along with a Javanese *'paep'* (*ulama*?), Tanu Patra, were prosecuted for negligence. They were suspected of disloyal concealment and tolerance of vagabonds, falling under the *sinalokan*:

> *gana-léna sura wiweka tan werroe ning baija*
> Careless persons [the district chiefs as defendants] setting aside caution, not knowing, [alternatively] ignoring the danger.[37]

This was not merely a clarification. As indicated by the preceding sentence, it was a serious offence. The two were reported as having been inattentive in observing the laws of the sovereign (*de wetten van den landsvorst*) and hence fell under the six-fold guilt (*sesderliej schulden*). The latter must refer

36 Hoadley, *Selective Judicial Competence*, Index.

37 *Ibid*, p. 81. Although a complete version has yet to be found, many of its parts originate from known *sloka* phenomena. '*Gana-lena*' is found in a half dozen *prakara*, among others from the Raffles *Surya Alam, Appendix C*, and the *Raja Niscaya* § 16. Winter interprets the term as meaning a 'careless person, like a bee seeking honey', *Javaansche Zamenspraken*, vol. II, pt. 3, no. 472. *Sur* (*ngesur* to push aside), *wiweka* (caution or prudence) and *tan weruh ing baya*, meaning 'not knowing' or 'ignoring the dangers' of the situation, are common expressions.

to the *sad-atatayi* (see Appendix IV), most likely that of 'betrayer of kings' (*raja wisuna*).[38]

A further development concerned local officials' retrospective repudiation of all knowledge of the intruding foreigner, Pangéran Bumi Nata and his entourage from the kingdom of Mataram. For this patently false repudiation – he had been living there for years and had taken three wives in the interim – they were prosecuted and ultimately fined. Their misdeed was expressed in the *sinalokan*:

> *hamiroeda gana-gana sandie hoepaijia tan werroe hing baija*
> To avoid or shun a powerful person [Pangeran Bumi Nata] alternatively 'not reporting to superiors in keeping with a secret strategy' [the repudiation], 'disregarding the danger'.

In addition to the ending *tan weruh ing baya,* which is a *sloka* in its own right, '*sandi upaya*' (a secret strategy) is also considered a *sloka* or near *sloka* from apparently an older era.[39] The *sloka* phenomena specifically named are more damning than the reasons for punishment specifically stated in the *salaran*. Under traditional circumstances the indigenous definitions would have led to further categories of crimes/misdemeanours.

The case's final *sinalokan* set punishments for the Regent, Kyai Demang Timbanganten (Bandung), Kyai Angga Yuda, and his ministers. These consisted of fines for their lack of vigilance on the Company's behalf. It called forth the *sinalokan*:

> *soera krama daratie seidem* [*sic sidhem*] *pramenen*
> Setting aside order/custom by rapaciously (*daratikrama*) saying nothing [about the nefarious activities] although it was known by all.

The final phrase indicates the seriousness of their crime. It revolved the 'crime of silence', a well-known *sloka* of the era.[40] More important it also demanded punishments by the sovereign without the necessity of judicial handling.

38 Apparently following the instructions of the Dutch Resident, the *salaran* adds to sovereign laws of '*ubaya ing nagara*', 'infringement on the Company's interdiction', de Haan, *Priangan*, vol. II, Bijlage XXV.

39 Suwarno, *Dictionary*, no. 1529 attributed to an Old Javanese origin.

40 Ngafenan, *Paribasan*, p. 124; Darmasoetjipta, *Kamus Peribahasa*, no. 992; Suwarno, *Dictionary*, no. 1185.

Kandurahan Panembong v. Suba Mangala of 1714/15

The *sinalokan* connected to the guilty verdict in the second case confirms use of suggestive, but not necessarily binding, identification of punishable behaviour. Suba Mangala, son of the Regent of Parakanmuncang, had attempted to frame his *kandurahan* (treasury official) by accusing him of corruption. As in the previous case, the accusation was strengthened by the (false) testimony sworn by nine subordinates. How the schema came unglued is not related. The translated *surat salaran* states only that the nine subordinates were found guilty. Their connivance fell under the *sinalokan*:

> *sur patra amigena sobaga awagé* [*agawé*] *dustha bahud tan weruh ing baya*
> Pushing aside documents makes hindrances with the character of becoming an expert evildoer, ignoring the consequences.[41]

Aside from what must be one of the earliest references to the corruption so characteristic of present-day Indonesia, the *sinalokan* is more suggestive than demonstrative. This is indicated by the used of *dustha* in the *sinalokan*, a term clearly associated with proven criminal activities.

Puspa Nagara/Wisa Truna affair of 1717

A third example is provided by the murder of a Company servant, Corporal Christian Kruger, while on duty in the eastern Priangan. He was stabbed during an inspection tour of the pearl banks at Segara Anakan by Wisa Truna, who fled. The Company's tentative hold on an outlying region with potentially valuable resources in concert with the potential danger this posed to its officials who often travelled unaccompanied in the region, ensured the case was closely monitored. For present purposes two legal issues are crucial. The first is the extent to which the murder had been arranged with the connivance of the local Regent, Puspa Nagara. Because there was no evidence for this, Resident Gobius turned to the general principles of Javanese law. The Regent was accused of being *een helder van moordeneers* (associate of murderers) amounting to one the *astha corah*. The Javanese term is not given. It could have been any one of the eight. 'Befriending' (*isaka*), 'knowing the actions of' (*sapratingkah*), 'assisting' (*tatrah*), or 'sheltering'

41 The second half of the phrase is found as a variation in the *Arya Dilah*, § 7, namely *sobanga agawé sadu, ambaud krama wicanté*, supplemented by Winter's interpretation that *bangga* means *budi* (character, properties).

(*goptah*) an evildoer are the most likely choices. The ultimate penalty was to be imposed by the sovereign. In other words, the *jaksa* left the choice of the specific law to sovereign authority.

The actual perpetrator, Wisa Truna, felt the full weight of the law. In a subsequent report to Batavia the Resident baldly stated that he was guilty of *raja wisuna* (destroying the peace between princely associates) and *wangkarita* [*sic waja wangkara*] (public or other misdeeds), two of the *sad-atatayi*.[42] As shown in a prior case before the Cirebon *jaksa* in 1696,[43] the labels were equivalent to a sentence of capital punishment. As with the other examples, the Puspa Nagara affair was closed with a succinct utterance (*ucapan*), i.e., a *sloka* or *sinalokan*, namely *purwaning nakira gandaning niata*. This has been translated as 'from of old an evil deed smells clearly', suggesting that the evil nature of the Regent's connection with Wisa Truna was obvious. The interpretation was attractive to Company officials. It provided an indigenous legal motivation for punishing an uppity Regent.

In common with the preceding cases, there were two groups of accomplices considered to share responsibility for the escape of Wisa Truna. The first group consisted of the local district chief (*ombol*) and his subordinates. They were considered as remiss in their duty to apprehend the fugitive. Their short-comings were summed up in the *sinalokan*:

> *anglila praya wiweka tan weruh ing baya*
> Turning from intention, [of the crime] to caution by ignoring the danger.

The second group consisted of acquaintances and neighbours, were held to be collectively responsible for the more serious offence, one redeemable only by payment of the *wergeld* of thirty-three *reals*. This was explained by the *sinalokan*:

> *lulurong buntuh dhusta mangilingaken kaloebet tarka baya*
> A dead end, allowing an evil doer to disappear causing danger of complicity.

Despite appearances, the *sinalokan* are more instructive than suggestive. *Lurung buntuh/buntung* is a modern Javanese *sloka*/proverb.[44] Through

42 Also cited in Hoadley, 'Sanskritic continuity', pp. 117-118.

43 Hoadley, *Selective Judicial Competence*, pp. 115ff.

44 The *sloka* is also cited by the *Wadigun Wangkara*, Add 18398, f. 62r. It means 'to accuse someone without evidence', which results in the accusation being rendered invalid, Ngafenan,

the *sinalokan* the *jaksa*, who must have been responsible for formulating it, indicated that the accusation was baseless. In this instance recourse to traditional forms constituted a subtle form of protest for skewing Javanese legal forms to serve the new sovereign, the Dutch East India Company.

In summary, the use of *sloka phenomena* as reported by the observations of Dutch officials operated on both the implicit and explicit levels. *Sinalokan* implied more serious crimes than those specified by the Dutch translations of the Javanese settlements. Not only were the *sloka* phenomena actively employed in contemporaneous litigation but also they provided key points in defining the transgressions. Under traditional, non-colonial, circumstances – only a small indication being available and that from textual law – the suggestions/indications named here would have led to more concrete, local legal responses. With reference to the 'diverse components' demands set by the *astha corah* and *sad-tatayi* were explicit. However, under the circumstances they were tapped only when they fit with Company aims. Nevertheless, even the few examples from Javo-Dutch cases help to clarify *sloka* phenomena's contribution to a type of case law.

Paribasan, p, 78; Suwarno, *Dictionary*, no. 796. A longer version, i.e., *lurung buntuh dustha mangilangaken,* is quoted by the *Luwangan* § 48 in connection with someone who falls under suspicion on grounds of circumstantial evidence (*tidharsa*). The most common form of *tidharsa* is a person who was the last to see an object before it went missing, i.e., was stolen. This could easily be applied to a person who went missing, thus raising suspicion of criminal complicity.

Section III

Character, Apparent Demise, and Context

Based on an assessment of available sources, Section II has reconstructed the major components of the Independent Kingdoms legal texts. Termed in this work the *sloka* phenomena, they not only dominate the contents of traditional Javanese written law but also provide a guide to deciphering them. Despite what on the surface appears to be a jumble of hopelessly disorganized and incompatible textual materials, guided by the *sloka* phenomena further study reveals a matrix of interrelated and consistent elements.

Section III opens with an attempt to summarize the nature of traditional Javanese law based on consideration of the *sloka* phenomena. The uniqueness of the phenomena to the Independent Kingdoms era helps to differentiate it from the preceding period usually termed Old Java. From there discussion turns to a chronology of the dismissal of traditional Javanese written law by the Netherlands East Indies government. This was in preference for either rule according to Dutch Indies law or an *adatrecht* which would be given its form and contents by C. van Vollenhoven and his disciples in the early twentieth century. That this was apparent is attested to by the continued popularity of traditional texts as attested to by their being re-copied, edited, and most likely revised by generations of Central Javanese scribes. More intriguing indications of the longevity comes from the apparent revival of many of the *sloka* phenomena among younger Indonesians and even some Islamic scholars in their quest for a public morality seen as lacking in today's Indonesia.

8 Character

At this point it seems prudent to remind ourselves that the *sloka* phenomena are instrumental. They constitute facets of law that both served the community and were created by it. With the knowledge gained of the *sloka* phenomena, discussion can turn to the broader significance of the law valid during the Independent Kingdoms era. A start can be made by emphasising its break from what we know of the law of Old Java.

Sloka phenomena as unique

Appreciation for the uniqueness of traditional Javanese law comes from comparison with what little is known of its predecessors. It has long been assumed that the law prevailing in the era of Old Java can be reconstructed from manuscripts copied, preserved, and edited by Balinese scribes. Much remains to be said on the issue. However, the present work is concerned with legal history only in so far as it touches on the *sloka* phenomena of the period under consideration. Nevertheless, any discussion of the subject must consider the accessible titles ascribed to Java and Bali as, for example, the *Agama* (of both Java and Bali), as well as the Balinese texts *Adigama*, *Kutara Agama*, and *Purwa Agama*.[1] Even a summary reading of the contents of those titles reveals the lack of expressions identifiable as *sloka* phenomena. The hundreds of paragraphs comprising those texts yield only some three dozen expressions even vaguely resembling those of the Independent Kingdoms era. The only *sloka* reference discovered to date comes from the apparently Old Javanese *Adigama* in connection with false witness.[2]

Because phrases resembling *sloka* of the Independent Kingdoms era are uncommon in titles of Java and Bali, a few examples can be given by way of illustrating their form and method of expression. Most of the three dozen terms repeated in several titles deal with *wak parusa*, literally 'verbal violence' illustrated by the Bali *Agama* § 295 and 297, as well as § 230-235. They concern scoffing and insults. Significantly, they are dependent on a strictly observed caste hierarchy, which does not seem to have characterised

1 The texts are discussed by Hoadley and Hooker, 'Laws of Java and Bali', pp. 274-346.

2 *Sloka* status has been erroneously assigned in *Ibid.* to three paragraphs from the Bali *Agama*, namely Art.s 295, 297, and 345. Further research shows them to be general statements (*ucapan*) roughly equivalent to *sinalokan*, see *Adigama*, LOr 3789, Sugiarto transcription LOr 10.441, p. 9, 10.

Old Java and certainly not that of the Independent Kingdoms era. That the parallel contents of the (Javanese) *Agama* are on a par is shown by the first of a dozen paragraphs on the issue.

> If a person out of anger scoffs (*anguman-uman*) at another (or) does him/her bodily injury (*angawakan mala ing awak*), scoffing at head, food, movements, behaviour, birth (*tojaman*), family, acquaintances, his/her knowledge such a person ['s action] is termed (*arané*) *wak-parusa* (§ 19).

Paragraphs 220 to 230 prescribe penalties determined by hierarchy of class and caste of perpetrator and victim. As direct translations of Manu (VIII: 267-87) it is not surprising that they are weighed in favour of higher castes, a characteristic supplemented by the contents of the other titles of Balinese origin.[3]

The Independent Kingdom's Javanese equivalent of *wak parusa* is *sabda parusa*. It is cited twice in the *Pepakem Tjerbon* where it is attributed to the *Raja Niscaya* and the *Jaya Lengkara,* (pp. 22 and 68 respectively). However, neither of the Dutch references are accompanied by the Javanese equivalent. Thus, it cannot be determined whether the terms employed drew on the vocabulary of the *sloka* phenomena or were just 'termed' so-and-so (*arané*). In the titles cited as constituting the *Pepakem* the term *sabda parusa* is consistently included as a *prakara.* These are found in, among others, the *Jimbun Slokantara I* (§ 7), *Jaya Lengkara* (§ 9), and *Arya Dilah* (§ 5), all from LOr 7440. An even earlier citation of *sabda parusa* as a *prakara* comes from the Berlin 402 *Surya Alam* (§ 41) from the late 1730s.

Crucial to the present argument is whether such phrases are designated by the specific terminology of *sloka* phenomena or are lumped indiscriminately under the heading 'named such-and such' (*arané*). As we have seen, the Independent Kingdoms era titles consistently express *sloka* phrases in their own special vocabulary. In contrast, the titles of Java and Bali consistently use for such terms *aran* (ng [...] 2. name (what s.th. is)) plus '-*é*' for the definitive article. Even the three dozen phrases which seem to resemble *sloka* phenomena are designated as '*arané*'. Moreover, none of the characteristic terms appear in the titles of Java and Bali, including the *Agama,* Jonker's *Kuthara Manawa,* optimistically accepted as representing Old Javanese law. More interesting, the appearance of *arané* citations in the texts of Java and Bali parallels citations from ostensibly younger, Senapati Jimbun

3 *Kuthara Agama,* Art.s 15, 48, 52, 68-72, 134-135.

era, Javanese titles.[4] Like the just named titles of Java-Bali, the paragraphs provided by RAS 33 and LOr 2125 consistently use '*arané*' to designate such phrases.

Further confirmation of a change in nomenclature comes from the fact that some phrases specifically cited in the Independent Kingdoms' texts as *sloka*, *sinalokan*, *aksara*, or *prakara* are in those of Java/Bali subsumed under the general term '*arané*'. The prime example is the oft-cited *prakara* from the Yogyakarta *Surya Alam* (§ 9:3) *amuk punggung* (meaningless violence). As noted in Table 6.1, no. 3, this concerns 'attacking one's own plantings', which has come down to the present as 'going on a rampage blindly causing damage and hurting persons'.[5] The *prakara* is mentioned several times by the *Pepakem Tjerbon* (pp. 24, 46, 68, and 90) citing as sources the *Adilulah*, *Jaya Lengkara*, and *Kontara Manawa* respectively. Yet it is cited in the titles Java and Bali, as well as in the Javanese Jimbun ones, as *arané* or *aranya*. The Balinese *Kutara Agama* explains it as verbal abuse escalating into physical violence, i.e., arguments becoming so heated that those so engaged reach a level of frustration provoking them to hack a fence or gate with a *kris*, or even attacking their own plantings. This is termed (*arané*) *amuk punggung* (Art. 83). The term appears often in the Jimbun Era texts. Examples are found in the *Gajah Mada*, f. 49, *Raja Niti.*, ff. 154, 156, 163, and *Undhang-Undhang Sénapati Jimbun* (ff. 80-81). It is even cited in a *sloka*-like context as motivation for a judicial decision attributed to the mid-seventeenth century.

Another example comes from the legal rubric in the titles of Java and Bali for what is termed (*arané*) the *panca-bhangga*, 'Skr [...] five ways of losing a lawsuit'.[6] Art 343 of the Bali *Agama* lists the remaining five. These include altering one's earlier testimony (*anya-wadi*), claiming differently than a witness (*krya-desi*), writing falsely a promise (*nopastayi*), not being able to reply to an opponent (*niruk-tirah*), and not appearing in court exacerbated by quarrelsomeness (*awuth-aprelaga*). *Panca-bhangga* is also named (*aranya*) in

4 Appendix III. 'Titles Left Out' terms these manuscripts the 'Jimbun Era texts' after the period's chief figure. Consisting of RAS 33, LOr 2125, plus an undetermined number of 'fellow travelers' as NBS 56, by date of acquisition they are nineteenth century copies. That their contents post-date mainstream titles used in this work in indicated by their unique titles, i.e., *Raja Niti*, *Gajah Mada*, and *Undhang-Undhang Sénapati Jimbun*; deviations in contents from 'standard' titles as the *Jaya Lengkara* and *Kuthara Manawa*; further developments of the *sloka* phenomena marking off a distinctive group of titles; and their near unique dominance of Kyai Senapati Jimbun.

5 Suwarno, *Dictionary*, no. 987.

6 Zoetmulder. *Old Javanese-English Dictionary*.

the *Adigama* (57.31, a romanised copy of LOr 3879 by Soegiarto). To the best of the author's knowledge the single reference to *panca-bhangga* in Java is found in IOL Java 90 (§ 50). More to the point, the first four of the five [*sic* six] items of the (Java-Bali) *panca-bhangga* correspond to the '*aksara* of the wrong' (*aksara salah*) or *uger-uger*, the eight fatal flaws of litigation (Chapter 4). During the Independent Kingdom era they were indelibly part of the *sloka* phenomena.

Other apparent likenesses to traditional Javanese law are found in the analysis section following presentation of the respective law texts of Java and Bali. They comprise several dozen *sloka*-like phrases designated as *arané*. A good example is *anumpak ing pang aking* (sitting on a dead branch). It applies to one suiting a dead person, the subject matter of the *Agama* Art. 18. In a slightly different version of (s)*lendhean kayu aking* (riding a dead branch) or *anggugat kayu aking* (accusing a dead branch), the phrase constitutes a common Javanese *prakara* affair, as well as a modern Javanese proverb.[7] Another example is provided by the *Agama* (Art. 66), the Balinese *Agama* (§ 280), and the *Kutara Agama* (162.4). This is the provision for a 'bedewed corpse' termed (*arané*) *katemu wangké kubuan*, meaning the discovery of the victim of murder by an unknown perpetrator. This entails collective responsibility for payment of the *wergeld* for those living within a fixed radius of discovery. No specific Javanese term is known for the phenomenon because the references come from Dutch reports.[8]

This short discussion has aimed at establishing that most unique features of Javanese law do not necessarily stem from Old Java. They have only been partially preserved in younger times. What remains to be done is to pin down of what these consisted. The characteristic features of the Independent Kingdoms law can be discussed under the rubrics of goal, selectivity, and autonomous law.

Goal

A characteristic expected of legal institutions is decisiveness. One party wins, the other loses; one reaps the rewards, the other pays the penalty,

7 Suwarno, *Dictionary*, no. 774, 1441, as well as no. 117 respectively.

8 Hoadley, *Selective Judicial Competence*, pp. 122, 125. Noteworthy, the transition from a title naming specific actions in the vocabulary of *sloka* phenomena to an all-encompassing general application of '*arané*' connects titles of the late Independent Kingdoms with those of Java and Bali. With further substantiation it even might provide the basis for grouping the latter with the Jimbun era titles as a younger level of texts from of the Independent Kingdoms era, including Bali.

materially, socially, or physically. Ideally through the instrument of law the original controversy is settled. The challenge was to ensure that those naturally divisive circumstances were only temporary. Former contestants must be reconciled, at least to the extent of being able to interact normally within the demands set by custom. In societies characterized by a centralized governmental authority recognition or sponsorship of a given solution ensures complicity of winner and loser alike. As a spin-off sponsorship tends to motivate state-provided means of decision through courts of law, rules and regulations, and even creation of a frame work for arbitrated settlements.

In this respect traditional Javanese law differs from expectations. Concern with preserving or restoring the *tata tantrem* was paired with decentralized of political authority. Not surprisingly, the function of *sloka* phenomena was attuned to Java's decentralized form of political authority, one rarely broken by short periods of concentration of political power in the hands of a competent ruler. The accomplishments of a Radèn Patah (aka Demak I, Senapati Jimbun), a Sultan Agung, or a Pangéran Mangkubumi was more than offset by the numerous examples of over-extending and overestimating the power of kingship, thereby bringing disaster to the ruler and ruled. This is exemplified by the rule of Mangkurat I (r. 1646-1677) and most of his successors.[9] This meant that centralized enforcement exercised by the state was not an option. It became so only with the imposition of Dutch political hegemony in the region beginning in the eighteenth century. During the transitional phase considered here foreign power helped to prop up indigenous authority only in so as far as it furthered Dutch East India Company ends.

Under the traditional forms prevailing during the Independent Kingdoms era, socially divisive threats inherent in legal contests had to be overcome without recourse to raw force. Such action took many forms. One was to show that the outcome of legal dispute was not dependent on decisive power exercised by the (state) court but stemmed from customary rules. A second was to secure acceptance by loser and winner alike, which demanded selectivity within legal rules. A final instrument was self-regulation in the form of surrendering certain types of punishments to the wronged party itself.

The clearest statement of the confluence of law leading to settlements and customary behaviour comes from the much-quoted § 50 of the *Luwangan*. Litigants are not defeated by the judges, but by their own utterances. As

9 Ricklefs, *Modern Javanese Historical Tradition*, p. 5ff.

the expression of generally accepted norms (*adat*), the core concept is captured (and preserved) in Classic *Sloka,* no. 24, a gecko that dies because of its own voice.

A second instrument was to secure acceptance of the solution by winner and loser alike. This is most likely the reason for duplicating the *surat kukudung* and *surat salaran* (letters of victory and loss). Nearly identical in content, they served as a means of ensuring not only compliance by former adversaries but also some degree of acceptance. As illustrated by the Japlak affair recorded by the *Serat Arok*, issuing such letters was preceded by verbal acceptance of the result by both parties.

> 183. Then all the *jaksa* ceremoniously signed [the documents]. Ki Raja Niti instructed Demang Undhang-Undhang, 'You announce both the *kukudung* and *salaran* which are subsequently awarded [to the respective parties]'.
> 186. ... Not long afterwards Ni Malandang Japlak [the loser] sat in a row with Malandang Kartiguna [the winner] before Rangga Nata Bhumi.
> 187. Then Ni Malandang Japlak was addressed by Ki Arya Raja Niti, 'The court gives you this *serat salaran* ['certificate of loss' ordering compensation] ...'
> 188. Ni Malandang Japlak answered, 'If this is in agreement with and expresses the wish of the country, these orders I then accept. [With regard to] the household [wives] of Kartiguna, yea, that is the sum of the debt, for which they became indentured, along with their two children.
> 189. Freed [are they now from] debt slavery'. Rangga Nata Bhumi calm was his speech, 'Ki Kartiguna do you not agree? If you do not accept this, please speak now!' Ki Malandang Kartiguna spoke while making a *semah* (gesture of high esteem made to a superior).
> 190. 'Yea, this humble servant accepts'. Demang Undhang-Undhang spoke soothingly, 'Finished is this case, not to be heard again (*bakah*), all that has been said is contained in the *serat kukudung* awarded to you, Ki Malandang Kartiguna, who has then humbly accepted it'.
> 191. *Tumenggung Jaksa Nagara* then acknowledged to Rangga Natabhumi, '[I am] satisfied with the solution made for Malandang Kartiguna, [who] readily accepts it at the Balé Watangan'. The court was dismissed.

Selectivity

The goal of settling such affairs once and for all was accomplished, 'Finished, not to be heard again'. Such verdicts required considerable selectivity.

Consequently, the deciding instance, a court of law under the sovereign or his surrogate, enjoyed a good deal of freedom in choosing among the options sanctioned by the texts in order to arrive at the one most likely to restore social harmony. Yet for outside observers this poses a problem. The choices offered by the textual tradition, which were dictated by concern with restoring or maintaining *tata tantrem,* is not matched by concrete examples of how they were made. One of the few examples provided by *pepakem*-era sources is the just-discussed Kartiguna-Japlak affair of the *Serat Arok.*[10] According to that title, the court drew its sanctions for arriving at the settlement from the Twenty-five *Prakara* (LOr 10.544, § 172). Specifically cited were *anggenuk pringga* (late with the payment), *amrat kara* (to kill an errand/order) and *apryuda* [?]. These, in fact, come from the Seventeen *Prakara* found in the Combi *Surya Alam,* § 14. Another paragraph of the *Serat Arok* (177) refers to sanctions stemming from the *uger-uger* (*aksara* of the wrong guaranteeing a suit's defeat), as well as three separate *aksara.* The named terms are said to fall under the *sloka: asangu papali,* which has not been identified or translated. Even more interesting is that the Combi *Surya Alam*'s § 14 no. 6, *akarya walang',* summarizes the case in abstract terms.

> [I]ts meaning, a person wounded through being stabbed by a thief sounds the alarm and suits before the *Bumi.* In the meantime, another theft occurs. The alarm is sounded, and traces are sought in the house where the stabbing is supposed to have taken place. He who investigates the tidying up and washing off traces of the thief's stabbing, along with other evidence (*cina bukti*) is presented to the village *Bumi.* The first who sounded the alarm is a *tekèk mati déning ulahé* a gecko who dies by his own admission.

The fact that the paragraph seems to be a condensation of the Japlak affair must mean that it is somehow connected, although there is no reference in the *surat* to that *prakara.* Any of the *uger-uger* could apply to the case, which according to the *Serat Arok* lacked valid proof. However, the *aksara* named in the *surat* – *aksara banyu,* (place of the court), *aksara kilat* (the king's will before it is uttered), and *aksara angin* (the intention of the court [?]) – fit the standard usage of the terms by the *Jaya Lengkara.*

10 LOr 10.544 Soegiarto transcription of KBG 47 considered in Chapter 7. The contents of the text of the *Serat Arok* is provided by Robson.

While the narrative confirms the active employment of *sloka* phenomena in legal settlements, the emphasis falls on the fact that the textual traditions provided several equally valid legal sanctions for punishing the same act. In the present case the *surat* does not specify which of the three *prakara* or *aksara* was chosen. The only clue comes from the last part of the *sloka* appended to the *surat kukudung*, namely *sima bangga rebut mangsa mati katiban taru* (disobedient/arrogant tigers die competing for prey, struck by a falling tree, alt. a falling star), Classic *Sloka*, no. 1. The disobedient/arrogant tiger would seem to apply to Kartiguna, whose arrogant behaviour in losing a cockfight was ultimately punished as a sort of divine retribution. This also brings us the full circle to the *mati katiban taru sloka/sinalokan* from the *Luwangan* (§ 18) discussed in Chapter 3 in connection with the first vignette of the *Jugul Muda*.

An analogous selectivity characterizes the Ki Awas v. Ki Samar dispute over two water buffaloes (vignettes nos. 13 and 18 from the *Pepakem Tjerbon*). In both examples the vignette was closed by a *sinalokan* composed of various parts of the well-known phrase, *adedamar tanggal sapisan kapurnaman*.[11] While reference to the affair in the narrative '*sinalokan*' section of the *pepakem* merely summarizes the case, a variant version found as a 'mock' *layang salaran* provides specific information on the decision's relation to underlying textual concepts. The key phrase providing a solution for the affair is:

> *unggakaken ing candi drigama ing uger-uger wolung prakara, ing titindhih salawé prakara,*
> The rise of the monument of *drigama* (worldly law) [as expressed] in the eight *uger-uger* and lead by the Twenty-five *Prakara*, LOr 7440, ff. 201-207.

Through the phrase, the court consisting of *jaksa*, *jejeneng*, and *nayaka* thereby identified the textual basis for the sanctions. These came primarily from the '*aksara* of the wrong'. Additional choices were provided by the 'Twenty-five *Prakara*', which should have been § 13 of the Combi *Surya Alam*, 'should have been' because it seems to be a mistake for the 'Twenty *Prakara*' (§ 11). The latter contains the *uger-uger* and both *sloka* used to end

11 Suwarno, *Dictionary*, no. 6. In the *Pepakem Tjerbon* vignette no. 13 (p. 78-79) closes with the *sinalokan*: *tanggal pisana dadamar yen kasamaran mantri den-asadaya*; while that of no. 18 (p. 83-84): *andamar lintang asulu taun awas mutuh cacad sambat ing nyata, yen kasamaran*. They build on the image of the darkness of the first days of the lunar month, i.e., the obscure claims, which are enlightened by the coming of the full moon, namely the inquiry.

the two vignettes found in the *Pepakem Tjerbon*. Tellingly the Japlak affair also refers to these sources.

At least five of the eight could have been used to decide the Ki Awas case. However, for reasons known only to the *kerta* two were selected. These were *anir yukti arah* (unclearness of accusations or plaint) and *toyamarta* (untruthfulness in the testimony) (Table 5.6). Their repetition as part of the Twenty *Prakara* would seem to reinforce the importance of legitimate alternatives, as does citing the proverbial endings within the two *Pepakem Tjerbon* examples. Unfortunately, the actual *sinalokan* given the loser (Ki Samar) and that awarded the winner (Ki Awas) have defied translation. All that can be said with certainty of the latter *sinalokan,* namely *catur sadarana amarti,* is that it appears in several titles as a phrase reflecting a victory in a suit.[12] Of the loser's *sinalokan* only the last phrase is recognisable. This is a variant of '*kantul di-unikaken dhandhang*' (a heron said to be a carrion crow), i.e., calling white as black and vice versa, a simile for distorting the truth.[13]

Autonomous law

A third and final instrument for ensuring both parties observed the settlement in a political environment generally lacking recourse to a decisive central authority was through the use of autonomous institutions. Of necessity these entailed a high degree of self-regulation. *Sloka* were a crucial part of this mechanism. A striking number of them are clearly self-fulfilling. Prominent examples are provided by *tekék mati déning ulahé*, as punishment for a self-acknowledged liar and provisions condoning private retribution in cases of *sanggraha/sanggama* (fornication, adultery) cited in §§ 15, 20 of the Berlin *Surya Alam* or Canto XVI, verse 10 of the Yasadipura version. Moreover, through being saddled with a specific (and negative) *sloka* losers were thereby burdened with epithets reflecting their misdeeds. Sembada was a 'shelter of thieves', and 'the same as a thief'. Dora not only stood condemned by his own words but also was branded as a 'liar' and thus shamed before the sun, moon, the heavens, etc. Although space does not allow more detailed exposition, there is more to it than just 'sticks and stones'. Being classed as an evil one (*durjana*) set the individual morally, if not physically, outside the pale of normal social relationships. He/she thereby became something else, i.e., a form of social excommunication. This constituted a condition that in

12 *Cacad* § 10, *Luwangan* § 20, no. 2 and § 39, no. 2.

13 Suwarno, *Dictionary,* no. 337.

important, if undefined, ways threatened the continuation of society's *tata tantrem*. Thus, the threat of social expulsion, often exacerbated by being weighed down by a *sloka*, constituted an important complement to the sporadic and often arbitrary exercise of executive authority, a psychological-sociological 'hue and cry'. Kings and kingdoms come and go; the rules of the game communicated by *sloka* and *aksara* were lasting.

Differing more in degree than kind, the self-regulatory tendency of Javanese law included several areas acknowledging injured party initiative. Self-regulation thus passed into an implicit delegation of authority for exacting punishments which were more usually monopolised by the state. Striking examples are provided by the special circumstances in which seemingly normal meetings between a man and a woman not related to him were construed as a form of sexual misbehaviour (*sanggraha*). As we have seen, *sloka* in the Berlin/Kartasura and Yasadipura *Surya Alam* dealt with of a man picking up a flower dropped from a woman's hair dress (*kembang baya*), relieving himself from the same place as a woman (*ketahi baya*), conversing with a woman outside of commercial activities (*kasela baya*), and asking a woman to wash his *sarong*. While such clauses may seem nonsensical, they were taken seriously in the legal texts as attested to by their repetitions in most of them. As implied by the Berlin/Kartasura text (§ 20) and specified by that of Yasadipura, Canto X, verse 15, if not acceptable to the woman's *wakil* (representative, deputy), the occurrence could lead to capital punishment for the man involved at the hands of the injured party. However, the title also specifies that if this was not carried out, he must be assessed a staggering fine. The point is that it was not a question of simply allowing the injured party to take revenge, but of delegating part of state responsibility to private parties, an early modern example of out-sourcing punishment.

A final example is provided by the numerous *layang buron* or 'letters of flight' of the late Independent Kingdoms period.[14] These were promulgated by the courts and awarded the plaintiffs as victors. It was a means of ensuring that the defendants as perpetrators/losers met the demands laid upon them by the court as private compensation and/or public punishment without the state's direct involvement. Through such documented acts the crown 'farmed out' authority to pursue, arrest, and demand payment from those fleeing by those deemed to be the injured party. The state had weighed the evidence and declared the guilt; the plaintiffs carried it out. Here a word of caution is in order. The extent to which the provisions of such *layang*

14 Hoadley, 'Javanese Case Law'.

buron were carried to fulfilment is not known. All the texts say is that if a declared fugitive is found, the prescribed fines or punishments shall be fulfilled. No information is available on how, or even if, such delegation was carried out in practice.

The above helps explain the generalist and non-specific nature of the titles. As denoted by the term *pepakem*, all Javanese legal titles are compilations, even compilations of compilations. Drawing upon various sources not cited in the paragraphs was the norm, not the exception. Rather than variations in degrees of evidence, guilt, etc., being provided by set texts, the tradition dealt with here provided multiple solutions for any given situation. Obviously differing circumstances required different provisions, not variations on a set piece of law. The choice was left to the sovereign's tribunal. Thus, a more accurate evaluation of Crawfurd's observation would be that his description is essentially correct. It is the interpretation or reasoning behind it that is misleading. Heterogeneity and inconsistency of legal titles' contents were strengths rather than weaknesses. They gave Javanese law the flexibility necessary to deal with a whole spectrum of affairs within a corpus of law drawing upon tradition/experience, which was thereby sheltered from temporary alterations by passing rulers. Law was composed of short, mutually consistent paragraphs, often represented by the *sloka* phenomena, which reflected the collective experience of society rather than the will of a human agent or that of a supernatural force. The aim was a self-governing society regulating itself through custom born of experience (*drigama*) rather than one tailored by mortal sovereigns (law books, constitutions, *undhang-undhang*, etc.) or a Supreme Being.

9 Context

The preceding chapter has argued that the law of the Independent Kingdoms was unique. Yet within the contextual perspectives of time and space considered here this was only partially so. What appears to be a break with the institutions of its immediate predecessor, Old Java of the Singosari-Majapahit era (c. eleventh to fourteenth centuries), seems to be due as much to lack of knowledge as the realities of institutional contrasts. Dated references to Old Javanese legal concepts as the *astha corah*, *astha dustha*, and *sad-atatayi*, as well as a law book termed the *Kutara Manawa*,[1] exhaust the available sources with established provenance and date. None of them, however, provide substantial information on the law of which they were a part or expressed. This is not to ignore the possibility that at least some of the Middle Javanese texts copied by Balinese scribes contain authentic selections of Old Javanese law. Yet which sections and how much of them are such remains unclear. The apparent gap, if indeed it can be proved to be such, is most likely connected with the rise of the Demak federation under Radèn Patah (aka Senapati Jimbun). A number of texts, whose contents are similar to those drawn upon here are attributed to just the Demak period.[2] Again, just how much of that tradition is retrospective or *ex post facto* attributions of younger material to older texts has yet to be established.[3] Moving forward in time, that is, from the Independent Kingdoms era, is somewhat easier due to the existence of more information, albeit as unprocessed raw material contained in manuscripts.

No matter how well or poorly the *sloka* phenomena performed within Independent Kingdoms society, they were doomed to be replace by something deemed more fitting by what had by the end of the period become Java's colonial master. In retrospect the reasons seem clear. Even under the form of indirect rule exercised by the Dutch East India Company down to its demise in 1799, traditional Javanese law did not fare well within the joint Javanese-Company legal system, one increasingly dominated by Dutch fiat and Company

1 See Appendix IV and discussion of the *Ku(n)tara Manawa* lawbook by Hoadley and Hooker, *The Agama*.

2 Either directly as attributed to Kyai Senapati Jimbun in Add 2125, ff. 172-299 or indirectly as those attributed to his companion Arya Dilah in LOr 7440 and 7442.

3 A striking example is that of the Indonesian poet, dramatist, and activist W.S. Rendra (1935-2009) attributing the *Slokantara* and *Jugul Muda* to the Demak period as introducing *shari'a* law. It was part of a speech praising the past heroes of the Republic entitled 'Pidato Megatruh' (Speech to/of the Great Soul) published in *Harian Bernas*, 7 November 1997, which has become popular on the internet.

innovations. De facto displacement of the traditional written law of Java took place well before the promulgation of the *Pepakem Tjerbon* in 1768 under the auspices of judicially inclined Cirebon Resident, *Meester* Pieter Cornelius Hasselaer. In fact, the last documented case handled by a semi-independent *jaksa* inquiry dates a quarter of a century before that compilation.[4]

Any concessions to or tolerance toward, or even attempts to utilize local legal concepts in colonial courts of law were prevented by the Congress of Vienna's decision in 1815. The island was to be restored to the Dutch. It followed the short British interregnum which provided much information of mixed veracity on Javanese law.[5] In any event, after 1815 territories which had been occupied by the British expeditionary forces would be returned to what had in the interim become the Kingdom of the Netherlands under its first monarch Wilhelm I (r. 1815-1840). The restoration was complicated by the fact that, among other things, the Dutch East Indies government in land transactions contracted during the 1810-1815 period provoked inadvertently a reaction on the part of the higher *priyayi* (bureaucratic nobility), ultimately resulting in the Java War of 1825-1830. This was followed in 1830 by the beginning of the Cultivation System, which not only exacerbated the already complicated Javanese land tenure arrangements but also contributed to declining welfare of the majority its inhabitants. A period of spontaneous lack of order due to armed hostilities was succeeded by a conscious one of literal 'lawlessness' in the service of maximising exploitation of the colony to the benefit of the newly founded Dutch monarchy. Despite the near revolutionary changes in land-man-ruler relationships, no discussion or negotiation of its conditions or even legality was permitted. Appeal from the decisions of its Dutch regulators, i.e., the Cultivation System administrators, was not possible. One scholar has gone so far as to characterise the first half of the nineteenth century on Java as relying more on men than law,[6] in other words a nascent 'police state'. This may be an understatement for Javanese law. Whatever law and order that existed was at the arbitrary discretion of the holders of power, Dutch officials and their tame Javanese *mantri*. The primary goal was ensuring the economic success the Cultivation System rather than adhering to the principles of either indigenous or European concepts of law.[7]

4 Sultan Cirebon v. Anom (Pinjalin), 1743, Hoadley, *Selective Judicial Competence*, pp. 121-125.

5 Among the more questionable reports are those suggesting that Javanese law derived from *The Koran*. Both Raffles and Crawfurd, as well as others, generally accept this, even though they cite Javanese titles containing purely local legal concepts.

6 van Niel, *Java under the Cultivation System*.

7 Lack of a functioning legal system on Java based upon any recognized laws for more than half a century is explained by the sweeping political and legal uncertainties that plagued both

If this was not sufficiently dysfunctional, the oscillations in Dutch policies had devastating consequences for the rule of law. During the first half of the nineteenth century as a period of constitutional uncertainty in the metropole few resources of time or energy could be expended on shaping the colony's laws, even if there had been interest in doing so.[8] At the same time, the restored colonial holdings' capacity to remit profits to the homeland, the sole reason for its existence under Dutch rule, had to be upgraded. This was accompanied by a great increase in the directly Dutch ruled part of the island. The 'native states' of the *Vorstenlanden* under indirect rule were reduced to a mere fraction of their

Java and the Netherlands during the first half of the nineteenth century. Tellingly, the colony's finances – more accurately remittances to Europe – had been in decline for decades before the bankruptcy of the Dutch East India Company in 1799. Java had become a liability rather than an asset for the Dutch economy. The following decade and a half of military defence policies in support of revolutionary France followed by British occupation of the island exacerbated the decline. The Java returned to the Dutch in 1815 was sorely in need of financial reorganization in order to provide for the minimal needs of the inhabitants and income for their Dutch masters. In Europe, the destruction of the United Provinces' governmental system resulted in the creation of a Dutch branch of the French Revolution. The subsequent repeal of French innovations by the Congress of Vienna led to the creation of a Dutch monarchy. Yet, heavy-handed measures taken to turn Java into a paying proposition ultimately provoked the Java War, which increased the monarchy's debts. Even more serious was the fact that the conflict on Java was followed by the revolt of the region that would become Belgium. The temporary union of the Dutch-speaking peoples, plus a minority of French speakers, resulting from negotiations at the end of the Napoleonic era was torn asunder by open warfare. The Netherlands lost a costly conflict, one which only increased the need to make its colony a paying venture. In very broad outlines this is the background for van den Bosch's genial invention of the Cultivation System, which turned out to be a uniquely effective machine for generating profits for the government, to the detriment of indigenous welfare.

8 Neglect of Java, which was coming increasingly under direct Dutch authority, was coupled by a more pressing concern with reinventing the Dutch state and its laws twice over. The United Provinces' governmental system – represented on Java by the Dutch East India Company – was a federal system. Political power was divided between that delegated to the collective centre in The Hague and that remaining under control of the seven individual units – six provinces plus the Bishopric of Utrecht. While the provincial entities generally recognized Roman-Dutch law, in each this was overlain by rules and ordinances from village, town, and even guild with a distinctly local flavour. Moreover, because Utrecht was a unit of the church it was governed by Roman law modified by concessions to the Protestant Reformation. The first transition was the French-style Batavian Republic which brought in Napoleonic laws to replace the various provincial ones. Overthrow of the French system along with its laws and the establishment of a monarchy, including what would become Belgium, meant that the older stratum of local laws had not only to be brought up to a 'national' standard. They also had to be integrated with those of the overwhelmingly Catholic (and partially French-speaking) population of the southern Netherlands. This was all brought to naught with the successful revolt of those provinces in 1840. The newly completed constitution had to be revised once more to eliminate earlier concessions to the southern provinces.

earlier land area and total population by successive acquisitions of the Dutch East India Company since the Treaty of Giyanti in the mid eighteenth century and even greater encroachments during the short British interregnum.[9] As a result, the greater part of Java's population came under increasingly direct European rule during a period in which its governance had decreasing ties to any form of law. What existed were the leftovers of rules and regulations of the Company time – Javanese law minus those parts abrogated by Company rulings, edicts, regulations etc., as well as the imperfectly introduced innovations of the British followed by a half decade of open warfare topped by the authoritarian arbitrariness of Cultivation System administrators.

Only in preparation for introducing a standard legal framework around mid-century did the lawmakers in The Hague attempt to come to terms with the legal limbo of Java. Provisions contained in the 'New Legislation' introduced in the 1846-1848 period would provide the legal framework of the Dutch colony for almost a century. However, these applied only to the Dutch and those accepted as such in the Indies. The Introductory Provisions (*Invoeringsbepalingen*) bringing the New Legislation into force abolished for those classed as 'Dutch':

> all decrees, provisions, publications, ordinances, instructions, edicts, statutes, customs, and all written and unwritten law then in force in the Netherlands Indies.

9 The already limited territories remaining under the Susuhunan of Surakarta and Sultan of Yogyakarta in 1799 shrank dramatically. Those annexed by Raffles in 1812 were surrendered to the returning Dutch four years later. In the wake of the Java War (1825-1830) the western extremities of Banjumas, Bagelen, Gowang and eastern areas of The Principalities proper were annexed by the Netherlands East Indies government. By 1830 the geographical territory controlled by the Javanese states amounted to a very small part of Java, some ten percent of the land area and probably a like amount of the population. This meant that the Javanese law which had been earlier influenced by Dutch presence was by this time valid for only a small, reservation-like area of south-central Java. For the remainder the successive European governments showed little inclination to apply the type of intensive direct rule which had become characterised of Dutch East India Company rule from Batavia. By default, the overwhelming majority of Java's population administratively and legally fell under a Javo-Dutch 'dominance' as that of Cirebon, West Java, Semarang, etc. Dutch territorial dominance had another consequence for the legal system. Defeat of the 'rebels' meant that by 1830 those with the will and means of resisting European encroachment were permanently removed from the scene. Only tame Javanese officials held positions with the Sultan of Yogyakarta, the Susuhunan of Surakarta, or the Dutch East Indies government. At the same time, the Dutch increasingly employed military means to enforce its will. The government henceforth enjoyed unprecedented powers of coercion, powers that were easily translated into legal fiat. What had been a political stalemate in the mid-to-late eighteenth century after 1830 took on the character of an authoritarian colonial state.

At the same time, it raised 'the religious laws, institutions, and customs of the indigenous people' to become the source of law applying to the *inlander* (natives).[10] This would replace the cumbersome legal system either borrowed from local law, as for example, the *Undhang Nitih Cirebon* and *Pepakem Tjerbon*, or had grown from judicial practice in Company times. More important, the 'New Regulations' gave concrete form to the key concept of the 'duality principle'. This was in practice a carryover from Company praxis that Dutch laws would apply for the Dutch and those choosing to be classified as 'Dutch' and local law for the natives (*inlander*). In fact, the regulations merely formalised principles that had been functioning in increasingly larger areas for the last two and a half centuries.[11]

Even this division was hedged by a provision axiomatically assuming that if the contents of native law conflicted with Dutch legal sensibilities, then European/Dutch law would prevail. Since religious law, the *shari'a,* was not acceptable to the colonial government, by 'institutions and customs of the indigenous people' the authors of the New Legislation must have had in mind what would emerge at the century's close as '*adatrecht*'. So much seems clear from the Council of the Indies 'consideration and advice' of 1853, which urged 'respect for the customary law of the people'.[12] This begs the question of how could the practitioners of law, i.e., judges, magistrates, and officials, know the contents of this customary law? Discovery of the *adat* and its systematic study under the leadership of Cornelius van Vollenhoven was half a century in the future.[13] Even further away was instruction in the subject at centres of higher learning in the Netherlands.

10 Ball, *Indonesian Legal History,* p. 215, § 12 (*Algemeene Bepalingen van Wetgeving voor Nederlandsch-Indië*), hereafter *AB.*

11 Passed by Royal Decree of 16 May 1846 and subsequently confirmed by Parliament, the package of 1846 came into force in the Indies on 1 May 1848. It predated the Constitutional Regulation of 1854 by some six years, but contained the most important legislation of the colonial period, including:

1. General Provisions on Legislation for the Netherlands Indies (*AB*)
2. The Civil Code for the Netherlands Indies (*Burgerlijk Wetboek voor Nederlandsch-Indië*);
3. The Commercial Code for the Netherlands Indies (*Wetboek van Koophandel voor Nederlandsch-Indië*);
4. Regulation on Court Organisation and Administration of Justice in the Netherlands Indies (*Reglement op de Regterlijk Organisatie en het Beleid der Justitie in Nederlandsch-Indië*);
5. Some Provisions on Offences committed during Bankruptcy, Insolvency and Suspension of Payment in the Netherlands Indies (*Bepalingen betrekkelijk de Misdrijven, begaan ter gelegenheid van Faillissement en bij Kennelijk Onvermogen mitsgaders bij Surseance van Betaling in Nederlandsch-Indië*), Ball, *Indonesian Legal History*, p. 209.

12 *Ibid.*

13 *Discovery of the Adat,* C. Van Vollenhoven.

At this juncture one could expect the end of story. After all, traditional Javanese written law was formally replaced by a combination of statute originating from political authority, native and foreign, and *adat* coming from custom. The former was supplemented by laws, ordinances, and regulations promulgated by the Dutch and, within reason, the recognized rulers of the rump states constituting 'The Principalities'. Similarly, as the newly-recognized law for the natives, *adatrecht* tended to amass studies, capped by a growing number of *adat* law decisions by local courts vetted by Dutch colonial officials. These provided precedents for subsequent cases of a like nature. To all intents and purposes law as contained in the *sloka* phenomena was a shadow of the past, one reinforced by lack of even academic interest.

'Rumors of my demise…'

But was traditional Javanese written law as dead as all that? That such rumours were exaggerated is suggested by occurrences in the century and a half following the New Legislation. For convenience's sake they can be considered chronologically. In the short run during the remainder of the nineteenth century, there was an active engagement on behalf of the supposedly abolished legal texts as witnessed by the number of copies and new editions of those texts produced by court circles. In the medium-term interest in 'implied law'[14] (customary or written) previously known via the written word – is attested to by the establishment and spread of *adat* law not only as an academic discipline but also as a living source of law. And finally, in the long range the untimely death of tradition is belied by the growing retro interest in the *sloka* phenomena as embodying a moral compass of exemplary behaviour seen as lacking in contemporaneous Indonesian society. Obviously, each of the topics could provide subject matter for a book or books. Until such is realised, we can content ourselves with a succinct sketch of the major points by way of setting this study in a temporal and spatial context.

A survey of manuscripts collections of Central Java shows that many of the titles of the Independent Kingdoms period continued to be copied,

14 As used by Lon L. Fuller in *Anatomy of the Law*, 'implied law' would fit both the contents of the texts under consideration and the *adat* which was to replace them. 'They find their implicit expression in [the] conduct itself […] the purpose of such rules never comes to explicit expression […] we have to infer what its [their] rules sought to accomplish', (pp. 64-65).

recopied, edited, and, almost inevitably, updated long after the promulgation of the New Legislation. At Yogyakarta the manuscripts forcibly removed from the *kraton* library by Raffles and company[15] were replaced by more modern copies of the standard works. Similar continuation of the legal tradition of the Independent Kingdoms period seems also characteristic at the Pakualam, Mangkunegaran, and Surakarta *kraton*-s. Interest in preservation of the legal lore analysed in this work continued unabated despite expectations stemming from the Indies government invalidating all previous written law.

But why did generations of practitioners and scribes devote scarce physical and temporal resources to copying, re-copying, and updating titles of a legal nature? That they were successively (re)-copied from predecessors is attested to by the near identical form and contents of the individual paragraphs. The number of catalogued exemplars of such titles held by public collections in Indonesia, Holland, and England comes to hundreds. To these must be added an unknown number in private collections. The accumulative efforts over time provide clear evidence that the contents of traditional Javanese written law were valued, if not esteemed, long after the end of the Independent Kingdoms.

Commandeering of resources is even more remarkable due to the absence of the most common initiatives for reproducing them. Two of them would be religious conviction and strivings for 'law and order' in the sense of codified and systematized normative behaviour. However, religious themes are all but lacking in these titles and their concern with ordering the state was superficial. Political power had long since passed to the Dutch. The striking contrast between effort expended and modest, if not disappointing, results achieved brings us back to the issue implicitly raised by Crawfurd and buttressed by the results of the present work. Why did the Javanese insist on preserving a body of manuscripts whose contents' practical value was nil?

A likely answer is that they constituted a repository of the law of Greater Java. They embodied *drigama*, experience manifested in custom. As such they functioned very much in the style of an '*adat* law book' (*adat wetbook*) postulated by the early practitioners of *adat recht*.[16] Attachment, undiminished by time, to the titles clarifying *drigama*, coupled with their

15 See Carey, *The British in Java 1811-1816*, Canto XIII, pp. 94ff, on the removal of Hamengkubuwana's palace archive to the British lodge and Behrend, *Katalog Induk* for a survey of its rebuilding.

16 *Adatrechtbundel I*, 'Adat pointer containing practical hints for the investigation of the *adat* law', pp. 16-20, first published by the Commission on Adat Law in 1910.

distinguishing characteristics, evokes parallels with the *adat* law, which became synonymous with the law of the 'natives' in the early twentieth century.[17] Collectively the contents of the Independent Kingdoms titles stood for a '*rechtsstad*' in a traditional Javanese sense. This included consolidating multiple solutions under a few major concepts (*Adilulah*, *Surya Alam*), clarifying *sloka* as the epitome of judicial ideas (*Jugul Muda*), setting the prohibitions of *drigama* and the *aksara* (*Jaya Lengkara*), and advancing general principles to be interpreted and applied to litigation (*Arya Dilah*, *Cacad*, *Slokantara*, *Raja Niscaya*).

Sloka and *adat*

In between the immediate reaction to the New Legislation or, more accurately, the non-reaction shown by the continuing commitment to traditional Javanese written law and the current retro-interest in the *sloka* phenomena is the middle ground of transition to *adatrecht*. Key here is recognition of the basic similarity between traditional written law and *adat*. A reasonable proposition is that they are two facets of the same law expressed in different media, written and oral. Due to limitations of time and space discussion is confined to a couple of points. One focuses on specialised vocabulary, which in turn raises the related issue of how tradition/experience could have been maintained over time; the other on the nature of their respective sources within the possibilities of change and/or innovation.

Any inquiry into the language of both traditional written law and its twentieth century oral equivalent in the *adat* literature must contend with a large number of terms and concepts that often differ from standard usage. For sheer numbers the index of the individual terms comprising *sloka* phrases in Winter's *Javaansche Zamenspraken* would be hard to surpass. Its equivalent, the 'Javanese *Adat law* terms' (*Javaansche adat-rechtstermen*) reproduced with explanation in separate volumes of the *Adatrechtbundels,* comes to some 600 items for roughly one-third of the ha-na-ca-ra-ka alphabet published in volume 23. These encompass those starting with 'ha' to 'ca' and in Volume 43 'ka' to 'da' making a calculated 1800 items for the entire alphabet. Following Keyzer, the contents of Winter's work have been advanced here as key to understanding traditional Javanese written law, the latter have been accepted as a 'standard' minimal list of terms crucial to the

17 This, one hastens to add, must be distinguished from the law for the 'natives' in the form of Netherlands East Indies codes, regulations, and special rules for specific groups, that is when the principles of the Dutch law of the metropole was not automatically applied.

understanding of Javanese *adat*(s). 'Minimal' seems warranted in light of the warning penned by the Commission for Adat Law preceding each list.

> It is not superfluous to remark that naturally in a list (or as that in earlier *Adatrechtbundels*) as there are dozens, sometimes even hundreds, of legal terms which could be lacking.[18]

To make matters more complicated, these terms often have meanings at variance with accepted norms.

Continuation of the Commission's 'note' in connection with the (partial) list of *adat* law terms is a case in point. It seems as valid for traditional Javanese written law of the Independent Kingdoms era as that of the *adat* in the late colonial one.

> Because which word and word form of the language have taken on the value of legal terms one can learn only through [the] practice, never from a dictionary. Naturally there are exceptions on rare occasions that such a book is constructed by someone that has made the law of the folk group under consideration a principle study… the intention with these lists is also only on the one hand to assemble what is practical and on the other hand to provoke the masters of language and *adat* law towards the communication of further legal terms that they had learned.[19]

The goal after more than a century remains unfulfilled.

A few concrete examples from earlier discussion suffices. That of '*aksara*' is most obvious. With the sole exception of a secondary meaning in Zoetmulder's dictionary, *aksara* is consistently defined as 'letter of the alphabet'. Yet as seen in Chapter 4, *aksara* as one of the dozen legal commands was already well established before Gobius' reference in 1717 to one of them ('*astra*', *sic aksara geni*) as providing the basis of a judicial sentence. This meaning was anticipated or reiterated by most of the original titles drawn upon to compile the *Pepakem Tjerbon*, with the *Jaya Lengkara* and *Cacad* taking a prominent place. That the era's legal literature was more catholic than the published dictionaries is shown by the fact that *aksara* is also used in two other manners. The first is the conventional one of letters, but in the legal context of, say, *sudra wacana* = 'leaving out letters in the *tutur* document in comparison with the *kendel*, i.e., forging the document as ruled

18 *Adatrechtbundel*, vol. 23, p. 67.
19 *Ibid.*

by the *Pepakem Tjerbon* quoting the *Undang-Undang Mataram* (p. 24). The other is as a collection of letters, a narrative, as found in, among others, the *Arya Dilah* (§ 1).

A close second is the term *luwangan*. Its conventional meaning is 'hole, pit, trap' or in the verbal form 'to dig' such. With some effort it can be discovered that *luwangan* also means 'example, pattern, etc'. and even 'proof, advice'. Clearly the latter fits better with the intention of the actual text. It is argued in Appendix I that the *Luwangan Undhang-Undhang* is a stand-in for the *Undang-Undang Mataram* cited as a major source of the *Pepakem Tjerbon*. Other accessible examples of variant readings include *sisiku* whose normal meaning of (*siku*) 'right angle' or by extension 'elbow' is better captured in present usage by the Sundanese '(expression of) anger/ wrath (of the ancestors or holy persons)' or 'punishment (in the form of sickness or misfortune as the result of overstepping a taboo)[20]; and '*ganda*' whose usual meaning of 'smell, odour' is modified by the *nakira ganda* [...] *nyata sloka* of the *Wadigun Wangkara*.

Sanghara occupies a special place, although confusion comes as much from the spelling in the various titles as from meaning *per se*. The original meaning within the enumeration of the four phases of the Hindu concept of the *kalpa* or cosmic decline should be '*sanghara*' 'destruction'. More specifically it comes at the end of the immortal cycle of birth-maturity-decline-destruction-rebirth and so on prescribed by Hindu cosmology. A common variation, allowed by the ha-na-ca-ra-ka spelling is *sang*(*h*) *ara*, alternatively *sengara* (1 curse; oath, 2 solemn oath) or in the verb form (*nyenger* to swear not to do s.t.).[21] Context here provides little in the way of guidance. 'Disaster' or more commonly *pralaya* fits best as the culmination of the four phases of the *kalpa*; 'curse' is appropriate within the Dora-Sembada vignette, which in the *Jugul Muda* motivated sovereign intervention in the form of a punishment, while 'an oath not to do something as (non-)action against an evil doer, brings us back to the *nakira ganda* [...] *nyata sloka*. Clearly a comprehensive compilation and comparison the respective set of terms would help to determine the extent to which traditional Javanese written law and *adat* are complementary, sequential, or exclusive.

Regardless of the outcome of such a juxtaposition, the existence of many marginally understood terms and concepts constituting traditional law, both written and oral, is clear. Its significance here is to suggest that the relative

20 Eringa, *Soendaas-Nederlands Woordenboek*.
21 Prawiroatmojo, *Bausastra Jawa-Indonesia*.

quantity acerbated by the demands of quality as the basic building blocks comprising both written law of the titles and those of *adatrecht* imposed an unrealistic burden on the practitioners of the latter. Lacking mnemonic devices to guarantee accurate reproduction over time on the model of the Hindu epics, nineteenth and twentieth century *adat* law 'sayers' faced an impossible challenge in keeping terms and concepts consistent. Common sense would argue that much of the learning must have been committed to writing. This seems particularly likely in that, as de Casparis has pointed out, the Javanese tradition, including that of law, was an uncommonly literary one.[22] This would strengthen the likelihood of written handbooks (*pepakem*) to aid the exactness of preservation of the legal tradition. In short, the oral nature of the *adat* as *adatrecht* seems overdriven, at least for Java.

Even more striking is the parallelism between *adat* and traditional Javanese written law in relation to basic sources. The latter, explicitly based on *drigama* (experience), can only have come from an extension of what has preceded, that is, custom. By its very nature custom/experience is not static. Although slower to change than that stemming from individual (sovereign) initiative, its 'senatorial' quality, custom must keep abreast of the changes society experiences over time. While van Vollenhoven freely recognized the ability of *adat* to change in tact with societal alterations, the implications of his successors, exacerbated by recording *adat* law decisions in Dutch, tended to fix its contents in time and space.[23] This was exacerbated by introduction of the European ideas of precedent and consistency in judicial decisions. For traditional Javanese written law, they were clearly alien and likely so for the *adat*. This, however, is far from certain because the very nature of oral sources does not allow comparisons over time. Hence one must assume that, as in the case with its written cousin, flexibility came from the existence of multiple choices for a given case, even ones ostensibly similar. Return to social order (*tata tantrem*) was the overriding aim, not abstract or ultimate justice. Hence the 'rule of law' departed considerably from that of the European concepts subsequently imposed on the legal system.[24]

22 deCasparis, *Indonesian Paleography*.

23 Hoadley, *Islam dalam*, pp. 520 ff., especially pp. 531-534.

24 A puzzling addition to references within the sources' contents is limited to a few titles of an apparently younger date. This is the phrase '*mangkana lwir/ling ing sastra*' (such are the words of the *sastra*) used to end virtually every paragraph of the *Raja Niti* and the last half of the *Gajah Mada*, both from RAS 33. Several interpretations of '*sastra*' are possible, including Sanskrit sources, titles of traditional Javanese law, but most likely a form of (written) tradition/custom. To complicate matters usage, apparently unique to the titles closely associated with a Senapati Jimbun (aka Radèn Patah), is found only in a half-dozen paragraphs of the *Agama*. While most

Thus, there seems good reason to wonder if the commonly-accepted juxtaposition of *adat* (oral custom) and *ubaya, undhang-undhang* (agreement of written governmental ordnances) was valid for the earlier period. More likely the legal tradition of the Independent Kingdoms period embraced both textual law as preserved in the titles considered here and an equivalent oral tradition to which we have no access. Hints from the sources and logic argue that they were compatible, if not congruent. Gobius' 1717 reference to the '*adat* of the *jaksa*' should not be ignored. The titles considered here, which continued to be reproduced well after the Dutch East Indies government invalidated all prior written forms, undoubtedly included what would emerge as *adatrecht* in the late nineteenth and early twentieth centuries. Hence dominance of *adat*, at least in its all-embracing authority, was an artificial product of Dutch fiat.[25] This does not, however, argue that its contents were not authentic. It is just that elimination of traditional written law contained in the titles analysed here allowed the oral version to dominate, carrying with it the danger of overestimating its significance.

To return to the question posed at the start of this section, the titles of what has been identified as traditional Javanese law collectively comprised a repertoire of legal principles proven by time and usage. Admittedly they varied in composition. In addition, it remains unclear what provided the basis for choosing which principles/concepts were to be reproduced in texts. By no means detracting from their validity, the heterogeneity and generalization must be counted as a *sine qua non* of a system in which precedent and consistency were not considered essential, despite that no single text constituted an all-encompassing law. Should an important principle not be found in the *pepakem* of one expert, the appropriate element would turn up in the collective memory, a written one, of another. Hence continuation of this collective legal memory, even after its validity was altered to the oral form of the *adat*, is understandable. Under the circumstances it would be illogical to abandon the written records of the legal tradition via the commands of the (temporary) authority of the Dutch East Indies government. The fact that its basic principles have continued or re-emerged in modern times attests to the longevity of the system.

of these are similar – *mangkana sasanané saking sastra* (§ 20, 136) or *mangkana sasana saking sastra* – §§ 53 (Jonker) and 70 are identical. They are even more noticeable in the non-vintage *Agama* (aka *Kunthara Manawa*) of §§ 221, 262, 267, etc. The possible connection is problematic in that the date and provenance of the *Agama* remains unclear, especially the extent to which it represents Old Javanese texts.

25 Jaspan, 'In quest of new law'.

Sloka phenomena today

Present-day Indonesia's interest in Javanese traditions is seen most clearly in the contents of the blogosphere. This encompasses pretty much everything from private opinion to reasoned presentation of scholarly evidence and much in between. *Sloka* composed of *aksara* found in vignettes are part of this trend. Evidence of direct usage comes from continuation as modern proverbs and the like. Equally striking are indirect indications manifesting themselves as part of other traditional concepts in which crucial features of the *sloka*, derivatives, or those associated with their compilation turn up repeatedly in modern dress. Addressing this somewhat diffuse subject opens by attempting to separate continuation from revival, or re-creation, of older traditions. Both have influenced the present. Of necessity, the points must be succinct. While the following observations are admittedly tentative, they would seem to be sufficiently weighty to show that neglecting the durability of traditional manners of legal/behavioural thinking can lead to misinterpreting contemporaneous Indonesian life. Put the other way around, greater understanding for and appreciation of the flavour of traditional Javanese ways of thinking leads to a more realistic view of the Republic's collective mentality dominated by the Javanese.

Arguments pointing to such continuities can be gathered into three points. The first point builds upon indications by modern Indonesian scholars that explanations of *sloka* and its derivatives have links to specific patterns in the present. Inherent in them are expectations that the message should influence for the better contemporaneous public morality. As a complement an attempt is made to show that significant modern phenomena are better understood via the innate qualities of the Javanese socio-legal tradition than by standardized and incompletely digested Western paradigms and expectations. The second point concerns the continued popularity of literal carry overs of the Aji Saka *sloka* tradition. Far from unique to the *Orde Baru* era, during which time such traditions were employed as part of the governing ethos, they have become even stronger in the post 1998 period of *Reformasi*. As spread and popularised by the internet's blogosphere and popular arts movements, they are possibly more widely distributed, albeit in 'Indonesian-ized' form, than at the time of their inception. The third point is the renewed interest in the Jayabaya predictions re-interpreted in Islamic terms. While the Jayabaya predictions are attributed to the Kediri king of the early twelfth century, in its present form the *Jangka Jayabaya* originate from roughly the same time and place of the textual traditions cited in this study (Chapter 7. 'Vignettes and Practice'). They were filtered through the court literati and *pondok-s* of the Independent Kingdoms era of the mid-eighteenth century. Tellingly, the predictions were expressed in *sloka*, some of which can be documented as current expressions.

Past in the present

It will be recalled that many scholarly explanations and interpretations of *sloka* end with very modern interpretations as to correct behaviour. Significantly the first *sloka* of the *Jugul Muda*, namely *sima* [...] *taru*, is interpreted in a modern context as 'a person who rebels and commits a crime, such as killing someone, in order to obtain what he wants'.[26] A similar interpretation is seen in the '*giri* [...] *tanu sloka*, also from the *Jugul Muda*, as is the case for the *denta-denti* [...] *sloka* from several of the texts (Classic *Sloka*, no. 16). Clearly, many of the *sloka* of proven origin in the Independent Kingdoms period, if not before, are still considered valid by modern Indonesian scholars and general public. In order to make the inherent message more explicit to fellow moderns, an extra paragraph of explanation has been added in these works couched in unmistakable contemporaneous terms. At very least one can discern recognition of *sloka* as applicable to modern life. Their original abstract contents are specified to modern times, a phenomenon that undoubtedly was used earlier in transforming moral *sloka* into legal prescriptions.

A variation of this past-in-present is the practice of using localized traditions to view the present in *sloka* terms rather than through contemporaneous, but foreign glasses. The issue has two aspects. The more obvious one is the unsurprisingly observation that much of public behaviour in Indonesia is 'traditional', that is in accordance with the thinking of traditional law. As an American proverb has it, 'You can take the boy out of the country, but not the country out of a boy'. No less an observer of modern times – and the keeper of mainstream economic traditions – *The Economist* noted the traditional character of President Susilo Bambang Yudhoyono's action in resolving a touchy political/administrative issue, i.e., corruption, at the highest national level. More to the point, that newspaper implied that application of a traditional Javanese approach resolved the issue better than more prosaic Western approaches using concepts assumed to prevail in

26 Suwarno, *Dictionary*, no. 1460.

modern nation states.[27] Other examples come readily to mind. One need not go so far as the favourite (Cornell) academic pastime during the Old Order of trying to match various ministers' behaviour with their counterparts in the repertoire of the *Ramayana* and *Mahabharata* shadow play stories with President Sukarno as the *dhalang*. Yet, it is common knowledge that Sukarno's successor, General Suharto, made extensive use of traditional Javanese instruments for running the country. His own biography abounds with slogans, *piwulang*, *paribasa*, and *sloka*.[28] Many items were, in fact, taken from the Old Order and skewed to fit *Orde Baru* conceptions of rule. In addition, there are many varieties of *pancasila* this and *pancasila* that, 'Asian values', and others are too numerous to cite here. Elements from 'tradition' (real, created, or pseudo)[29] not only gave character to the New Order but also contributed to its longevity.

Aji Saka lives!

Aji Saka's *aksara/sloka* are prospering in today's Indonesia. Interpretations have been advanced by serious and frivolous scholars, commentators, bloggers, etc. What is common for all of them is that the uncompromising loyalty of Dora and Sembada to their master's conflicting wishes (*setia* v. *durhaka*) have given way to a more nuanced version of various degrees of chicanery. Modern versions also tend toward moral philosophy and mysticism. No less a figure than Pakubuwana IX (1861-1893) is said to have created a moral philosophy from the *aksara* comprising the Dora-Sembada story. It was resuscitated and commemorated in a new building in the Yogyakarta *kraton*, the 'Historical and Traditional Values Hall' (*Balai Kajian Sejarah dan Nilai Tradisional*) dedicated on 13 July 1992. The philosophy is introduced by a classical Javanese verse, which translates as:

> There lacks neither instruction nor teaching
> for the people of Java.
> [As for meritorious] behaviour in life, if they wish to follow it,
> then the Javanese *aksara*
> are their true teachers.

27 *The Economist*, 28 November 2009.
28 Suharto, *Soeharto. Pikiran, Ucapan, dan Tindakan Saya. Otobiografi.*
29 Pemberton, *On the subject of 'Jawa'*.

In keeping with the tradition of the original, the philosophy expounds the true meaning of the five stanzas composed of *aksara*. For our purposes, we can content ourselves with the observation that Pakubuwuna's *sloka* repeats the message of Aji Saka's, but in moralistic terms redefined by Javanese Islam.

The dedication date of the *Balai Kajian Sejarah dan Nilai Tradisional* was not fortuitous. President Suharto had opened the Javanese Language Congress a year earlier with an address on the 'affirmation of the relevance for the modern Indonesian nation of the noble values contained in the philosophical means of the letters of the Javanese alphabet' according to *Suara Merdeka*.[30] Nancy K. Florida continues:

> In April 1994 the Yogyakarta Center of Research on Traditional History and Values, a division of the Indonesian Department of Education and Culture, hosted the National Seminar on the Meaning of the Letters of the Javanese Alphabet ('*Seminar Nasional Pengkajian Makna Ha-na-ca-ra-ka*'). The official invitation to the seminar explained its mission: 'to unearth the noble cultural values of the Indonesian people and to realise (*merealisasi*) the speech that President Suharto presented on 'The Hidden Meaning of the Letters of the Javanese Alphabet'.

Following this vein, many variations on the Aji Saka *aksara/sloka* have emerged. As they are more than adequately represented in the blogosphere, it seems unnecessary to consider them at any length here.

Showing both the widespread nature and its flexibility is the example of a popular movement meditation called *amerta*. The founder and principle *guru* of the Amerta Movement, Suprapto Sudarma, feels that the Aji Saka *sloka* was too authoritarian, thus giving the wrong idea of what it means to be Javanese. In 1991 he created a new variation of the concept by liberating it from narrow tradition.

> Somehow, I don't like this. I don't want to see fighting and death. That's why I refused to accept the usual order of the Javanese alphabet. I changed the composition into a new order which gives a different meaning.
>
> *Batara sada pada jaya ghaca wahana maga kala nyata*
> Two independent persons meet. They are equals. They contemplate the facts of the situation. That is the way to reach the truth.

30 *Suara Merdeka*, 21 July 1991, cited by Florida (1995), p. 37 n 71.

> With this composition, I can have a new idea for my life: that I always have the mirroring of the truth, of the space, the line and the time and I mediate so as to become equal.[31]

A common characteristic for all movements to modernise is that they tend to depart from literal restatement of the original references to *sloka* in order to arrive at an interpretation felt to be more attune with what being Javanese, Muslim, or Indonesian should be. The original message has become divorced from the original vignettes of *aksara*, thus re-creating *sloka* as the bearer of new Javanese traditions. Undoubtedly as a result of law's function being usurped by alien European concepts, they have moved increasingly toward moral teaching and even more characteristic formulations of religious and mystical philosophy. As pointed out by many observers, this often approaches views characterised as 'Sufi'. In historical terms this can also be a re-incorporation into a parallel branch of law/religious expressions which goes back to the time of our earliest texts. Within the Independent Kingdoms era Kartasura produced the Berlin *Surya Alam* showing a direct line of development toward Islamic Javanisms characteristic of Yasadipura I & II and Rangga Warsita, as the dominant *pujangga* of Surakarta. That they have had an impact on the Yogyakarta literary world is indicated by association with the *Suluk Sloka Jiwa* works of Sufi mysticism.[32]

Hence, the answer to our rhetorical question as to relevance and continuity is ambiguous. Interest in the literal *aksara* and *sloka* continues. As one blogger put it, 'the Aji Saka story continues to fascinate Javanese youth'. This is with the qualification that its flow has changed directions. One of the more modern versions is its use within the growing phenomena of 'Netizen-ship' (from internet + citizen) for those spending a lot of time on the internet and consequently being influenced by its contents. The aim seems to be neither to return to traditional values or concepts by upholding the traditional loyalty of authoritarianism endorsed by Aji Saka nor to emphasize modern moral philosophy through Islamic thought, thus aimed more at reforming society than preserving it as, for example, turning to the *ramalan* considered below. Rather it seems to aim at constructing a version of a cyber-world, itself not unaffected by the retro interest in among other things the Dora-Sembada relation within the Aji Saka tradition. Of interest in the present context are the ideas advanced by Ario Seta. In Chapter 5 entitled 'Netizenship: Between Ignorance and Prudence', a subchapter is

31 Lavelle, *Amerta Movement*, 'Modernizing the Javanese warrior concept', pp. 219-220.

32 www.jawapalace.org/suluksaloka.html, Ahmadi 2002.

devoted to explanation of prudence couched in terms of the Dora-Sembada vignette.[33] Without going into the intriguing details of the presentation, its significance lies in confirming just how much the *sloka* phenomena remain a part of the modern scene, despite having their roots in the at least a far back as that of the Independent Kingdoms era.

Ramalan: contemporaneous Islamic moral wisdom

Islamic lessons of morality can be drawn from Jayabaya prophecies as part of the *yuga* cycle, although whether this points to continuity or renovation is unclear. Particularly attractive are the prophecies illustrating the misery of the *Sengara* Age expressed in eighteenth century Javanese Moslem dress. Google-ing 'Jayabaya' '*ramalan*', or '*Kitab Musarar*' results in hits too numerous to be dealt with here. The essay confines itself here to the laments-as-morality identified by Kyai Mochtar Adam, a highly respected *ulama* living and working in Bandung. In a recently published work[34] the Jayabaya *ramalan* are matched with strikingly similar verses in the Koranic literature. In this respect it should be noted that the *ramalan* are not only descriptions of the low level to which life has sunk in this *Sengara* Age but also signs of the impeding end of the world. Deviating from the Hindu/Buddhist original, by implication the logical end can be avoided, or at least delayed, by 'cleaning up one's act', a form of moral rearmament. As Kyai Adam says

> From the results of the investigation is forged the essence launched in the form of a new work in the hope that it will become a source of enthusiasm for the struggle of our grandchildren in the future. The ideals of the *pujangga*, which portrayed a golden age, are clearly a source of inspiration from the spiritual images of Sultan Agung. If we investigate in a chronological manner, it becomes obvious that that moment points to the image of a great and fully sovereign nation, namely *Negara Kesatuan Republik Indonesia*![35]

The relevance of the age-old descriptions of the *Sengara* Age to the present as found in among others the *Kitab Musarar* is heightened by the fact they are reflected in the *Sunna*. A good example is provided by '*Ramalan* no. 7.

33 Ario Seto, *Netizenship, Activism and Online Community Transformation in Indonesia*, pp. 134-138.

34 Kyai Muchtar Adam, *Ramalan Prabu Jayabaya*.

35 *Ibid.* p. 17, (my translation).

Menjulang Menara-Menara' (The Soaring Towers,[36] which encompasses the first half-dozen *ramalan* of the *kitab.*

> In the future there are wagons without horses, Java is ringed in steel, boats sail in the sky, rivers are of tears, markets lack voices; these are the signs that the time of Jayabaya is neigh (*Ramalan* nos. 1-6).

This parallels the *Hadith* of Hr. Bukhari:

> Abu Hurairah tells that the blessed Prophet said, 'Among the signs of Doomsday are the race to build ever higher buildings'.

More characteristic for the remaining two-hundred plus *ramalan* are descriptions of the deplorable state of social life. Only a few of examples can be given. Number 5, 'Permitting Lies' reads: *Jangka Jayabaya: Timah dianggap perak, emas diarani tembaga, dandang dikandakake kuntul* (tin is considered as silver, gold is seen as copper, a crow is seen as white egret).[37] The latter phrase is, in fact, a Javanese *sloka*/proverb meaning 'a bad thing or person that is considered to be good'.[38] This is reflected in the *surah al-Mumtahanah* [60]:12. Number 6 on 'Bloodshed' reads *Jangka Jayabaya*: *ana peperangan ing jero, timbul amarga para pangkatakeh sing padha salah paham* (the inner struggles come about because among the elite many lack understanding).[39] '*Perangan ing jero* [*batin*]' is also a modern Javanese proverb/*sloka* meaning ' at war with one's inner self or feelings.[40] This has a number of predecessors in the literature surrounding the Koran, among them, Hr. Muslim citing The Prophet: 'Truly the signs of the nearness of annihilation are: disappearance of knowledge and the even spread of stupidity, and manslaughter spreads everywhere, and this manslaughter is murder',[41] followed by examples of the bloodshed in many parts of the world. Number 10, 'Daring to have a weak law' reads: *Jangka Jayabaya*: *Ukuman Ratu ora adil* (the king's law is not just), which in Kyai Adam's interpretation has an anti-corruption message for Indonesia's rulers.[42] Finally, Number 42 on 'Dysfunctional Regulations' reads: *Jangka Jayabaya*:

36 *Ibid.* pp. 85-92.
37 *Ibid.*, pp. 71-75.
38 Suwarno, *Dictionary*, no. 337.
39 Kyai Adam, *Ramalan*, pp. 75-85.
40 Suwarno, *Dictionary*, no. 1290.
41 Kyai Adam, *Ramalan*, p. 76.
42 *Ibid.*, pp. 98-104.

Pedagang akeh alangane (trade suffers great blockages),
Akeh buruh nantang jurangan (many workers challenge the bosses),
Juragan dadi umpan (Bosses become bait),
Sing suwarane seru oleh pengaruh (the one with the loudest voice has influence),
Wong pinter diingar-ingar (the clever are pursued)
Wong ala diuja (evil ones are spoiled),
Wong ngerti mangan ati (those who understand eat their hearts out),
Bandha dadi memala (wealth becomes a sickness).[43]

Judgment as to truthfulness of the utterances and degree to which they supplement or are preceded by the wisdom of the Koran and *Sunna* is best left to the reader. In any event, Kyai Adam's book captures in print what many Indonesian bloggers are saying on the cyber net.

43 *Ibid.*, pp. 201-202.

Section IV

End Material

Appendix I The Problematic *Pepakem Tjerbon*

The *Pepakem Tjerbon* publication

In keeping with earlier publications of ostensibly local law, the Semarang and Freijer compendiums in respectively 1750 and 1760,[1] the *Pepakem Tjerbon* of 1768 was intended for East India Company officials. Had it been directed to the other members sitting on the Javo-Dutch courts – *jaksa, pangulu, tumenggung,* and Cirebon princes or Priangan Regents – a Javanese text on the model of the *Layang Ubaya, Surat Cirebon,* or *Undang-Undang Nitih Cirebon*[2] would have been more appropriate. The Company needed an accessible, consistent, and concrete law text in order that its officials could claim consistency with local custom in reviewing judgments and subsequently accepting, modifying, or invalidating them. Company policy dictated that the legal decisions, vetted in order to keep them within the bounds of Dutch priorities, follow Javanese law 'in so far as it is compatible to us [the officials of the Company]', so often stated in the Company records. The ambition with the *pepakem* project was to be attained through a selection of paragraphs from existing, heterogeneous titles, a *pepakem* of *pepakem,* which would embody Javanese written law. In this regard the comprehensiveness of titles chosen by 'team Hasselaer' is indisputable. Any listing of relevant Javanese legal traditions matches that cited by the *pepakem's* introductory rubric.[3]

The *Pepakem Tjerbon* should have provided the ideal source for reconstructing traditional Javanese written law. However, despite drawing upon most important of the era's legal titles, several factors argue against accepting its contents as representative of the era's law. The most striking failing is suggested by the contrast between the *pepakem's* contents and that of the *Wadigun*

1 The Semarang compendium is formally named 'Compendium der voornaamste Javasche wetten, nauwkeurig getrokken uit het Mohometaansche wet-boek, Mogharaer', published in van der Chijs (ed.) *Nederlandsch-Indisch plakaataboek,* vol. V, 1750-1754, pp. 14-37 and Freijer compendium, after its compiler, 'Compendium der voornaamste Mahomedaanshe wetten en gewoonten nopens erfenissen, huwelijken en echtcheidingen', *Ibid.*, vol. VII, 1755-1764, pp. 392-407.

2 Hoadley and Hooker, *The Agama*, pp. 258-269.

3 Specific references to the same titles by early scholars are found in Winter, *Javaansche Zamenspraken*, vol. II, pt. 3, p. 143; Crawfurd, *History of the Indian Archipelago*, vol. III, pp. 78-86; and Raffles, *History of Java*, pp. 279-280. 'Traditional law' as used here excludes the Javo-Dutch legal texts as the *ubaya* of the Cirebon-Priangan, as well as the *prajanji* and *angger-angger* of Central Java belonging to the transitional period from traditional Javanese to Dutch European law, Hoadley, *Islam Dalam*, Bab 5, *'Perjuang untuk Supremasi'*, pp. 275-327.

Wangkara which opened this work. The latter, as all relevant legal titles, is dominated by *sloka* and *sloka* derivatives. Yet these key components are conspicuously absence in the Dutch compendium. A partial exception consists of the unique formulation of *sinalokan*. Two other factors counsel caution in accepting the published *Pepakem Tjerbon* at face value. The first concerns the supplement to the original Dutch text of an apparently younger Javanese manuscript unencumbered by information on origins or date requisitioned in connection with preparations for the *pepakem's* publication in 1905. The second is the lack of congruence between the contents of the *pepakem*'s paragraphs and those of the titles from pre-existing Javanese manuscripts cited as its source.

Dutch v. Javanese texts

The *Pepakem Tjerbon* publication is composed of unequal Dutch and Javanese components. At its core is the original archival act written in Company era Dutch and officially promulgated in 1768. This means that the compendium of translations of Javanese texts lacks reference to the sources of information. Only titles are provided, which as we have seen, are unreliable due to disparity between title and contents. The Javanese component has an even less solid pedigree. It consists of a manuscript of unknown date and provenance, the 'de Nooy manuscript' after the Cirebon Resident who supplied it. For the 1905 publication the editor, G.A.J. Hazeu, paired the de Nooy manuscript with the archival text. In accordance with the request of the Bataviaasch Genootschap, which sponsored publication, the eighteenth-century Dutch text is reproduced in the left-hand column and the corresponding paragraphs from de Nooy text in the ha-na-ca-ra-ka script in the right-hand column. The Dutch archival act is longer and more explanatory than the compressed, nearly cryptic, Javanese of the de Nooy manuscript. In addition, many Dutch paragraphs lack a Javanese counterpart in the published work, never the reverse.[4]

Although a Javanese source had thus been made available for the *Pepakem Tjerbon* publication, concordance between the contents of the de Nooy text

4 According to Hazeu, that the Dutch version was so true to the original deserves unqualified praise. 'With amazement one observes the fact that in the second half of the 18th century there were [Dutch] personnel in Java who knew enough Javanese to be able to reproduce rules often difficult to understand. Although the actual power of some of the terms is not always felt, the meaning is seldom misunderstood. Beside the in many respects pioneering work accomplished by Raffles we can point to this in 1768 created Dutch translation of the *Pepakem Tjerbon* with some satisfaction', 'Introduction', p. vii. Praise of Raffles' contribution, undoubtedly referring to the *Surya Alam* translation, as a positive model seems ironic. As we have seen, the weakness of both publications lies in the uncertainties of the exact relationship between Dutch or English translation and the equivalent paragraphs in the Javanese sources.

and the Dutch text are not as clear as its editor would have us believe. At issue is the apparent incongruity between their general similarity and a lack of a one-to-one correspondence between the contents of their respective paragraphs. In short, the relationship between the de Nooy text and the Javanese *pepakem*-s, which are said to be its source, is tenuous. The implicit assumption is that the contents of the de Nooy text are identical with that which team Hasselaer had to work with in the second half of the eighteenth century. In practice this means that attempts to go beyond the Dutch text and to compare its contents with the (more) original expressions are frustrated by the uncertainties of date and provenance of the Javanese language part of the *Pepakem Tjerbon* publication.

The issue is exacerbated by hiatuses and differences in length of respectively Dutch and Javanese renditions of the same paragraphs. The de Nooy manuscript was found only in 1895 after a search in the Cirebon archives the preceding year proved to be fruitless. Although not conclusive – it could still be an older text, which remained undiscovered in some collection – lacunae and mismatches between the two do not inspire confidence in its authenticity as reflecting the pre-1768 contents of Javanese *pepakem*. No folio numbers are given for the Javanese text with which to ascertain the source of the relevant passages. In any event, several other manuscripts cited in Chapter 2 have better credentials. Even the solution suggested here of checking the de Nooy contents against the manuscript versions drawn upon in this work proves to be more work than is justified.[5] It seems more profitable to concentrate on the manuscript versions and use the Dutch text to supplement the information thus provided.

Contents

The *Pepakem Tjerbon* publication consists of three sections. The first section consists of an introduction to legal procedure entitled 'Manner of Procedure at Cirebon under the direction of the Seven *Jaksa* and the Sultans Collectively'. This eighteen-page treatise on procedure (pp. 1-18) is characterised by considerable legal formalism, particularly in the use of written documents and the requirements of consistency, absent from both Javanese texts and the few case examples from the period. No Javanese text is cited as the source to match the Dutch paragraphs, resulting in blank spaces in the right-hand column. This means that the 'Manner of Procedure' was not part of the de Nooy manuscript. As indicated by the folio

5 Preliminary comparison of supposedly identical paragraphs between the de Nooy text and relevant manuscript texts as the *Raja Niscaya* and *Jaya Lengkara* show that considerably less than half match. Most of them come from sources other than those cited by the de Nooy text.

numbers in square brackets provided by the published work, the original text begins on page nineteen of the printed version. Pages one to eight seem to have been composed immediately prior to the proclamation in 1768 by way of summing up the procedural rules scattered throughout the body of the *Pepakem* with sporadic references to the contents of the respective Javanese titles. That it is a foreign innovation is not surprising. Summaries of legal procedure are virtually unknown in Javanese manuscripts of a legal nature. This strengthens the argument that they belong to the legal literature produced under and likely influenced by Dutch rule.

The summary of Cirebon legal procedure is followed by a second section constituting the *Pepakem* proper. This covers pages nineteen to seventy-one, which correspond to folios one to forty-two of the archival text. According to Hazeu's calculation, the proportion of the contents contributed by the diverse *pepakem* was as follows. The *Raja Niscaya* accounts for fifteen per cent of the total length and twenty per cent of the substantive section, an *Undang-undang Mataram* with respectively eight and sixteen per cent of ditto, a *Jaya Lengkara* with thirty-eight and forty-five per cent, a *Kontara Manawa* with thirty and zero percent, and an *Adilulah* with zero and c. one per cent (p. 124). As a departure from local legal traditions, the substantive section of the *Pepakem Tjerbon* has been organised topically under rubrics apparently coined by the compilers. This has resulted in imposing order on the apparently arbitrary choice and sequence of paragraphs found in the Javanese titles.

A third and final section (pp. 71-114) derives from the *Jaya Lengkara* and the *Kontara Manawa*. Paragraphs attributed to the *Jaya Lengkara* include animal parables and illustrative vignettes tacked on the end of the compendium proper (pp. 71-85). These provide several short legalistic sketches. A dozen or so end in *sinalokan,* which derive solely from the de Nooy manuscript (see Chapter 6, under '*Kinawi*'). The paragraphs attributed to the *Kontara Manawa* (pp. 85-114) consist of a mixture of animal fables in the *Pancatantra* tradition, a few paragraphs reminiscent of the (Balinese) *Agama*, and many of an unrecognisable character. Sections two and three are discussed systematically by Hazeu in an informative note apparatus. The publication is concluded by a few comments on the text's colophon, a copy of its proclamation in 1768, and an invaluable index to the work's technical legal vocabulary in both Company Dutch and romanised Javanese.

Most relevant to present discussion is the second, substantive part of the published text. It follows directly the Introduction's list of *pepakem* drawn upon in compiling the *pepakem* cited in Chapter 1. Its heterogeneous paragraphs have been gathered under the Dutch rubrics of: 1) rules of procedure (pp. 19-30) summarised in the first section, 2) evidence (pp. 31-36), 3) witnesses (pp. 36-42); 4) legal categories (pp. 43-53), and 5) punishments (pp. 54-71). Just how much re-arranging of the original texts' contents was undertaken by the compilers is shown by a closer look at the disparate origins of the subsections one to five. Noteworthy here is that the contents of the cited *pepakems* were not re-written for incorporation in the text on the model of the first section. They are quoted literally, constituting blocks of undigested text, albeit in translation, cut from the named *pepakem* and pasted into the *Pepakem Tjerbon* under rubrics created by team Hasselaer to identify the contents. Many are recognizable from specific titles and not a few are identical to them. However, their contents tend to uphold Crawfurd's negative judgment of Javanese law as a mixture of rules, competence, authority, etc. For example, the first section on procedure (p. 20ff) starts with the rubric 'From the *Pepakem Raja Niscaya*'. Then follows an under rubric '...nine articles which decide law suits'. The factual contents of the nine are built around a short phrase in transcribed Javanese after a colon followed by a Dutch translation of the explanation provided by the manuscript. The first nine begin with

> Anya Wadie [*sic anya wadi*]: difference in contents between the *kendel* and *tutur* documents...Akarje deesie [*kirya desi*] after having submitted the *kendel* letter, asserting things that do not favour the case and are not in agreement with the *pisaid* [complaint] and *kendel* letters.

They continue in a similar manner for the entire list, their contents showing similarities with equivalent Javanese paragraphs found in other manuscripts containing legal prescriptions. These are followed by '13 articles which decide suits'. They, in fact, consist of the *Surya Alam*'s 'Thirty *Prakara*' listed in Table 6.1 above. They are decisive in a negative fashion; presence of any one of them results in defeat (*kalah*). The section then turns to fifteen similar points taken from an *Undang-Undang Mataram* (p. 22ff), plus nine more from the *Adilulah* (p. 25), one from a *Salokantara* three more from the *Raja Niscaya* (p. 26), eight again from the *Jaya Lengkara* (p. 28), and one again from the *Raja Niscaya* (p. 29). They finish with three from an *Undang-Undang Mataram* (pp. 30-31). Most of them reflect the contents the *uger-uger* and *andhih-andhihan* (p. 34ff), as the *aksara* of the wrong and right respectively, even though *aksara* are named within the work only once and then in the accepted meaning of letters of the alphabet. A few *sloka* are found in the *Pepakem*.[6] None are specifically termed *prakara*. In short, the proper

6 These include Classic *Sloka*, no. 17.1, *sragala lumumpat ing papalang*; no. 17.2 *tebu-tuwuh ing socané* from the *Pepakem Tjerbon* (p. 26), citing the *Solokantara*; no. 20, *estri lancah, toya,*

Javanese terms for the *sloka* phenomena are nowhere mentioned directly in either the Dutch or Javanese versions of the published text.

Late date

A second point arguing against accepting the *Pepakem Tjerbon*'s contents as authentic Javanese law comes from the relative late date of the compendium. By 1768 the Dutch East India Company's representatives had been dispensing law for the subjects of the principality, as well as the regencies of the neighbouring Priangan region, for close to eighty years. Study of cases handled by the Javo-Dutch courts has documented the type of changes in procedural and substantive law brought about by the existence of alien hegemony. In fact, the last case in which the *jaksa* participated dates from more than two decades before the promulgation of the *Pepakem Tjerbon*, namely the Sultan Cirebon v. Anom (Pinjalin) of 1743.[7] By 1768 the text no longer reflected autonomous Javanese law, but one characterised by a relative high degree of alien accretions. Supporting arguments concentrate on two points, namely artificial innovations and literal authenticity

Artificial Innovations

Several radical changes in the fabric of law appear without warning in the Dutch publication. These contrast with the legal tradition established on the testimony of its own texts. The first and most obvious example comes from innovations within judicial authority for assigning capital punishment for criminal activity. Citing the *Raja Niscaya* as its source (pp. 54-59) the *Pepakem Tjerbon* cites the 'six points', actually the *sad-atatayi* (Six Tyrants) discussed in Appendix IV. The provision is found in neither the West nor Central Javanese examples of that title.[8] Even more remarkable, the *Pepakem* states that these crimes lead to capital punishment under the authority of the *pangulu*! By this time the *pangulu*, originally a leader from *'ulu'* (*lit.* head; a leader), had taken on the meaning of chief religious official in the community. To the extent this was realised in practice it would signify a shift from princely authority (backed by the Company) to that exercised by religious functionaries, which it otherwise consciously excluded. Not only is there no evidence of the existence of institutionalised *pangulu* courts but also license to punish transgressions of the *sad-atatayi,* along

p. 39 citing a *Jaya Lengkara*; *candra tirta sari cakra*, p. 52 citing a the *Raja Niscaya*; no. 18, *sloka dursila*, i.e., *kusuma wicitra*, p. 53, also citing a *Jaya Lengkara*.

7 Hoadley, *Selective Judicial Competence*, p. 121-125.

8 Rather it is found also in the *Jimbun Slokantara* I (§ 2) and *Surya Alam* (§ 15).

with the *astha dustha* and *astha corah,* had always been a monopoly of the sovereign.[9] Hence their transfer to a new instance in the form of a tribunal composed of Islamic functionaries must be a textual innovation of the *pepakem.* Motivation can have come from either a concession to what the Dutch felt to be a growing Islamic identity among the 'natives' or an attempt to undermine potential Islamic, anti-Dutch sentiment by bringing tame *pangulu* into the Company-dominated administrative system.[10] A third possibility is that it was a 'paper tiger', being only for show. Throughout the eighteenth century, Dutch East India Company officials kept the assignment of capital punishment firmly in their own hands.

A second example of innovations reported by the *pepakem* as though they were accepted practice concerns the water ordeal (*toyagama*). It was added to the original *agama-drigama* (religion-custom) dichotomy. The innovation is found only in the printed *Pepakem Tjerbon* (p. 43) citing as its source the *Jaya Lengkara.* The *Jaya Lengkara* is well enough known to be able to observe that the *Pepakem*'s attribution only partially matches the reality of its contents. *Drigama* (experience, custom, etc) lies at the heart of the entire *Jaya Lengkara* tradition. Implicit here is that it was also true for the related *Jimbun Slokantara,* and even much of the *Surya Alam.* '*Agama*' (set, fixed), which would become *agama Islam,* is rarely found in the any of the titles, including those associated with Senapati Jimbun. The tenets of Islam are almost exclusively found in the package of imported texts from the international world of Islam. Moreover, there are no documented references to *toyagama* in the titles used in this study.[11] Even a newly-translated Banten text from 1820, 'History of Majapahit' (Art. 1) mentions *agama-drigama,*

9 For example, the *Agama* (§ 56) states that 'these three guilts of malefactors (*dustha*), tyrants (*atatayi*), and thieves (*maling sic corah*) are capital crimes (*dosa pati*), this is the *agama* (set rule) of princes' and § 176 stating that homosexuals, thieves, and tyrants (*atatayi*), if proven, must all be executed by the prince. This is reiterated in § 181, adding that their children and grandchildren must be executed by the prince.

10 See Mahmood Kooria, 'The Dutch Mogharaer'.

11 What seems to have happened is that the (Koranic) oath (*sapata*) administered by the *pangulu* became coupled with a pre-Islamic 'gods ordeal', here remaining under water (*silem*). Some support comes from the fact that the term used in the de Nooy text is '*ipat-ipat*' (curse, malediction; *ngipat-ipat* to forbid s.o. to do s. t. on pain of invoking a dreadful curse). The *toyagama* concept was subsequently adopted by the Dutch officials as a means of resolving time-consuming and often inconclusive legal process seen as counter-productive. While only vague textual references to the use of *toyagama* are found in, say, the *Gajah Mada* of RAS 33, ff. 66, 82-83, there was a threat of its application in an actual case in 1734. When the court decided that the lack of decisive evidence could be made up for through evoking the 'god's ordeal', the defendant refused to undergo the ritual. Refusal to undergo the ordeal provided a self-enforcing outcome, Hoadley, *Selective Judicial Competence*, Suta Darta v. Wira Utama, p. 166ff.

with *karinah* as a third rather than *toyagama*.[12] Both examples, as well as others that could be cited, show the willingness of the *Pepakem's* compilers – possibly the authors of the de Nooy text – to embroider on existing legal traditions, thus skewing the contours of Javanese law.

Literal Authenticity

A third source of controversy is the lack of congruity between the *pepakem*'s contents and those of the titles specifically named as its sources. To gauge the extent of the discrepancy between citation and actual employment of the titles as the *Pepakem's* building blocks, an analysis of the compendium's composition is helpful. Table 1 lists the specific pages of the printed compendium as compared with the contents of the individual titles. The task has been facilitated by Hazeu's detailed comments on specific paragraphs, supplemented by an index of both Javanese and Dutch terms appended to the publication (pp. 132-187). Arranged in the order given in the introductory rubric, the left-hand column gives the respective titles and their percentage of the *pepakem*'s substantive text. The second column provides the page numbers where the titles have been cited as sources in the printed version. The third column indicates the respective manuscript titles. The far right-hand column adds comments on the sources. All things being equal, the contents of the named titles should correspond to the citations in the printed *Pepakem Tjerbon*.[13] That they do so to a very limited extent is noted after presentation of the necessary background.

The titles have various degrees of accuracy.[14] This leaves us with the two major texts cited by the *Pepakem Tjerbon* introductory rubric. The first is

12 Ayang, 'Undhang-Undhang Banten', under '(8) Sajarah Majapahit', p. 209ff.

13 To ensure that the lack of correspondence between the *pepakem* text and the originals of the cited titles is not a product of drawing upon variant sources, those cited for the *Raja Niscaya* and *Jaya Lengkara* – some seventy-four per cent of the *pepakem*'s contents – come from differing sources, both as regard to context and place of origin. More detailed information on the respective sources is found in Chapter 2.

14 The strike-out ~~marks~~ indicate that not all titles cited by the *Pepakem Tjerbon* are available in manuscript form. Two must be modified or eliminated. First, there seems to be no autonomous source for a *Undang-undang Mataram*, which comprises some sixteen per cent of the Cirebon *pepakem's* substantial text. What exists is a fragment originating from the Cirebon *Kaprabonan* without date published with a translation in anom., '*Undang-Undang Mataram*', pp. 349-355. As far as name is concerned the closest example comes from the contents of the *Undhang-Undhang Luwangan*, a title known from the two West Javanese manuscripts, namely LOr 7440 and 7410. '*Luwangan*' means (hole, pit) with a secondary meaning of 'antecedent, precedent', Pigeaud *Javaans-Nederlands Woordenboek*. The title could then be read as 'antecedent' or 'precursor' to an *Undang-Undang Mataram*, or even '*Model/Example* (Prawiroatmojo, *Bausastra Java-Indonesia*) *of the Laws of Mataram*'. The two versions are nearly identical. LOr 7440 contains

Appendix I, Table 1 Manuscripts v. the *Pepakem Tjerbon*

Title	Citation on page	Manuscript source	Comments
Raja Niscaya 29%	7-8, 20-22, 26-28, 29-30, 32-33, 38-9, 41, 42, 47-49, 51-57, 62-63, 68, 71	LOr 7410, ff. 2_v-8_v/ Add 12 303, ff. 35_v-38_r	near identical texts
~~*Undang2 Mataram*~~ 16%	22-24, 30-31, 37, 49-51, 57-9		no known text
Jaya Lengkara 45%	28-29, 31-37, 38, 39-40, 42-44 53-54, 59-62, 63-68, 69, 70, & 71-85	Add 12 303, ff. 19_v-31_r/ RAS 38, ff4-98 LOr 7410, ff. 28-41 LOr 7440, ff. 208-244	identical texts variant example
~~*Kontara Manawa*~~	47 & 85-114		controversial title
Adilulah/(Surya Alam?)	24, 343-6	LOr 7440, ff. 117-113 LOr 7442, ff. 1-42	near identical texts
(Single citation, i.e. >1%)			
Salokantara 26			
Jugul Muda	44-45	LOr 7440, ff. 315-401 LOr 7410, ff. 71v-113v RAS 6, ff. 23-52	exemplars identical 'Classic *Sloka*'
Raja Niti 47		[RAS 33, ff. 86-115]	

eight extra paragraphs, i.e., §§ 47-54, which in contrast to the preceding forty-seven do not end in a *sinalokan*; LOr 7410 prefaces each paragraph with a short phrase identifying the subject and it is attributed to Wangsa Diraksa in the year Dal. Otherwise both examples are composed of short legal vignettes. Each is closed by a *sinalokan*, often two, one for the winner and one for the loser. Several of them or parts thereof are either repeated in other titles or are identifiable as *sloka* or *sloka* fragments, see Chapter7. '*Sinalokan*'. Despite its *bona fides* in the form of date and contents, the title remains something of a mystery. Why do none of the paragraph contents match anything in the pages cited in the *Pepakem Tjerbon* as coming from the *Undang-Undang Mataram*? Surely a 'model/example' of an *Undang-undang Mataram* must have had some relation to its source. Alternatively, why was not the *Luwangan* included in the compilation? This is specially puzzling because it is found in manuscripts containing not only the other titles contributing to the *Pepakem Tjerbon* but also manuscripts pre-dating the publication by several decades. A third issue is that the title itself points to Mataram administrative regulations (*undhang-undhang*) as a generic source of the *Pepakem Tjerbon*. A second casualty is the much-discussed *Ko[n]tara Manawa*. The title provides the last third of the Cirebon *pepakem* (pp. 85-115). It resembles no other manuscript. Despite suggestions of a connection with the *Kuntaramanawa darmasastra* cited in the *Nagarakṛtagama* (*sic Desawarnana*), its contents have nothing in common with those representing the Java-Bali legal tradition in Middle Javanese. As pointed out by Hazeu in 'Tjeribonsche Wetboek', p. 163ff, its contents reflect more fables of the *Pancatantra* genre than law *per se*. The modern Javanese *sloka kunthara ora pakra* is an 'ideal that does not materialise', Old Javanese according to Suwarno, *Dictionary*, no. 749 and similar ones. This suggests that in the Independent Kingdoms era the term '*kunthara* (*manawa*)' was used as a generic description the *Raja Niscaya*, some twenty-nine per cent of the substantive part of the printed text. As indicated in the 'manuscript' column, it is found in near identical copies originating from West and Central Java, respectively LOr 7410 and Add 12 303. Division of its contents into numbered paragraphs is an external exercise based on the appearance of *'Punika'* (This is) or an equivalent term *'Yén'*, *'Lamon'*, *'Anapun'*. Yet the singular name given it by the *Pepakem* is belied by its own pedigree. The first sentence of the manuscript reads,

> This is the *panggrayangan* (group/criticism) of the *Raja Niscaya*, *Wadhigun Wang*[*ka*]*ra*, *Salokantara Talaga Ening*, which show the truth of all the *padu* [cases], 1507 [which reduced] to eight affairs (*prakara*) of *cina*. (§ 1)

It continues by listing well known eight *'aksara* of the right' (*ikral/andhih-andhihan*) discussed in Chapter 5. *'Aksara'*.

By far the greatest contributor to the compilation is the *Jaya Lengkara*. It accounts for roughly forty-five per cent of the *Pepakem*'s substantive contents. The *Jaya Lengkara* is a Java-wide title found in manuscripts from Banten, West Java, to Central Java. Along with the *Jugul Muda* it is one of the more consistent titles in terms of contents. Yet there are notable exceptions. One is the version contained in LOr 7440, whose middle section – thus after the standard listing of the *aksara* – is built up of a dozen or so paragraphs identical to those of the *Jimbun Slokantara I*.

With this excursion into the building blocks of the *pepakem* we can return to the issue at hand. This is the fact that the contents of the cited paragraphs from the *Pepakem Tjerbon* correspond poorly or not at all to the available manuscript sources. While this does not necessarily undermine their veracity, it shows that they could as easily come from one or several other titles than that cited. *Pepakem* titles were not intended as legal texts in the European sense with resultant expectations of consistency and exclusiveness. One of the primary motivations for the compilation project resulting in the *Pepakem Tjerbon,* was to standardize and centralize the contents of all

of something 'not sufficiently concrete' rather than an autonomous law book. References to the last four titles contributing to the *Pepakem Tjerbon*, namely the *Adilulah, Slokantara, Jugul Muda*, and *Raja Niti,* are summarily dispatched in few lines. Because they account for less than one per cent of the contents, the last three receiving only a single citation, discussion of their contents is found in Chapter 2 within the context of other manuscript sources.

> their [the respective *jaksas*] *pepakem* or law books [which were to] be collected into a single book.[15]

These were undoubtedly what Gobius in 1716 meant by his comment on *jaksa* 'miscellany books', a reference to the differing *pepakem* possessed by individual *jaksa*. From this an important point emerges, namely that even *pepakem* bearing the same name could have varying contents. Most commonly they have taken the name of a notable particularly memorable in the field of justice as a *patih* (Jugul Muda, Arya Dilah), a sovereign (Jaya Lengkara, Surya Alam), or a war leader (Senapati Jimbun). Some titles suggest their subject matter as the *Luwangan Undhang-Undhang, Cacad*, and *Slokantara*. Yet there was no one-to-one correspondence between title and contents or even complete congruity between titles bearing the same name.

15 *'Memorie Hasselaer'*, cited in Hoadley, *Selective Judicial Competence*, p. 139.

Appendix II Classic *Sloka*

The legal *sloka* considered in this work are 'classic' in the sense of 'remarkably typical: outstandingly important'.[1] Frequency of occurrence and usefulness in clarifying the *sloka* phenomena of the Independent Kingdoms era provide the criteria. In this respect some two dozen *sloka* are particularly relevant to the present study. They come from the *Jugul Muda*, *Jaya Lengkara*, and *Surya Alam*, plus those found in related 'minor titles', all cited as sources of the 1768 *Pepakem Tjerbon*. The twenty-four chosen for further consideration may seem an inadequate representation of even legal *sloka*. They contrast with some fifteen-hundred *sloka* and *sloka*-like phrases contained in *Javaansche Zamenspraken*. In defence it can be pointed out that the present work is a study of their function as examples of a code rather than the entire body of such phrases. Consequently, their number suffices to establish the importance of the *sloka* phenomena as tools for delving into the vast number of *sloka*-phrases, legal and non-legal, contained in the Javanese manuscripts.

At the outset it should be noted that attempts at consistency in the organization of this appendix are thwarted by the contrast in available and comprehensible information concerning individual *sloka*. Here they are ordered after their appearance in respectively the *Jugul Muda* (nos. 1-13), *Jaya Lengkara* (nos. 14-22), and *Surya Alam* (nos. 23-24), although they are repeated in the other titles. For ease of reference an appropriate name has been assigned to every *sloka*. Afterwards the *sloka* are cited in the most usual form and their source provided. This is followed by Translation (literal or literary) and references to Copies and Variations. The latter consist of both literal phrases from other titles and longer explanations. In instances where the title provides its own complementary explanation, this is recorded in my translation under the rubric Textual Explanation. Given the importance of *Javaansche Zamenspraken* the rubric 'Interpretation of' quotes when available Winter's contribution translated into English from the Javanese in ha-na-ca-ra-ka script. In many cases a Modern Translation is available which draws from one or more of contemporary Indonesian authors as Suwarno, Darmasoetjipta, Ngafenan, and Hariwijaya. In special cases, as no. 2, an Analysis added. More commonly such considerations are relegated to the specific chapters focusing on respective *sloka* phenomena.

1 *The Concise Oxford Dictionary.*

Jugul Muda

1 Patih Jugul Muda citing the 'Dora-Sangkara *sloka*'

Sima bangga rebut mangsa mati katiban taru (LOr 7440, f. 341)
Translation
A deviant/disobedient tiger seizing prey dies, struck by a falling tree [an un-expected fate].

Variations
gana ina, arebut mangsa, mati katiban taruh, a dastardly young buck in searching for prey dies, struck by a falling tree, *Wadigun Wangkara* § 8, Add 18398, f. 62r termed a *sinalokan.*
sima bangga andurkara amet mangsa, Suwarno, *Dictionary,* no. 1460, 1461.
sima bangga tanpa karana, Winter, *Javaansche Zamenspraken,* vol. II, pt. 3, nos. 318, 319.

Commentary
For unknown reasons a royal follow-up to the Dora-Sangkara affair is lacking in the three complementary sources of LOr 7410, RAS 6, and the published *Serat angger: Jugul Muda*. They are otherwise nearly identical to the LOr 7440 version used as the primary source in this work. Were it not for the alternative version in *sinalokan* form from the *Luwangan* § 18: *padhu bangga rebut mangsa katiban ing taru*, a disobedient suit (*padhu*) competing for prey [i.e., victory] is struck by a falling tree, one would be hard put to include it as a Classic *Sloka*. In any case, nominal variants have come down to the present in proverbial form.

2 Tumenggung Raja Sasana quoting the *saloka agama 'dustha pandung'*

Mustika bramara corah titir penajaraken surak ing ampuhan mati déning ngalun-alun (LOr 7440, f. 331)

Translation
[The presence of] mice and bees as *corah* (1 thief, bandit; bad person) [discordant elements] triggers the alarm, [even with] supernatural powers [they] die due to their own actions.

Textual Explanation
P(m)usthika is the name of a mouse, if it is present (*saba*) in the dwelling (*wisma*) it should be killed; *brahmara* is the name of a bee, if this bee is present in the dwelling it should be killed.

This is the utterance of Kyai Tumenggung Raja Sasana, 'A person who carries out a theft against Your Majesty should be killed at Your behest (*lungguh*?)'.

Copies
Jugul Muda: LOr 7410, f. 77v; RAS 6, f. 34; *Jaya Lengkara*, Add 12 303 f. 25r; *Luwangan* § 5; *Cacad* § 4; *Pepakem Tjerbon*, pp. 94/170; *Surya Alam*, Berlin 402/van der Hout § 14; and Yasadipura, *Surya Alam*, Canto IX, verses 12-14.

Variation 1
Mustika ing kang rumiyin brahmara, cora malih titir penajaraken iku lan surak ing ampuhan mati déning ngalun-alun, Serat angger: Jugul Muda, p. 16.

Variation 2
If a person suiting before the *jaksa* opens [i.e., offers] food or promises gifts, this results in loss of the suit. A steadfast and virtuous *jaksa* is loyal to the process as a minister (*patih*), day and night performing the role of dedication (*tapas*) to the words of the king expressed as [the *sloka*] *adadamar téngga pisan kapurnaman* (Darmasoetjipta, *Kamus Peribahasa Jawa*, no. 3). 'Silence [absence] of the complaint' (*sepi abawa rena*) is not valid, resulting in loss of the suit. The meaning of '*sepi abawa rena*' is complaint without a document [signed by a *jaksa*] which is of no use, (to accuse someone without witness or written report, Suwarno, *Dictionary*, no. 1442) [hence] the *jaksa* declares for defeat in the case because it does not agree with [lit. it is a danger to] just governance [as expressed] by the *sloka*: *anirna parusa* (to reject or disobey the rules or orders of authorities, Suwarno, *Dictionary*, no. 140); *sudakir araja-parah*, being like [the *sloka*] *mustika brahmara corah surak ing a(m)puhan titir pinajaraken mati déning ngalu(n)-alu(n)*. Its meaning: *mustika* is a mouse, brahmara is a bee, if a mouse is found in the house day or night it may be killed, but not if found in the forest; *surak ing ampuhan* is the sound of bee as *durjana*, if found in the house they must be killed and *lambéné* [?]; [*titir pinajarakan*] is just the expression of a person who wants to shift [change testimony or stray from righteousness]; *mati déning alun-alun* means he who rules the country [parallel with owing the house] who discovers a mouse or bee [i.e., *durjana*], yea he who rules must kill them! (Berlin 402, ff. 404-403/LOr 1832, ff. 28-30)

Van der Hout translation
If someone suiting without written proof or witnesses loses a case, he may not demand right from the *fiscaal* (*jaksa*). Should he attempt to do so, he must be repudiated and felled.

No witness without a supporting document is acceptable. Although [such is the case] one anticipates this if the paper is not immediately ratified by the *jaksa*. He must be defeated because such does not conform to the way of law.

[King] Surya Alam cites the conversation of a certain two rulers concerning [cases of] thievery. They had sketched them by saying the following: 'The *jaksa* serves the necessity of knowing [the *sloka*] *mustika brahmara* [...] *alun-alun*. *Bromara* means a bee, *Moestika* a mouse. The householder should destroy bees when they fly in. *Surah ampuhan* means the noise of mice which are by nature malignant. They also must be destroyed. *Titir Pinadjarakan* means the bustle and turmoil of folk in apprehending or executing a thief or thieves (§ 14).

Variation 3: Yasadipura Surya Alam, *Canto IX, verses 12-14*

12. Furthermore that not pleasing to the country is the *sloka*
belonging to *pradata* [namely]*: mustika* and *bramara*
corah ya, which *kapyarsi*, *soerak ngampoehan*, *pina-*
jaraken titir (*M*)*ati déning aloen-aloen* to this person,
the reason for death [is that] a bee [and mouse], [raise]
the responsibility of being killed. The one who kills is he who owns
the house, he is the one who kills.
13. A mouse/bees destroy the walls of a house, because of that
they are killed as miscreants. Thus, he who owns/rules
the realm is authorized to kill, even bees
if they are present in the residence.
14. Presence in a garden is not proper to kill, only if
in the house, or invading the roof frame, breaking the rules, a mouse
inevitably destroys the contents of a dwelling, thus is a miscreant.
15. Yea, this is what has become the magic (authority) of the realm, thus able to be completed, even in denying, if there are remains (indications), the alarm is sounded, *soerak* [*ing*] *ampoehan* (possessing supernatural powers), this is what kills.

Interpretation of: *Musthika bramara corah, surak ing ampuhan, titir pinajarakan mati déning alun-alun,* (Winter, *Javaansche Zamenspraken,* vol. II, pt. 3, no. 442).

This is the *sloka* of miscreants. The meaning of *mustika* is mouse, *bramara* a bee, *corah misuwur* a well-known thief. Miscreants have become as a mouse continually destroying or as a bee constantly making its presence known. Their evil nature is well-known. The meaning of *surak ing ampuhan* is possessing supernatural powers [alternatively gale with mist and rain in the mountains] by a miscreant, who from the news of his evil deeds comes to his apprehension. The meaning of *titir pinajaraken* is the sound of the gong which spreads the news. The miscreant, which has become the subject of the alarm, is allowed to/must be executed. The meaning of *mati déning alun-alun* is that a miscreant dies as the result of his own actions/ utterances, which are known for their evilness.

Modern interpretation
'A *durjana* who is well known to have the character of continually (happily) destroying [property] and damaging others is condemned to death. The meaning: a person whose fate is misfortune occasioned by his own actions'.[2]

Analysis
Typical for the genre, the significance of a *sloka* extends far beyond the textual explanation. In the present instance this covers only the first part of the *sloka*, namely that concerning mice and bees as unwanted guests with well-known evil characteristics, which occasions sounding the alarm (*titir*). While this provides motivation for ending their destructive activities by allowing them to be killed, it leaves out the more important part of the *sloka* as law. License to punish consists of two parts. The first – *surah ing ampuhan* – remains unclear. Suwarno, *Dictionary*, no. 948, gives 'a person 'applauded by a storm', an alternative dictionary meaning is ((1 to possess special (supernatural) power (weapons, words)), that is, someone with supernatural powers. Prawiroatmodjo, *Kamus Jawa Indonesia* gives for *ampuh* 'a storm and misty rain', while the van der Hout version maintains that it is the sound of mice.

The second part – *mati déning ngalun-alun* – conveys its intention. This cannot be derived from the literal meaning of the *sloka*'s contents, even though it is crucial to the phrase's function. The literal meaning of 'dying by the grassy town square', is negated by the presence of the causal conjunction *déning* (1 (done) by; 2 because of). A solution is provided by a version found in LOr 7410, f. 77v. There a textual explanation clarifies the phrase as 'dying because of his acts'. This is seconded by Winter, *Javaansche Zamenspraken*, vol. II, pt. 3, no. 442, who provides a parallel of 'dying by his own utterances'. In other words, *alun-alun* has a non-dictionary meaning of 'deeds, behaviour' as reflected in the modern translation by Ngafenan, *Paribasan*. The point is crucial to the self-enforcing character of Javanese law. However, without the existence of an alternative title the phrase must either be left unexplained or

2 Ngafenan, *Paribasan*, p. 88, see also Suwarno, *Dictionary*, no. 948.

its deeper meaning dependent upon internal logic linking act with appropriate response. Evil creatures as mice and bees, which 'carry out damages to others' (Ngafenan, *Ibid.*, p. 88), deserve to be eliminated. The *sloka* context is explicitly applied by Raja Sasana in the *Jugul Muda* to human beings with the equivalent results, which comprises its purpose within law.

More intriguing is the Berlin *Surya Alam* paragraph which seems to link attempted bribery of a *jaksa* to the importance of valid evidence from witnesses to the *mustika* brahmara [...] *alun-alun sloka*. This is done via the transitional *sloka sepi abawara,* which is a form of false or unsubstantiated accusation. This is punishable because it is a threat to a righteous system of law. Hence it could be interpreted as meaning that corruptors and those attempting to suit without valid documents are the same as *mustika* and *bramara*.

3 Senapati Raja Gondala citing the *saloka agama* 'snake in the house'

Sarpada awésma adhustem pajaletnam prabem wisesa pakreti (LOr 7440, f. 332)

Literal translation

A miscreant (*dustha*) snake in the dwelling *pajaletnan* [?] is killed on the king's authority (*wisésa*).

Textual explanation

ula iku yén sata wisma waneng paténana rahina wengi, wus tan amani durjana, kaya ta durjana ing alas ing ngumah wenang paténana (LOr 7440, f. 332)
This snake, if inside the dwelling one has the authority to kill by day or night so that there is no peace for miscreants. Likewise, a miscreant in the jungle [or] in one's house may be killed.

Variations

Apem apjah awéhsam pa...mi séjapakhati ula hi kulamonana sabawés mawang patyanana ratu wira ina awileng patyanipun (LOr 7410, f. 77v)
Sarta amejah ana wasem wiku durgamem madhutha majem tanana patyansem (RAS 6, f. 36)
Sarpem liripun amejahan, wismen prabeha wisesa, pakerti liripun nenggih (*Serat angger: Jugul Muda*, p. 17)

Interpretation of: *Sarpem ana wismem prabem wisésa pakerti mati*

The meaning of *sarpem* is snake, *ana wonten* in a house, *prabem* king, *wisésa*, authority, *pakerti* deeds, *mati* death. The sequence of the paragraph is as such: a snake in the house must be killed as an example of the authority of the king who owns the house/realm. This is to clean up by killing the snake (evil-one, *durjana*) which has entered the dwelling.

Tuan Anu: A snake in the house with the king is a figure of speech, verbal symbol [for exercise of royal authority vis a vis *durjana*], (Winter, *Javaansche Zamenspraken*, vol. II, pt. 2, no. 270).

Modern interpretation of: *Sarpen ana wisma* [*em*], *prabem wisésa prakreti mati*
'A snake in the house dies because of the power of the king or of the owner of the house'. This is clarified as 'a thief caught committing a crime within a home must be killed, and the owner has the right and power to do so', (Suwarno, *Dictionary*, no. 1415, see also Ngafenan, *Paribasan*, p.121).

4 Demang Lembu Jawa citing the *saloka agama* 'a tiger dies'

Sardu pejah durgayem prabu ak dati(?) sadula macan ky (?)macan iku rahina wengi ingalas ing we[*na*]*ng sawenang pinaténan karana durjana* (LOr 7440, f. 332)

Literal translation
A tigers dies as a dangerous obstacle [on the orders of] the king. A *sardula* is a tiger. That tiger by day or night in the forest [or in the town] must be killed having no regard for him, because it is a miscreant.

Variations
Sardulem pjah durgemam reyanem suknatya arinem pasu pradutem macaniku gahin awengiwa patyanana (LOr 7410, f. 78r)
Sardulem pjah adurgamen sarka durgamendem, prabhu kertine diyem (RAS 6, f. 37)
Sradulem ing kang rumihin pejah durgayem malih, ya nepsuka arinum lan malih pasuhapa durgayem kalawan malih iya prabhu akerti widéyem iku (*Serat angger: Jugul Muda*, p. 17)

Interpretation of: *Sardula* [*sima*: tiger] *pejah durga mayem ywanem sukreta arinem pasu apa durgeyem prabhu akerti widéyem.*

A tiger dies in its evil deeds plaguing deer; how can a king feel uneasy in thus doing right. This is a *sloka* of thieves exemplified as a tiger plaguing human beings just as a tiger preys on deer or livestock in the city, countryside, or forest. A king's responsibility is to sentence as justly as possible (Winter, *Javaansche Zamenspraken*, vol. II, pt. 3, no. 263).

5 Pecahtanda [Pecotandha] citing the *saloka agama* of 'thieving monkeys'

Kutilem gatem culikem anem prabem arti dhustem durgamem culika namaning kethék lewih ing durgama ora kaya duratmaka, wenang pinatenan king durjana ika (LOr 7440, f. 333)

Variations
Kutilem écolikem inem sangem atrigi dhustem durgamem culikutilem pratem amcah kutilem lewisuka embojanadiketéka lewihi durgama boya kadiyurat maka wong patipun kang durgama iku (LOr 7410, f. 78r)
Kutilem culikem artiné dhustem durgamem culikem kutilem (RAS 6, f. 38)
Kothilem culikem iku, prabem atri dhustem lan culika ika thilem lan mali, durgamem kang langkung culika punika (*Serat Angger: Jugul Muda*, p. 17)

Interpretation of: *Kothilem aculikem prabem atri dusthem culika-kutilem durgamem, kotilem aculikem prabem dustem kutilem durgamam.*

This is the meaning of what is said: Encountering difficulties, i.e., untrustworthy/dishonest monkeys, makes a commotion for the king. The intention of the *sloka* concerns thieves exemplified as monkeys which are difficult. These untrustworthy monkeys have made a commotion. If [confronted by] evil, it is appropriate for the king if he feels uncomfortable with this or the responsibility to execute. (Winter, *Javaansche Zamenspraken*, vol. II, pt. 3, no. 215).

6 Jaksa Raja Niti citing the *saloka agama* of 'leeches and worms'

Kremi [*-krema*] *smapékan duratmaka wruh duyaga sardula prikidit kremi geteting ing angawak-grak, gegeting manuk duratmaka iku geteting ing sami ja* [...] *ma sredu naming lintah angganaminging banyu, lintah iku gegeting ing banyu, macan iku gegeting ing sami buron wrtei namaning uler, dita naming suket ksay ta uler, gegeting ing suket duratmaka gegeting ing jagat* (LOr 7440, f. 333)

Variations
Krami sampéka duratmaka nradu angnka serdula wreki dita kremi gegeding awaké (LOr 7410, f. 78v)
Kremi, sampéka duratmaka, werdu, sardula, kangka kremi (RAS 6, f. 37)

Kremi sampéka lawan durmaka lawan malih, werdu ongga saradula wikriditra (*Serat angger: Jugul Muda*, p. 18)

Interpretation of: *Kremi sampéka wreki kaka duratmaka wredu ongga sardula wikridita*

This is the *sloka* of thieves. A thief is the same as parasitic worms, intestinal worms, snakes, carrion crows, leeches, and wild tigers. Truly such must be killed (Winter, *Javaansche Zamenspraken*, vol. II, pt. 2, p. 269)

[compare: Yogyakarta *Surya Alam* § 26
These are the scourges of all those who mind the realm
The scourge of the town, these are the *dustha*, i.e. tigers, jackals, etc
The scourge of the forest, worms
The scourge of one's own body, intestinal worms
The scourge of the grass, snakes
The scourge of water, leeches
The scourges of the crown are many]

7 The Kanduruwan citing the *sloka agama* 'walijem pradhustem…'
Walijem pradus(th)em pejah kandana tumanem durgayem pejah awésnem duratmaka ana cinanipun pejah juga kramaya (LOr 7440, f. 334)

Variations
walijem tridusthem atri duptem, pjah agantu letu manem duratem den sawiya durgampem duratmaka. (LOr 7410, f. 79r)
[lacking in RAS 6]
jalitem tradhustem malih, pejah kendi datumnem durgamema, pejaha wésma kalawan dasa wisa catur gayim (*Serat angger: Jugul Muda*, p. 38)
[Defies translation]

8 Rongga Panjang Sora citing the *sloka agama* of kings
Giri [suci] jaladri surya pawaka sasa[m]ka, anila tanu [mangen] (LOr 7440, f. 335)

Literal translation
A mountain, the sea, sun, fire, moon, wind, and ink [on paper].

Variations
Giri suci jaladri pawaka serya, sakra ka nila tanu wulan (LOr 7410, f. 79r)

[lacking in RAS 6]
Giri suci lan jaladri, pawaka lan surya sasongka anila, tanu telas sing sasongka (*Serat angger: Jugul Muda*, p. 19)
Giri jaladriya pawaka candra tirta yama resi (*Sunduk Prayoga* § 1)
Pragi wilis kusuma warsa giri jaladri surya pawaka (*Kuntharakara* § 11)

Textual explanation
Your Majesty [should be] as a mountain, not subject to shifting [opinion or judgment]; as the sea, accommodating as water, such is Your Majesty; as *surya*, the name for the sun, the king is named as the 'steamer'; as *pawaka*, the name for fire, a king is as fire, annihilating all miscreants; as *candra*, the name for the moon, a king is like the moon in lighting up the entire world: as *tanu*, the name for ink, [a king is like ink] steadfast (*angun wesi*) for all the world's folk.

Interpretation of: *Giri suci jaladri pawaka surya sasongka anila tanu.*

The meaning of *giri*: mountain, *suci*: holy, *jaladri*: the sea, *pawaka*: fire, *surya*: the sun, *sasangka*: the moon, *anila*: the wind, *tanu*: ink [not] vacillating.

This is the *sloka* of kings. Its meaning: a king in furthering justice is steadfast as a mountain, calculating within righteousness as pure water, savouring justice as the sea is patient and wise in everything and spreading culture, powerful towards miscreants as fire, not shunning his function/duty, even including children and relatives following the ways of miscreants, indeed under his authority, investigating all affairs and evil ways as the sun, which means being clear as to the intentions in searching for miscreant as the moon, with the intention to be quick in apprehending *durjana*; as the action of the wind, in sentencing miscreant; as ink which has fallen on paper is indelible (Winter, *Javaansche Zamenspraken*, vol. II, pt. 3, no. 479)

Modern translation
'An ideal king is firm and just (like a holy mountain), caring and forgiving (like the sea), punishing (like fire), enlightening (like the sun), forbearing (like the moon), able to accomplish tasks thoroughly and complicatedly (like the wind), and decisive and unchanging once he takes his stand (like ink)'. (Suwarno, *Dictionary*, no. 465).

Jimbun-era variation
(*giri*) *jaladriya pra*[*waka*] *candra* (*Gajah Mada*, f. 7)

9 Pandelegan [Titi Mantri] quoting the *saloka agama* of the eight thieves' wives

Astha dusthem adu[r]gayem istri wiwiyoda culikem adusthem rajem wiradawuh atas triyem (LOr 7440, f. 336)

Textual explanation

The eight miscreants and their wives, [along with] Pun Makaka and his wife can be executed for accompanying her husbands. The reason for these words: Makaka had brought his wife [into the plot to steal].

Variations

Astha dusthem adurgayem istri wiroda culikem adusthem pjah istriem rajem wiruda pjah dusthem istriyem (LOr 7410, ff. 78v-80r)
Astha dusthem pjah ing durgamem, istri wirodra culikem adusthem estriyem pjah arodra,adustem (RAS 6, f. 43)
Astha dusthem durgayem, astri wirodra lawan acukem dhusthem malih, pejah éstriyem malih, rajem mawirodra lampus dhustem astriyem ika (*Serat angger: Jugul Muda*, p. 19)

Interpretation of: *Astha dusthem durgayem astri, wirodra dulikam dusthem rajem wiroda, pejah dustem éstriyem*

Its meaning, the eight thieves deserve the death sentence, along with their wives ... the reason why the wives follow in death is because their actions planted shame on them. The viciousness of the theft exceeds the sternness of the king's power (Winter, *Javaansche Zamenspraken*, vol. II, pt. 3, no. 65).

10 Patih Jugul Muda citing the *sloka 'tataneman ashta orem...'*

Tataneman astha orem bogini istri wadakahem maling urip kanayakah padarma kang sinatriya (LOr 7440, f. 337)

Literal translation

Tatanem nyusa orem means that as far as what is planted there are no differences. His Majesty has been created by the gods and there is no difference with the common masses. The difference is only in name and status, which is recognized or not [short phrase to the effect that women cannot be equal]

Textual interpretation

A king executes a body (*babandan*) of the wives showing [the consequences] of failing to recognize the riddle of one struck [by misfortune]. Thus, were the utterances of Kyana Patih Jugul Muda, expressing the curse of missing the God's [prohibitions], which fall under the '*tribaga muka*'.

Variations
Tataneman orem gogdah istri wagradakah maling urip kanayakah sang sinatriya (LOr 7410, f. 80r)
Tataneman nusya urem bugena estri, wadakem balenggu estri wadaka, maling urip kanayaka panandara kang sinatriya. (RAS 6, f. 45)
Ataneman sya orem goning, maling ngurip kanayakah lawan pradepa kang satriyané, Serat angger: Jugul Muda, p. 40.

Other texts
Tataneman ashta orem bogini isi wadatah maling urip kanayakah paladarma kang sinatriya (*Cacad* § 2 and *Jaya Lengkara* of Add 18 398, f. 3r, both citing the *aksara bumi*)

11 Patih Jugul Muda citing another *sloka agama*, '*mawat prabhu...*'
Patawatik prabu tanca prabu dilok awat drimatamatika, parabu wang uwapan duka Batara, aningali anak rabiné ing wong den-kadi aningai wong ngatuwa, prabu dilok awatika Panduka Batara, yén aninggali raja darma ning wong den-kadi aningali wingka, batmawata prabu tani (LOr 7440, f. 338)

Variations
Matrewat prabhu tanih paradrabya nilog tawat atmawat aparabutanih madrawa garani wong ngabuwa (LOr 7410, f. 80r)
Mawat paré butané, paladerbit nilo tawat yan magat parebutané pasétipa barané (RAS 6, f. 47)
Matra ya prabhu aning para dretni lot awat lan amawat, parabu anirewéng daranih, matreyat daranih tegesira. (*Serat Angger:Jugul Muda*, p. 20-21)
Apasih apa daraning nenggih (*Ibid*, p. 21)
[Defies Translation]

12 Patih Jugul Muda citing the *sloka ratu gama* '*anrayo bracaca*'
Anrayoga braca[ji] karajahit, asura [-sura siri] widagda prataméwira sadarana (LOr 7440, f. 339)

Textual explanation
Andra(i)yoga [braca] ratu watek anganggaji, tan pegat angulah kabecikan candra, wulan, sang prabu den-asih ing wong larang, karahita kaloka (famed) ing wong katah, asura wani, sang ratu den-wani (agile) kétén, widogda

[*pratamé*] *bisa ngucap sang ratu aja mimisus waro(i), sadarana, sang ratu angampura wong kang luputan, ken damo alidha paseh.*

There is a *sloka* of my master, King of Medhang Kamulan. The first is *adriyoga*, a king complete with esteemed character; *abracha karahita*, a king compassionate to his servants and who watches over the kingdom; *prasama*, great and small are equated; *asura widagda*, brave whom none dare to challenge, not publicly shameful, generous not stingy; *bobotan sikara* not to mishandle/plague [his servants/subjects]; *anukma bramacari*, handsome, not feminine; *adoh ing raja tamah*, far from evil passions (compare: Add 12 303, *Jaya Lengkara*, f. 31r and *Jimbun Slokantara* § 3)]

Variation (Jaya Lengkara)
Adriyoga, abracah karahita, pra(sa)m(a) asura widagdya, anukma bramacari.

13 **Patih Jugul Muda citing the *sloka ratu* (*wong kang anudukandur, wongé amatang, wong tiba*)**
Makutem makutatahan makuteteran, makuti pako (RAS 6, f. 48)
[Defies Translation]

JAYA LENGKARA

Slokaning aksara:
14 **Authority for *aksara bumi*: *tatateman astha orem* ...** [see no. 10]

15 **Authority for *aksara banyu*: *triyeksa agunem-gunem jroning wespa tarinayem wadu sosyarunem anamunide wayah* (Add 12303, *Jaya Lengkara*, 20r)**

16 **Authority for *aksara srengengé*: *denta-denti kusumah warsa sari cakra* (Add 12 303, *Jaya Lengkara*, f. 20v and LOr 7440, f. 214; *Luwangan* § 25; Berlin 402, *Surya Alam*, f. 49; *Cacad* § 2; *Arya Dilah* §§ 4 & 6; *Sunduk Prayoga* § 41.**

Variations
denta-denti si cepet sibener si duga si ora sih (*Sunduk Prayoga* §§ 9, 31)
denta-denti srenga srengi kusuma warsa (*panca wisesa*) (*Raja Niti* §§ 87, 92-93)

Interpretation of: *'Sloka adil'* (Righteous *Sloka*) *Denta-denti kusuma warsa sarira cakra*

This is the *sloka* of justice exemplified by ivory or a tusk, which if extracted cannot be replaced, a flower bloomed cannot be closed again, rain which has fallen cannot be returned, such also is righteous which once declared right cannot be said to be wrong, once said to be wrong cannot be declared right. (Winter, *Javaansche Zamenspraken,* vol. II, pt. 2, no. 217)

Modern translation
'True justice that cannot be negotiated, modified, or changed: a just decision, situation, or action described as being like ivory or teeth growing naturally, a flower withering in the rain, or a weapon striking and killing a person' (Suwarno, *Dictionary,* no. 328).

17 **Authority for *aksara kilat/thathit* (Add 12303, *Jaya Lengkara*, f. 20r and LOr 7440, f.214; Cad § 2, *Jimbun Slokantara* I, f. 206; *Luwangan*, § 23; *Pepakem Tjerbon/Slokantara*, pp. 26, 46)**

1) *sragala lumumpat ing papalang*

Interpretation of: *kebo lumumpat ing palang Ngibarat priyantun utawi jaksa anggagahi prakawis ing sanak prasanakipun*

A metaphor of a bureaucratic nobility or *jaksa* facing up to the [legal] affairs of friend and relatives. (Winter, *Javaansche Zamenspraken,* vol. I, p. 164)

Modern interpretation
'A buffalo jumps over a wooden barrier at the entrance of its stall [...] a judge who defends his family members or who decides in favour of his family members despite knowing that they are guilty' (Suwarno, *Dictionary,* no. 673).

2) *tebu-tuwuh ing socané,*

Variations
Tebu tuwuh ing sucané (*Raja Niti,* f. 164, § 175) (*dustha* = talking badly of one suiting = no case. compare: *kidang melempat papalang mangsa tandu* from the *Undhang Senapati Jimbun,* f. 25) and *teboe toewoeh sosotjanja, ing salokané winarni, kalawan ninoempang kara* (Yasadipura, *Surya Alam,* Canto VIII, verse 28)

Modern interpretation
'Sugar cane that begins to sprout will grow new cane from the old [...] a deal that had been struck has to be renegotiated; a project that had been stopped has to be started again' (Suwarno, *Dictionary*, no. 1526)

3) *tumanem ing sunuké*
[Defies translation]

18 *Sloka agama*, the '*sloka dursila*' (*sloka* of miscreants) for *jaksa*
Kusuma wicitra, griba, saji aweh trinara gina majarawasé tawasa

Translation: from the *Pepakem Tjerbon*

Koesoema Witjitra, [...] of which the clarification is that judges must be experienced in the artifices of *durjana* and *duratmaka*: evildoers and thieves, because they are as pleasant of mien as a flower; their practices are as fine as water which always finds a way and cannot be held in the hands, as the wind which comes so subtly everywhere, as a *tapa*, that is a poor devoted anchorite, who comes begging for alms but who has the intention of spying on one's house, or as clouds or smoke on distant mountains so great is their daring. These are the practices of the *durjana* and *duratmaka*. Such with right are subjected to *jara* and *kukud*: confiscation of goods and forfeiture of wife(s) and children's freedom.

Textual explanation
This originates from the *pepakem Jaya Lengkara*. You *jaksa* in your deliberations take as your point of departure (*miyos*) the *sloka-agama*: *Kusuma wicitra, griba, saja, awéh trinaragina, majarawasé, tawasa,*

Its meaning: to be alert (*awas*) [concerning] activities of *durjana* [and] *duratmaka*. The meaning of *durjana*, a person evil in his actions; the meaning of *duratmaka*, an evil person who has stolen, though it be as a flower (*kembang*); its meaning, fragrant to the senses. There are those like water (*sumbapé* [?]). There are those like the wind in their invisibility and deception, continuously filling spaces [both] large and small (*anrusi*), [this] is the essence of wind. There are those as a *matiraga*, who plans in advance by assuming the guise of an anchorite or of a mythical god (*batariman* = *batara*), but [in reality] spying on one's house marked for burglary (*dhodhok acung-acung*) [in this] deceiving (*angakali*). There are those like the mountain mists, its meaning: arrogant (*angkuh*) in their daring [of which] no one can exceed or surpass.

Such are the practices of *durjana-duratmaka*. Thusly it is best for all to know that for evil persons it is fitting that they be punished by confiscation of goods and forfeiture of wife's and children's freedom (*jara kukud*) (citing the *Jaya Lengkara*, p. 5).

Copies
Pepakem Tjerbon/Jaya Lengkara, p. 53; *Jaya Lengkara* 7440, f.219; *Jimbun Slokantara II* § 2, f. 133-4; Yasadipura *Surya Alam*, Canto X, verses 7-8, *Undhang Senapati Jimbun*, f. 80 (compare Berlin 402, § 14, § 23 and *Luwangan* § 43).

Variation 1
Surya Alam of Yasadipura, Canto X, verse 8.

There are *durjana* like the sky, there are *durjana* like water, as an ascetic, as clouds,
etc [these are] the disguises of *durjana*. A *durjana* [can] pose as an ascetic, called a
pandita (holy hermit), who is in touch with [other] *durjana*, as a traitor *pandita* who
prays often [to hide his] miscreant [soul].

Variation 2
Jimbun Slokantara II, § 2

Translation
This is the *sloka* of miscreants (*dursila*): *kusuma* [...] *tawasa* drama. Its meaning: the court must be alert to the character of *durjana* [namely] as a flower, as the wind, as water, as a holy anchorite, as the smoke of fire, these are the many characteristics of *durjana*.

Variation 3
Surya Alam, Berlin 402 § 23

A righteous king is brought to ruin by two causes, [namely] *kapir* and *durjana*. These destroy the nation. If the king does not right the evil doers' crimes, [he] shares in those evil deeds. And whosoever is apprehended (*angilawan*) as a durjana, any kind of *durjana*, his crime [must be considered by] the *pradata* court taking as it point of departure (*amiyosaken*), the *sloka*: *kinir diya*.

Its meaning: to be in one's guard against *durjana*. Of the *durjana* there are those like water, those like the wind, or like *matiraga* (anchorite); *durjana* as water or mists [such] are the guises of *durjana*.

Variation 4
Surya Alam, van der Hout § 23

Two things that can bring ruin to the king's land. First is the great extent of marauding and the other *kapir* (non-Moslem) nations. Therefore, must the smallest indication of these be punished immediately in the measure of the exigencies of the affair. If not, the king himself is tarnished.
When a thief is apprehended and brought before the king and he denies his misdeeds then he, says the king, cannot as such be marked, after which one must immediately be bound and be carefully examined and decided on by the *jaksa* of the realm of Surya Alam.
Upon which Jaksa Adi Kara and Raja Pradata given the following expression: *kusuma* [...] *katinggla*, that is one who serves must know in advance which sort of thief this is. One has among thieves various terms, namely water thief, wind thief, an anchorite thief, etc. The first signifies a hidden hate against the king, the second a holy person that goes over to thievery, and the third is through a priest becomes a thief.

Variation 5
Undhang Senapati Jimbun (LOr 2125, ff. 79-80)

Ring Medhang Kamulan amiosaken sloka: kusuma narcita, sari angangis agni macing rawisé wacandra majang sudrama,

Translation
[after a list of the *astha corah, astha dustha, sad-atatayi*, etc.]
The meaning: the *jaksa* must be alert to *durjana*, there are those as water, as wind, as anchorites, as clouds, etc. these are the disguises of *durjana*.

19 *Sloka* of the *kerta* (court)
Srengéngé piné, banyu kinum, bumi penendem geni pinanggang (*Jaya Lengkara*, f. 23r)

Copies
Kuntharakara, § 6; *Surya Alam*, Add 12323, § 2. See also Darmasoetjipta, *Kamus Peribahasa Jawa*, no. 1005 and Suwarno, *Dictionary*, no. 1485-1486.

Interpretation of: *Srengéngé piné, banyu kinum, bumi penendem geni pinanggang*

This is the *sloka* for the four [namely] king, *patih, pangulu, jaksa*. Its intention is thusly, in judging justly an investigation into some one's crime [it must be as] the rays of the sun, nothing is to be furtive or secret (*kasilib*) [*srengéngé piné* = the sun bakes]. Within the investigation as to the justness of the crime [it must be as] water in a damn (*wawadah*), transparent and direct as clear water [*banyu kinum* = water emerges]. The order (*tata*) [must be as] the earth, its meaning is baseness to avoid (*singkiri*) chaos (*tembung sari* = xylophone noise?) [*bumi penandhem* = earth buries]. The judgement with authority (*wisésa*) [must be as] fire (*latu*), if burned it must not be by parts [incomplete], its meaning even to embrace blood relatives or friends [*geni pinanengen* = fire burns], such is the true application of authority which is authorized (Winter, *Javaansche Zamenspraken,* vol. II, pt. 2, p. 274).

Variation 1
Jaya Lengkara, 23r. and *Undhang Senapati Jimbun* (LOr 2125, pp. 81-82)

The meaning of *banyu kinum* is litigation thus immersed so that the court utters neutral (*padhem* = dead, neutral) judgements, which are pure (*weningé*); the meaning of *srengéngé piné* is litigation baked so that the court expresses a view clear and clean; the meaning of *geni pinanggan* is litigation burned so that the court expresses all that is warmed [i.e. actual], if there is a passionate expression of the gods [i.e., a prejudiced judgement] uttered in the court's sentence, the fine is *asta-wara*.

Variation 2
Kuntharakara § 6, no. 2

This is the purity of *pradata* affairs, vanquished by the court which knows that: *bumi...kinum*: The sun is for sun-drying, the water is for submerging [...], that is, the person in authority must make a decision that is as just and appropriate as possible (so that it can function like the sun or water. Its intention: greater from being settled, greater from the brightness/clearness, like that named *nukma krama carik* (immortal soul of a scribe) he who knows a document before it is written.

Variation 3
Surya Alam (Add 12323, § 2)

Another expression of His Majesty Surya Alam, those named/appointed as king, *pangulu, jaksa, patih, mantri*, [must know the significance of] *banyu kanemu bumi* (Darmasoetjipta, *Kamus Peribahasa Jawa*, no. 1005) *pinendem sargnéngé pinangan kang atat.*

Modern Interpretations

Ibid.: *Srengenge pine banyu kinum:* – srengéngé = sun; *piné* [*sic pépé*] = to dry s.t. in the sun; banyu = water; kinum = immerse in water

Raja, patih, jaksa, and *pangulu agama*, when deciding an affair must be as just as possible (*tidak pandang bulu* = not discriminating against, regardless of who or what it is) [meaning] the sun dries, water immerses

Suwarno, *Dictionary*, no 1485; *Srengéngé piné banyu kinum.* 'The sun is for sun-drying, the water is for submerging [...] the judge or person in authority must make a decision that is as just and appropriate as possible [so that it can function like the sun or water]' *Ibid.*, no. 1486; *Srengéngé piné, banyu kinum, bumi pinendhem, geni pinanggang'*: The sun is for sun drying, water is for submerging, earth is for burying, and fire is for burning or roasting'

Undhang Sénapati Jimbun

Thusly Tumenggung Jaya Komala spoke to His Majesty the king of Medhang Kamulan forcing to heighten the group of all kings, cited the magical protection of the court, [namely] '*srengéngé piné, banyu kinum, bumi pinendhem, geni pinanggang'* (LOr 2125, ff. 81-82, under *walat*).

20 Demang Jaya Gondala citing the *sloka* of *aksara* intentions for king and ministers

Éstri lancah, toya lancha, maraga lancha, lata lancha (*Jaya Lengkara*, f. 23v.) [Suwarno, *Dictionary*, nos. 413, 412]

Literal Translation

Women are crooked, water bends, roads are crooked, stalks are bent. The meaning: there is no woman straight/just in her speech. Trust (*andel*) in her utterances [are as likely as] a river without bends, a road without curves, a straight plant stem. [Only] then is a woman just in her speech. Persons suiting must be just in their utterances.

Variations

Jaya Lengkara

Sloka of one suiting with a woman: flower stems are crooked, fire is crooked, roads are crooked, stalks are crooked, *béwéh* [a fruit] is crooked (RAS 38, f. 50).

Kuntharakara

Estri nacah, adi nacha, anyabawa kusuma nacah, uda wicaté, dramara puspa wicaté granayada (§ 5)

21 Kyai Arya Jaya Samodra
Brana wiséta wicatih, bramara kusuma, wicatih krapapayuda wicatih speta giri wicatih (*Jaya Lengkara,* f. 26r)
[Defies translation]

22 Kyai Arya Jaya Samodra citing the *sloka agama*
1) *Sekar tunjung bang tumuwuh ing séla* [cf. *tunjung tuwuh séla = jamur amét kadang.*

A lotus (alt. mushroom) growing on a stone [...] something that is impossible (Suwarno, *Dictionary*, no 3, 1591)

2) *Pethak mekar ing karsa* (*Jaya Lengkara*, f. 28v) (see also *Ibid*., no.1591).

SURYA ALAM

23 *Angon-angonaken* (*alt angus-angus*) *ngadu pucuk eri* (*Raja Niscaya* § 2)
Copies
Surya Alam, Add 12 323, § 8; Berlin 402/van der Hout, § 73) [Darmasoetjpta, *Kamus Peribahasa Jawa*, no. 84, Ngafenan, *Paribasan*, p.18]

Variation
Anggonang ina angadu pucuk ing eri, manawi dora sambada, angungingani liring bukti, sapanga temen (*Kuntharakara* § 2)

Interpretation of: *Angon-angon angadu pucuk ing éri,*

The *sloka* of a person aiming to apply *kalédasan* (?) of intelligence [one must] beware of that which are lies and those which are the truth, as well as actions and words of those who suit and those who are suited.

Tuwan Anu: What is the meaning of *angun-angun?*

Kawitana: The meaning of *angun-angun* is a wild buffalo, that which is exemplified is the *jaksa*. [As regards] *angaben lilincipan* [this is] a parable of actions and words which are compared in utterances in legal cases [which must be weighed in an ordered process]. (Winter, *Javaansche Zamenspraken*, vol. II, pt. 3, no. 96)

Modern Interpretation
'A wild bull pitted against the tip of a thorn...two powerful men (usually judges or lawyers) match skills and intelligence to win a court case' (Suwarno, *Dictionary*, no. 134).

24 ***tekèk mati déning ngulahé* [Yasadipura, *Surya Alam*, Canto XII, verse 42; *Combi Surya Alam* § 14, no. 5 (*akaraya watang* = Japlak); *Jimbun Slokantara I*, f. 188 [Darmasoetjjipta, *Peribahasa Jawa*, no. 1023, Suwarno, *Dictionary*, no.1527; Ngafenan, *Paribasan*, p.130] [continuation: *ing a(m)puh titi pinajaraken mati déning anglu-alu(n)* (Berlin 402, § 14) *mati déning aloen-aloen wong ika* (Yasadipura, *Surya Alam*, Canto IX, verse 12)**

Interpretation of: *tekèk mati ing ulané, ngibarat tiyang ingkang bilahi saking wicantenipuin piyambak.*

Parable of a person who comes into difficulties from his own utterances (Winter, *Javaansche Zamenspraken*, vol. I, p. 188).

Modern Interpretation
1) 'a gecko that dies because of its voice, i.e., to suffer or to fail because of one's own words' (Suwarno *Dictionary*, no. 1527); [compare: *tekèk mati ing ulahé, lir sima [bangga andurkaka] amét mangsa* 'a tiger that struggles to rebel and commits a crime in order to capture is prey [...] a person who rebels and commits a crime, such as killing someone, in order to obtain what he wants' (*Ibid.*, no. 1460).

Appendix III Titles 'Left Out'

The point of departure in discussing the sources used for this study is the fact that legal titles, even those bearing the same name, vary markedly in content. This contrasts with the consistency of their component parts – the *sloka* phenomena – regardless of title or provenance. Recognition of the basic inconsistency comes from study of the era's earlier manuscripts, namely those containing the titles cited by the *Pepakem Tjerbon* as their source attested to by the Introduction. They thus provide a benchmark for identifying the era's most significant titles. Because the Dutch publication has a known provenance and date lacking for most Javanese legal titles, '*Pepakem* Era titles' seems an appropriate notation. Without such a cannon it becomes difficult to defend choice of the sources used to study various facets of Javanese law. In that case one is confronted with many untapped, but relevant, manuscripts whose date and provenance can only be established imprecisely. Uncertainty can arise as to whether a title has been chosen to fit pre-formed assumptions or are the result of judgments based on study of titles relevant in time and space.

Because the issue only indirectly concerns the subject at hand, discussion has been relegated to this appendix. A start to bringing some order to the daunting number of unpublished sources can be made through distinguishing layers of textual traditions. It provides a way of breaking down the total number of texts into smaller groups in order to make analysis more manageable. In this context it can be observed that sources for the inquiry fall somewhere in the middle between precursors and successors. These are examined within the heterogeneous nature of the textual material at our disposal.

Precursors

A rule-of-thumb criterion for identifying precursors to *Pepakem* Era titles comes from the juxtaposition of titles' contents and the respective manuscripts' probable date of origins. Fortunately, the special relation existing between *sloka* phenomena and text provides a means of eliminating from further consideration titles included in the manuscripts cited in this study. Close reading of these titles reveals that their contents, that is, those discussed in this appendix, do not fit within the matrix of title, paragraphs, contents, and terms characteristic of mainstream texts. Significantly, these were likewise omitted from the *Pepakem Tjerbon's* Introduction.

Four titles whose potential value is not at present realizable take a prominent place in the manuscripts drawn upon for this study. Three are from LOr 7440 and one from Add 12 303. It will be recalled that LOr 7440 identifies three titles as coming from the pen of an early eighteenth century Sumedang *jaksa*, Candra Yuda, which precede the mainstream titles. They include a *Niti Sruti* (ff. 1-34), a *Niti Praja* (ff. 34-72) – both with an apparent Old Javanese flavour – and a *Sunduk Prayoga* (ff. 73-100). The latter is also found in a variant version in Add 12 303 (ff. 35r-35v) and Add 18 398 (ff. 40r-47v). The fourth title of interest here is the *Kuntarakara* from Add 12 303 (ff. 31r-35r). More than just rounding out a list of manuscript sources, the *Sunduk Prayoga* and *Kuntarakara* provide some challenging variations on the usual forms of *sloka* phenomena contained in *Pepakem Tjerbon*-era sources.

Niti Sruti

One of the more problematic titles under consideration contained in the first thirty folios of LOr 7440, is the *Niti Sruti*. It is not only one of three titles attributed to an identifiable author, Candra Yuda, but also one of the earliest titles, somewhat predating the early eighteenth-century *Saloka* of RAS 33 from 1727 and the Kartasura *Surya Alam* from the 1730s. The author in question is a Sumedang *jaksa* named in the Dutch East India Company records of the 1720s. The last sentence in the *Niti Sruti* text reads '*titi tulis kawula Candra Yuda* (The end (of) the writing of your humble servant Candra Yuda)'. That he was indeed one of the Sumedang *jaksa* is confirmed by the LOr 7440 manuscript:

> text (*kitab*), the heritage from the elder, your humble servant Candra Yuda, *jaksa* of Sumedang' (f. 74).

The titles provided by the respective manuscripts are by no means the originals. LOr 7440 was copied by a single hand, most likely closer to the random dates from the nineteenth century found in the manuscript than the era of Candra Yuda. Yet the use of the term '*kitab*' (text) is significant. Standing in contrast to *tulis* (writing) of the first quotation, it would seem to indicate that the whole manuscript was part of the heritage associated with Sumedang's past. This is spelled out by the immediately following notation in a different hand, thus one foreign to most of the manuscript's contents.

> [A] reminder, the time of recreation of this text (*kitab*) from His Royal Highness, Adipatih Suriya Nagara by this humble servant Nyatanu (?)

> on Thursday the 28th of the month of Jumadilawal in the year Jimawal 1219 [1804].

Suriya Nagara has not been identified. However, the similarity of regent titles in Sumedang and that of *Adipati* argues that he was mostly likely the Regent there in the late eighteenth or early nineteenth century.[1]

The *Niti Sruti* is composed of over a hundred paragraphs of roughly equal length. Each is separated by the *pada luhur* sign indicating a break in the narrative. This suggests that it was written in verse, although it lacks the compulsory indication of the specific verse form usually incorporated in the last sentence of a canto. Only in the beginning of the third paragraph is the title indicated, namely, 'This is the instruction *Niti Sruti* imitating the *pandita*' (*punika ing wasita Niti Surti* (*sic Sruti*) *pinda pandita*). The language seems to be an archaic form of modern Javanese. Although individual words and terms are recognisable, it is difficult to construct a consistent narrative. That it belongs to the world of Javanese law is attested to by specific mention of evildoers (*dursila* § 20 and *durjana* § 21), as well as terms familiar from the other texts of this nature as, for example, *agama, jaksa, mantri, maling retna,* and *maling jiwa* enumerated in the *Surya Alam*. The title's penultimate paragraph mentions a *Niti Praja*, which may be an introduction to the following text bearing that name. As part of the genre the title is not unique within the era's legal literature. The first line is identical with the opening lines of several of the texts from the Yogyakarta collection.[2]

An interesting variant of the *Niti Sruti* was re-written and published nearly one and a half centuries later by Rangga Warsita (d. 1860), the last of the famed Surakarta *pujangga* (a master of the literary art; poet). For convenience sake, an internet version is considered here. This is hardly the place to consider why a text which seems to belong to the earliest category of Hindu (Vedic) literature was 'written' by a prominent *jaksa* in the Independent Kingdoms period characterised by a growing Islamic identity. '*Sruti*' is a piece of divine revelation 'heard' by the *resi* of the Vedic period. *Sruti* literature not only pre-dates the *smriti* (man-made) literature – including among others the *dharma-sastra-s* of which Manu is the best known – but also the revealed source of *dharma*. Candra Yuda's eclectic interest was not unique. There are other, seemingly similar, *sruti* texts originating from Yogyakarta.[3]

1 See Hardjasasputra, 'Bupati di Priangan'.

2 Ricklefs and Voorhoeve, *Indonesian Manuscripts*, Java 22, ff. 74-95; 13, C., ff. 30-45; 43, B., ff. 59-113.

3 For example, IOL Jav. 38, D: ff. 565-97, dated 1764; Java 34 and 43

Indeed the relatively numerous copies, which contrast to the few references from the Hindu-Javanese period of early Mataram and Majapahit, might argue that the title is significant more for antiquarian interest than a living legal tradition. In any event, the title raises more questions than it answers. Crucial here is that if it is only a historical fossil, how do we determine which of the other titles in, say LOr 7440, are likewise dead and which represent living law? Again, we are thrown back on the authority of the *Pepakem Tjerbon* for identifying the period's most relevant titles.

What stands out in the manuscript version in comparison with the later version by Rangga Warsita and the internet source is that there are apparently only two points of contact. These are the six points distinguishing a person arriving at spiritual enlightenment and specific references to the *Astha Brata* from the *Ramanyana*. The concise, almost cryptically compact manuscript version has been embroidered by subsequent texts. The latter consist of specific verse meters, i.e., *Dhandhanggula, pada* (verse) ff. 16-22, and *Pucung/Kinantu pada* ff. 33-36 and ff. 1-22 respectively. While the message, as far as can be determined, is similar, the texts differ in form and language. *Krama* is used in the manuscript version, *ngoko* in the later one.

Perhaps even more noticeable is the introduction of specifically Islamic elements in the later versions. These consist of references to *agama Nabi, Kang Jeng Nabi, Sang Apatya*, i.e., Koja Jajahan in Egypt, the superiority of Islam via the *Serat Sruti*, etc. As a documented and dateable phenomenon, this seems to parallel the 'rewriting' of the *Surya Alam* by a subsequent generation of Surakarta *pujangga* as Yasadipura I. With the documented rewriting of the *Niti Sruti* there would seem to be a good case for an Islamisation of existing texts in the vernacular, one which most likely preceded the reception of more general works from the international world of Islam conveyed though the vehicle of Classic Arabic.

Niti Praja

The *Niti Praja* which follows in LOr 7440 (ff. 34-72) also shares the first lines with the Yogyakarta texts now housed in London collections. Complete versions are found on the internet (http://kandjengpangerankaryonagoro.blogspot.com/). The opening lines read: '*kadi asilem (ing) sagara geni/rasa ing driya duk lingyaken panyariké Niti Prja ingapus*'. The first part can be translated as 'Like diving into a sea of fire, the feelings of the heart' followed by a past *sangkala* (chronogram) equivalent to AJ 1634 or 1712. The date fits Sultan Agung's reign to which the title is attributed. While this seems to be an afterthought, the conversion would also reasonably fit for the manuscript of Candra Yuda named in the lines immediately preceding the *Niti Praja* title. Comparison of the contents of LOr 7440 with the internet version shows that the titles are nearly identical. This is aside from relatively small differences in spelling or wording in which the LOr 7440 version makes the more reliable impression despite challenges of transliteration. One of the few major differences is that the internet version imposes order on the contents by numbering the seventy-two paragraphs and adding descriptive rubrics in Indonesian. The translation from Indonesian given below is supplemented by comments on their contents.

Under 'Responsibilities of the state apparatus' (equivalent to §§ 1-15, LOr 7440, f. 34ff.) several characteristics attributed to the legal sphere are recognisable. For example, the sun (*surya*) as looking over all and the seas (*samudra*) as cleansing the earth, have been met with earlier.[4] In addition there is a consistent concern with change (*gingsir*) or more accurately the lack of unfounded change or shifts in pleas or decisions, as well as the assumption that the ideal *mantri* 'is mindful (of the king's wishes) before they are uttered'.[5] The section marked 'Relationships between people within the state' (§§ 16-30) understandably makes many references to *jaksa,* especially in §§ 22-28. Many of them emphasize the necessity of weighing (*timbangan*) the contents of *pepakem* without deviation (*gingsir*) from the truth (*bener*). Another is that *jaksa* should not be tempted by worldly matters to the detriment of the realm (§ 23). Moreover, the *jaksa, jejeneng,* and *paliwara* must be clear in their thinking on the *ratu adil* ('righteous king' of prophecy) and the expressions of the *Niti Praja,* which keeps them from going astray and falling into corruption (*ruruba*). However, all this comes after mention of the king of Egypt sending out of Moslem merchants to *nusantara* (*Koya jajahan,* which is associated with the *Yudanegara* (administration of the country).[6]

Unfortunately, little can be added in connection with the following three rubrics of 'Decentralised authority' (§§ 30-45), 'Integrity of the bureaucracy' (§§ 46-60), and 'Creation of a prosperous country' (§§ 61-72). They are suspiciously more in tune with the concerns of present Indonesians than those of Java under Sultan Agung. While the LOr 7440 *Niti Praja* makes some references to the titles of *jaksa* and *paliwara,* etc. and even cites a

4 Mainly in the much quoted Classic *Sloka,* no. 8, '*giri* [...] *tanu*'.

5 Knowing the sovereign's wish before it is uttered is the hallmark of *aksara kilat* discussed in Chapter 4.

6 The *Koya Jajahan* is found in LOr 1817, which Pigeaud, *Literature of Java,* p. 33 has added that 'Cod. 10.867-A contains a list of initial lines of cantos by Soegiarto'. See also RAS 22, which contains a *Niti Sruti* (ff. 74-95) in Canto VI and a *Niti Praja* (ff. 95-113) in Canto VII, followed (ff. 113-54) by a *Yudanegara.* Cited in Ricklefs and Voorhoeve, *Indonesian Manuscripts in Great Britain,* p. 80.

puzzling *sloka* – *geni murat tirta suda sagara geni* (f. 38) – the contents only to a small degree match form and content of 'Classic *Sloka*' identified in the present work. As with the *Niti Sruti*, which it follows, it is difficult to place the *Niti Praja* within the context of traditional Javanese written law and more specifically to harmonise it with the latter's most distinguishing feature, namely congruence with *sloka* phenomena set in vignettes.

There seems no satisfactory answer to why the titles were ignored by Resident Hasselaer's team in the 1760s. This is especially so because they were part of the repertoire of a *jaksa* active nearly a half century before the promulgation of the *Pepakem Tjerbon*. One possibility is that they were too closely identified with either Hindu legal/moral concepts – elements of the *sruti* literature formed the basis of the later *dharma sastra*-s – or too foreign to key concepts within the *Sunna* and *Koran*. While the Dutch officials of the East India Company were for practical purposes willing to make concessions to the island's religious predilections, a conspicuously religious orientation was unacceptable in the secular courts envisaged by them. All this, of course, begs the question of why ignore the *Niti Praja*. One would think that a source of wisdom on how best to manage the realm would be welcomed. It is possible that Dutch strategy was to skew the traditional legal system toward acceptable working principles in which reference to hallowed local tradition had no place, except as subterfuge.

Sunduk Prayoga

Standing in juxtaposition to the first two, the third title to be considered here is the *Sunduk Prayoga*. Its omission from the *Pepakem Tjerbon* is even more puzzling. A Patih Sunduk Prayoga is frequently cited in the mainstream titles, especially so in the *Jaya Lengkara* where the *patih* is named as belonging to the exalted group of kings and ministers introduced by the legal texts. In common with many of the titles drawn upon in this work, the next step would be creation of a law book bearing the name of its principle figure as, for example, the *Jugul Muda* or *Arya Dilah*. For some reason this did not happen. Moreover, radically different versions are found in LOr 7440, ff. 73-100; Add 18 398, ff. 40r-48r; and Add 12 303, ff. 35r-38r. This would suggest that it, like the preceding titles discussed here, was not considered sufficiently mainstream to be included in major compilations of contemporaneous legal works.

Despite this, the title's contents confirm its position as an, albeit variant, version of the legal literature focused on here. This is particularly true with reference to *sloka*. In the opening paragraph (LOr 7440, f. 73) immediately following the assertion that the *kitab* was part of the Sumedang heritage it commands:

> Know this! [the contents] of the *Sunduk Prayoga* [which is] from he who watches over the realm, a Sang Arya Wuwuh, whose ordering is *giri* [*suci*] *jaladri pawaka surya sasangka anila taru* (Classic *Sloka,* no. 6).

Indicated by the '*punika*' (this) following the *pada luhur* sign for a change in subject, the work can be divided into some nineteen paragraphs, ending on folio 100 with the usual *tammat//titi* (The End). As in the case of the other titles considered here, paragraphs marked off by *Punika* have been given a number for ease in reference not included in the original text. At first glance the *Sunduk Prayoga* seems to repeat or possibly provide the origins of Classic *Sloka,* no. 6. As we shall see, it was cited in the *Jugul Muda* as defining the sovereign ideal, namely

> firm and just (like a holy mountain), caring and forgiving (like the sea), punishing (like fire), enlightening (like the sun), forbearing (like the moon), able to accomplish tasks thoroughly and complicatedly (like the wind) and decisive and unswerving (*tan giring*) once he takes his stand (like ink on paper).[7]

Yet upon further consideration, the *Sunduk Prayoga*'s explanation (*arané* = the name is) of individual terms adds more to confusion than clarification. On the positive side the repetition ensures that there is no mistaking the spelling despite challenges in interpretation of the ha-na-ca-ra-ka text. On the negative side the lack of explanation the *sloka*'s significance as found, for example, in the *Jugul Muda* leaves the reader at a loss in attempting to arrive at its deeper meaning. Touching on specific *sloka*, it can be noted that the present version gives a variant interpretation of 'forbearing moon (*candra*)'. It also introduces three items apparently left out of the *Jugul Muda* and Winter versions. Alternatively, it could have been added depending upon which version is the eldest. These introduce among others *tirta* 'the name for water which cleans the unclean' and *yama*, 'the name for awakening suspicion'. Both are frequently encountered in the mainstream literature, most notably in the naming of the five (*sic* four) *yuga* or cosmic time periods leading up

7 Suwarno, *Dictionary*, no. 465.

the present one of 'deceit'.[8] A third item, *resi*, 'the name of a hermit' is seldom encountered in the literature but does turn up in the *Niti Sruti*. Adding to the challenge, a somewhat confusing passage follows, apparently by way of clarification of additional demands of a good sovereign. Thus, he should be like a *pandita* (Javanese for *resi*, 'one learned in the texts'), i.e., without spitefulness (*sengit* encountered in the introduction to the *Surya Alam* as a demand), with an attitude of knowledge (*idhep*), and the giver of boons (*nugrah*). These are followed by a couple of unclear attributes, ending with that of '*ésthotaken*' or steadfastness. Only if he fulfils these demands does the title concede that he will be renowned as 'The Prophet' (Mohammad?). The criteria are capped by further exhortations defining kingly virtue.

Even though only partially understood, the *Sunduk Prayoga* additions to the *giri* [...] *tanu sloka* raise some interesting points. Does it reflect a precursor from which the classic *sloka* was composed or a later, more complete explanation, including oblique references to Islamic kingly virtues? The current state of knowledge allows only speculation on the point. That it is modest is witnessed by the handling of other Classic *Sloka*.[9]

Aside from these two *sloka*, whose explanation is greatly helped by reference to similar expressions, it is difficult to make sense of the remainder of the title. What is striking is the number of seeming Arabic terms in the text for the apparatus of Islamic ritual. Paragraph 3 expounds on the *tasbeh* (rosary) and among others *ijab-kabul* (marriage contract, offering of the bride by her *wali* and acceptance by the groom) to avoid the snares of the

8 The *tirta, karta, yuga, dopara, sangara* reworking of the Hindu cosmic cycle of *yuga* is discussed in Hoadley, 'Javanese Case Law'.

9 For example, with reference to the *sloka dursila* (Classic *Sloka*, no. 17) the LOr 7440 *Sunduk Prayoga* adds a phrase immediately preceding the usual '*kusuma wa(ra)sa cakra*'. This addition consists of the phrase *cala tirta* (*sari cakra*). These are explained as: *cala*, the name of *pened* (good order of steadfastness or firm (*tetep*)); Suwarno, *Dictionary*, no. 255, 252 maintains the *cala* is 'something that stands up, a deliberate action, even 'light, torch' no. 954); *tirta*, the name of water, the good order of cleanliness, purity; *sira*, the name of a flower, the good order of its scent; *cakra*, the name of a deity, the good order of watchfulness. After these additions comes the standard explanation for *denta-denti kusuma warsa*, the total being called *sura panggeh* (?). At the end of the paragraph is repeated *cala* [...] *cakra* with different meaning, namely *cala* = firm, *tirta* = intellect, *sari* = sweetness, and *cakra* = speed (alt. 'firm, enlightened, appealing in speech[?]'). It would seem to modify the bald observation as to the finality of a judgment – an indirect admonition not to *gingsir* (change) so often encountered – with a strategy for that expression. The shortcoming is compounded by the fact that only the first *sloka* is identifiable with those of the 'Classic *Sloka*'. Those of §§ 8 and 10 seem to be a variation of the well-known *denta-denti* (no. 15). The remainder either have a tentative connection or are couched in what seems to be archaic, or at least obscure, Javanese phrases, apparently not found in the contents of the main stream legal titles.

devil (*sétan*); § 4 deals with *iman*; § 6 contains the *sloka* of '*ratu istiyar*'; § 8 refers to the *salat* (ritual prayers and actions performed five times daily); § 9 concerns the *tohid* (affirming inner religious conviction) and *mukmin* (the believers, the faithful); § 10 concentrates on the *sura panggeh* (?); while § 18 raises the threat of condemnation to *naraka* (hell). The number of terms in the *Sunduk Prayoga* that can be associated with Islam is admittedly relatively small. However, in comparison with the almost a-Islamic contents of titles dealt with in this work, they stand out. In any event, the striking mixture of what seems to be terms from both Islamic and Hindu legal concepts raises the possibility that the title might provide fertile grounds for investigating 'colloquial Islam' or reflection of a growing Islamic identity via modification of traditional Javanese texts.

Variants

Additional witness to the general lack of consistency between title and contents comes from the Yogyakarta manuscript versions of the *Sunduk Prayoga*. Because the Add 12 303 provides only a fragment, discussion can centre about that found in Add 18 398. Whatever the case with the other exemplars, the *Sunduk Prayoga* found on folios 40-48 of Add 18 398 has little discernible connection with either the contents of the *Pepakem* or, more importantly, the literature considered in these pages. Only a small number of terms or concepts match recognizable ones in this study. Of the half dozen *sloka* cited only two nominally fit those of the Classic *Sloka*. The *denta-denti sloka* (Classic *Sloka*, no. 16) found on folio 41r, is also quoted by LOr 7440, f. 214. Here the *sloka* is brought into connection with the *karta malakarta* (prosecuting court of law), the essence of which are contained in six *prakara*. Of them only the last, i.e., *aksara* 'guidance of the government' (*warsitan ing parentah*) is recognisable. The second *sloka* is '*sima* [...] *taru*' (f. 47r) cited as a '*sloka* of violence' (*walat*), but without further explanation. Other *sloka* cited are unknown in the literature so far explored in this enquiry. Still other apparently random terms fit the standard list, for example the reduction of 1507 *prakara* to 144 (f. 41r) of the *Surya Alam* or the *uger-uger* (f. 48r).

Kuntarakara

The fourth and last title – *Kuntarakara* (Add 12 303, ff. 31r-35r) – straddles several standard sources of information.

> This is a fragment of the *Kuntarakara*, twelve affairs (*prakara*) which are proper and just [alt. in agreement with the *Adilulah*] named Talaga-Ening. Of the 1944 [144?] *padu* cases which were contested in the time of Purwa

> Carita, all *padu* cases were compressed to become five affairs, which are contested by the *mantri* of Purwa Carita. That which is first [is] *tirta*, the second *karta*, the third *kali-yuga*, the fourth *dopara*, the fifth *sengara*. The meaning of *tirta* [is] water (*banyu*) whose character is to overflow the earth, the meaning of *karta* [is] not to be struck by deceit (*sikut/siku*), the meaning of *kali-yuga* [is] action, the meaning of *dopara* [is]lies, the meaning [of *sengara*] is called sin (*dosa*).[10]

The title consists of three parts. The first fourteen paragraphs start and end with the *andhih-andhihan* or *aksara bener* (of the right), which ensure victory in a suit as discussed in Chapter 5. Paragraph 14 ends in a *sinalokan*. In between the title deals with comparable concerns of the standard sources of the era. This with the addition of half a dozen *sloka* in § 5, no. 6, a *sloka karta*: *srengéngé* [...] *pinanggang*, Classic *Sloka*, no. 19; § 8, *sloka karep aksara*: *Éstri* [...] *lanca*, no. 20; and § 12, the *giri* [...] *tanu sloka*, no. 8. The middle part of the title consists of five paragraphs associated with Talaga Ening, including several *sloka*-like phrases. A final section, some sixteen paragraphs claims the *Adilulah* as its origin. They deal with a variety of subjects, mainly as clarifications (*tegesé*) of various terms. There are also cross references to other titles.

> [This is] the meaning of the *undhang-undhang*, together their message, coinciding with the message of the *undhang* of truth, the meaning of *Raja Pralambang* (prophecy) enumerating that spoken by the king. The meaning of *Praniti Sastra*: he who knows the *Dasa Nama*. The meaning of *Jalarang*: he who knows the true past [tradition], the fire before it flames, and the flower before it blooms. The meaning of *Raja Kapa-Kapa*: he who knows the circumstances true and false. The meaning of *Jugul Muda*: true, not going astray, disappear, not being touched. The usages of Patih Jugul Muda: willing of trust, the goal of custom. That which is the usage of Patih Raja Niti, [is] attentive, not forgetting. That which is the usage of *Raja Kapa-Kapa*: to know the actions of each person. That which is the usage of *Raja Kunthara*: the law court and power of the olden days (§ 6).

Successors

To date only a small number of titles have been examined from which to construct the outlines of a post-*Pepakem* layer of titles/texts. Common for the manuscripts in which they are contained is that they were acquired late

10 Compare these terms with those named by the opening of the *Wadigun Wangkara* (p. 23).

in the Independent Kingdoms era and thus overlap with that which would become a period dominated by the Dutch East Indies. More specifically, these titles include RAS 33, LOr 2125 and LOr 1832, as well as Netherlands Bible Society [NBS] 56. The title page of RAS 33 bears the provenance and date of 'Sumenep, 4 Febr 1814'. It was thus not a part of the Raffles collection, which were taken from Yogyakarta directly after the conquest of Central Java in June of 1812. Whether this differentiates it from the others, which were in existence prior to that date, remains a question for subsequent research. What is striking is that its contents to a considerable extent tally with those identified as belong to this group. The latter also contrast with those of the *pepakem* era to the extent of marking off a separate category.

RAS 33, comprising some 250 folios copied by the same hand, consists of three titles. The first title, apparently named by the cataloguer, is

> The Gajah Mada (a papatih of Majapahit) by Begawan Sukarti, a Pandita usually called Jogo Muda'.[11]

The opening paragraphs relate the frame story built around Patih Gajah Mada being tutored on the contents of law by his grandfather Begawan Sukarti. The title mixes recognizable legal terms, phrases, *sloka* phenomenon, etc. from the Independent Kingdoms period with new departures. These come in the last thirty folios (54-84), which contain among other things summaries of five didactic cases.[12] These are repeated nearly verbatim in several other titles of the era, most particularly those of LOr 2125, the second manuscript of interest here. A more important title is the second title, a *Raja Niti,* identifying itself as

> a song of praise to the descendants of the *Raja Niti,* the *panca wisudya* descended to become the *Nagara Krama, panca wisésa* descended to become the *Raja Niti,* the *panca wyawara* descended to become *Kutara, panca wisya* descended to become the *Salokantara,* becoming the *Nawa Natya* and the *panca upaya* descended to become the *Kamandakan.* The five have descended to become the song of praise of the *Raja Niti* to be the authority in this world, from which is best to punish (ff. 88-89).

11 This is found at the top margin of folio 3. However, the attribution is only partially correct. More accurately the quote applies to ff. 208-234 of the last title in RAS 33, one called 'Sloka' dated 1727. The folios indeed constitute a copy of the *Jugul Muda* considered the earliest tradition of the period.

12 Hoadley, 'Javanese Case Law'.

Although little can be made of the introduction, is its use of terms from the Majapahit era and the specific reference to a *Nawa Natya* title, which also cites the *Nagara Krama* and *Pancawisaya, are* striking.[13] Without transition folio ninety-two turns into a collection of seemingly random legal paragraphs, most of them attributed to the 'words of Kyai Senapati Jimbun' (*Kunang kang pangandika Kyai Senapati Jimbun*). The rest of the 200 paragraphs follow a common pattern. After a reference to Senapati Jimbun the substantive part opens by describing a legal situation which calls for an appropriate punishment, ending with 'such are the words of the *sastra* (*mangkana lingé sastra*). A modest number of *sloka phenomena* are quoted.[14] Scattered throughout the title are additional case summaries, not infrequently termed '*layang ubaya*' (a letter of agreement, usually issued by a prince). An idea of the volume of the material comes from the fact that the ninety folios each contain two to three paragraphs per folio making between two and three hundred paragraphs for the title. The frequent mention of Kyai Senapati Jimbun belies the identification of the text as a *Raja Niti* in the cryptic introduction.

This material is supplemented by three titles contained in LOr 2125, namely, a *Jaya Lengkara, Kutara Manawa,* and *Undhang-Undhang Senapati Jimbun*, respectively ff. 1-40, 41-171, and 172-299. The provenance and date of LOr 2125 is far less certain than that of RAS 33. Before its acquisition by Leiden University Library it belonged to the collection of T. Roorda (d. 1874). Most likely it was Roorda, who added the titles on the top margins (in Dutch) of the first folio of each title, i.e., folios 1, 41, and 173 respectively, as well as the pencilled numbering in the left-hand margin of the first 190 paragraphs of the *Kutara Manawa*. Unfortunately, no further information from which to derive a convincing date or origin of the work is available, although in general the manuscript appears to be younger than those of RAS 33. Moreover, LOr 2125 was copied by two or possibly three hands in what Pigeaud has asserted is a 'cursive West Javanese script, ink faded'.[15]

Content-wise the title closest to the *pepakem*-era texts is a *Jaya Lengkara* variant. Its first six folios summarize the standard frame story of the great durbar held at Medhang Kamulan convened in order to agree upon the contents of the law. The crux of that law is epitomised in the dozen *aksara*

13 Pigeaud, *Java in the 14th century*, vol. III, p. 119.

14 Examples include the *sloka*: '*denta-denti kusuma warsa*...' (Classic *Sloka,* no. 15), '*Gana angrusa bangga*...', '*Anir yukti*', as well as references to many of legal issues characteristic for the Independent Kingdoms era.

15 Pigeaud, *Literature of Java*, vol. II, p. 71.

clarified in turn by respective *patih* of the kingdoms which had submitted to King Jaya Lengkara. The folios also contain some Classic *Sloka*, among others, nos. 2, 3, 6 stemming from the *Jugul Muda* and *Surya Alam*. Folios 7-11 tend to paraphrase §§ 2, 11, 13 of the Yogyakarta *Surya Alam*, as well as § 20, 21 of Berlin 402. They also include the essence of the Ni Guna v. Pun Tarka case found in the *Raja Niti* and *Kuntara Manawa*. By 'the essence' is meant that only the main points of the case are repeated, without reference to the specific litigants or the court lead by Senapati Jimbun. A similar reference is made on ff. 34-35 to the Pun Diwal case. The rest of the folios frequently repeat paragraphs from the *Gajah Mada* and *Raja Niti*, including a couple of their (non-Classic and undecipherable) *sloka*, as for example '*gagak katulung kunerpa*'. Most of the paragraphs fall in line with the contents of their sister manuscripts. Moreover, on the basis of the frequency of citation – well over half the hundreds of paragraphs – the group as a whole can be termed the Senapati Jimbun titles.

The longest title of LOr 2125 is the second, a *Kuntara Manawa* (ff. 41-171). This too seems to consist of a mixing of paragraphs, most of which can be traced back to or otherwise fit the content of the *Gajah Mada* and *Raja Niti* from RAS 33. A suggestion that this is indeed a younger text, or at least post-dates them, is the fact that repetition of the case summaries are gathered into consecutive folios rather than being scattered throughout the title. For example, cases nos. 1-5 of the *Gajah Mada* are placed consecutively on folios 123-130 in the *Kuntara Manawa*, the essence of the Pun Dalu case on folio six, while the two new case summaries – the Ki Bantara and Ki Sangung affairs – are on found in §§ 167-168. The contents of the remainder of paragraphs fall within the general context of the titles.

The final title, an *Undhang Senapati Jimbun* (ff. 172-299) is only a few folios shorter than the *Kuntara Manawa*. Leaving no doubt as to the key figure, on the top margin was added:

> *Reglement oft oendang van Senopati Djembon. Policie Reglement, criminale zaken straffen enz* (Rules or *undhang* of Senapati Jimbun. Police ordinances, criminal affairs, punishments, etc.)

Its contents are of a mix of legal terms, precepts, and definitional paragraphs interspersed with a repetition of eleven of the fifteen cases contained in RAS 33, plus four additional ones of its own. What stands out is that five of the *Raja Niti* cases are repeated verbatim, but without the year or source of authority, i.e., '*sastra*' or 'according to Kyai Senapati Jimbun'. Although only superficially examined by the author, there are indications that NBS 56 is of a similar character. It contains all the just-named titles, plus another. However, it must be admitted that the precise relationship to the titles just mentioned needs further research. The author's microfilmed reproduction of the manuscript was in some places not legible. According to Pigeaud,[16] NBS 56 includes a *Jaya Lengkara*, a *Kuntara Manawa*, 'the judgments of Senapati Jimbun' (*Undhang Sénapati Jimbun*?), a *Gajah Mada*, whose frame story fits that of LOr 2125, and a *Raja Niti, Panca Wisuda* mentioning among others a *Nawa Natya*.

Despite the similarities with *Pepakem* era titles, they have been drawn upon only sparingly by this study. This is due to the shortage of information concerning date and provenance acerbated by a lack of satisfactory correspondence of their contents, especially concerning *sloka*, with those of the former group. The fact that they also contain case summaries of what has been argued elsewhere are actual cases, or very close paraphrases, containing dates and place names, as well as the overriding proximity of Kyai Senapati Jimbun, raises several apparently unanswerable issues. Hence, this study has chosen to focus on those titles most closely identifiable with the historical *Pepakem Tjerbon*.

16 *Ibid.*, vol. II, p. 723.

Appendix IV Diverse Components

Tatayi-dustha-corah

As carry-overs from the preceding era, the concepts of *tatayi-dustha-corah* – comprising a set of particularly abhorrent transgressions – continued into the Independent Kingdoms era, albeit with modifications. That they were operational before the infusion of Indian concepts is suggested by the fact that one result of 'Sanskritization' was to formalize pre-existing concepts under borrowed rubrics. In this form they continued to play an active role in Javanese legal administration through the eighteenth century. The first listing of such transgressions comes from the Kaladi inscription of King Balitung (r. 900-928). It enumerates undesirables who are forbidden to enter the freeholds established by the grant. The relevant part of the inscription reads:

> 7b 6. The advantages and disadvantages were as follows: Sharing and dividing, all sorts of fines (*dhendha*), reviling, the corpse covered in dew (*wangkey kabunan*), blood flowing, spattering of saliva
> 8a 1. *moliha maling amuk, maqyana lawang, mati amamumpang*, these were the 'Eight Kinds of Misconduct', (my italics)[1]

Despite challenges of deciphering the contents, several of the transgressions are recognizable. Among them are *wangkey kabunan* (finding a bedewed corpse), *maling* (thief), *amok* (weaponed attack), and (*a*)*mumpang* (molest/abduct women). As Javanese terms they very likely pre-date the Hindu era. According to the inscription these with the others mentioned constituted a category known as the *astha corah* of the 'Eight Kinds of Misconduct'. The Canggu inscription of 1358, better known as 'the Ferry Charter', also refers to these transgressions.[2] In it the good character of the ferry men was established by their freedom from contamination of transgressions of the type listed in Balitung's Kaladi inscription. However, instead of listing individual 'crimes', the Canggu inscription mentions freedom specifically from 1) the 'Eight Larcenies', the Kaladi inscription's 'Eight Kinds of Misconduct', *astha corah*, 2) *strisanggrahana* = *mumpang* (molester/abductor of women), and 3) *tanggapi* (receiving stolen goods), which belongs to the category of (*astha*) *dustha,* i.e., the 'Eight Miscreants'.

1 Barrett Jones, *Early Tenth Century Java from the Inscriptions*, Appendix 4, p.189.

2 Pigeaud, *Java in the 14th Century*, vol. III, pp. 160, plate 9, verso, lines 1-6.

But what were the *astha corah* and *astha dustha* to which should be added that of the *sad-atatayi* or Six Tyrants? They constituted transgressions which entailed the severest punishments ordered directly by the sovereign and normally did not require judicial process. Found only in younger texts dating from after the period of 'Indianization', the three categories can be summarised.

Sad-atatayi or Six Tyrants consist of:
1. arson (*agnida*), 2. weaponed attack (*amok/waja wangkara*), 3. molest/abduct women (*daratikrama/murugul/strisanggrahana*),4. betrayer of kings (*p(w)isuna*), 5. poisoner (*wisada/upasi*), and 6. sorcerer (*neluh*).

Astha corah or Eight Kinds of Misconduct, consist of:
1. evildoer (*karta*), 2. collaborate with an evildoer (*karhitah*), 3. befriend an evildoer (*apritikah*), 4. give food to an evildoer (*bhaktadah*), 5. relative with an evildoer (*sahacaraha*) 6. know the actions of an evildoer (*talayah*), 7. Assist or gives weapons to an evildoer (*tritah/tulung*), and 8. shelter an evildoer (*goptah*).

Astha dhusta or Eight Malefactors, consist of:
l. murder of an innocent person, 2. order the murder of an innocent person, 3. wound an innocent person, 4. accompany a murderer, 5. befriend a murderer, 6. give shelter to a murderer, 7. eat with a murderer, and 8. help a murderer.[3]

The evidence suggests a process of the institutionalization of original Javanese crimes into categories derived from Sanskrit models. *Amok* (blind attack) and *mumpang* (molester/abductor of women) of the Kaladi inscription were incorporated into the category of the *sad-atatayi*, *maling* (thief) remained under the *astha corah*, while *wangkey kabunan* (finding a bedewed corpse) was dropped from that category, although it retained its serious character by demanding answerability for those living around the site of a murder.[4] By the time of the Canggu inscription in the mid-fourteenth century the categories had taken on sufficiently concrete form to be cited under the Sanskrit rubric of *astha corah* without needing to name the contents. Alternatively, a single reference, explicitly in the case of the *astha dustha*

3 The *sad-atatayi* and *astha corah* have been discussed in Hoadley, 'Sanskritic Continuity', based upon the *Salokantara* and *Wratisasana*; the *Adigama*, in Hoadley and Hooker, 'The Law Texts of Java and Bali', pp. 326-331; and *The Agama* §§ 56, 176, 181.

4 *The Agama*, Art. 66.

and implicitly in the case of the *sad-atatayi,* represented the entire category. At an unspecified time after the Majapahit period the three categories were codified into a generally accepted list, as that given above.

The contents of heinous crimes retained their validity well into the eighteenth century. For example, the provisions of *sad-atatayi* and *astha corah* were utilized in 1717 to condemn a Javanese Regent to exile with forfeiture of rank, property, and the freedom of wife and children.[5] Two decades earlier the *raja wisuna* and *waja wangkara,* part of the *sad-atatayi* felled the *Shahbandar* of Cirebon.[6]

Yet in the Independent Kingdoms period their use was selective and even then, in modified form. The oft-cited *astha dustha* provides the point of departure because it dominates the first half-dozen paragraphs of the law books of Java and Bali.[7] The Eight Malefactors as they are translated here – alternatively The Eight Murderers or The Eight Wicked Ones – tend to focus on those actively carrying out illegal acts. These include, for example, 'to kill an innocent person', 'to order the murder of an innocent person', and 'to wound an innocent person', as well as various degrees of complicity. Despite their prominence in legal texts of ostensibly Old Javanese origin preserved on Bali, by the time of the titles considered here the *astha dustha* were all but forgotten. The single reference comes indirectly from the *Jugul Muda*'s main vignette. It will be recalled that a Ki Dustha instigated a theft of King Mahapunggung's golden image, itself symbolic of the wages of sin brought down upon the realm by the greed of Dora and Sangkara in the title's opening vignette. That it was no ordinary theft (*corah* or *maling*) but an act of defying royal order is signified by its being termed *dustha* (bad, wicked, evil, sinful, Prawiroatmaja, *Bausastra Jawa-Indonesia*). Ki Dustha was accompanied by eight *duratmaka* (criminals), several of which bear the names of the *astha corah* (Eight Thieves), as (Sa)Pratingah, Bojakah, Tatrah, and Codékah explained by § 1 of the *Jimbun Slokantara I.* After being apprehended on the complaint of Dustha's wives, deliberation via *sloka* by the realm's highest ministers counselling the sovereign on his rights and duties provides the core of the *Jugul Muda.* In the end all the *duratmaka* received the harshest of punishments, at least as far as could be meted out by the king's surrogate, the *patih.*

While the concept of the *astha dustha* was to all intents and purposes neglected by the titles of the Independent Kingdoms period, the *sad-atatayi*

5 Hoadley, State v. Puspa Nagara, *Selective Judicial Competence,* pp. 91-92.

6 Ki Aria Marta Ningrat case of 1696, *Ibid.,* pp. 25-26.

7 These include the first half-dozen paragraphs of the *Agama,* or §§ 1 & 2 of the Jonker version. The same holds true for the Jimbun-era *Kuntara Manawa* LOr 2125.

show a high degree of consistency in form and content. Almost the sole modification from the Old Javanese was that they are frequently cited as only five in number, that of sorcery being omitted. There seems no satisfactory explanation for the contrast between rubric and actual number of facets, although sorcery (*neluh*) appears in separate paragraphs in the Jimbun era titles.[8] Again cited by the *Jugul Muda*, an overriding consistency is introduced by the '*tatayi*' vignette immediately following the explanation of the dozen or so *sloka* arising from the Ki Dustha affair. The principle actor of that vignette, Ki Tatayi was guilty of arson, poisoning, running amok, sorcery, abduction, and slander of high persons. At some point in time the concept was developed into a *sloka*. The LOr 7440 *Jaya Lengkara* specifies the crimes allowed the sovereign to punish through confiscation of goods and even death. The six were expressed as the *sloka*: *awisadah-angupasi* (poisoning), *agnenidah-anunomi* (arson), *angékawara wong anelu* (sorcery), *waja wangkara* (*amok*), *angadoni ujar pada wong agung* [= *raja wisuna*] (slander of kings), and *angi(ti)wat* (kidnap), *amaling* (theft), *anudiki* [*supaladara*] (abductor of women) (§ 4). The wording shows traces of Modern Javanese usage, although the respective meanings parallel the originals. With some variations the *sloka* is repeated in the *Jimbun Slokantara I* (§ 2). The *sad-atatayi* also constitute §§ 7-11 of the *Luwangan*, complete with relevant *sinalokan*.[9] At least one of them, the fairly common *raja wisuna*, has become a modern idiomatic expression indicating 'a king with a problem' i.e., false accusations.[10] The latter continues in a modern vein:

> For a secret agent to inform a powerful minister about a secret report given to the king that contained information about this minister's mistakes is the same as *raja wisuna*.[11]

Although use of the *astha dustha* floundered and the *sad-atatayi* maintained its validity, the *astha corah* blossomed during the Independent Kingdoms era. At the same time the concept shows a great deal of variation, especially

8 *Neluh* in Jimbun Era texts, mainly the *Raja Niti* and the *Undhang-Undhang Sénapati Jimbun*, provided the terms of prosecution in the Ni Janggur case, see Hoadley, 'Javanese Case Law'.

9 Relevant *sinalokan* from the *Luwangan* read: § 7, *sima wirodha amasang jiwa dhadhang angilopati, gana-gana tan weruh ing baya, pati krama yojana*; § 8, *kakah célah…ér sapih kew nyaning puspa* (?); § 9, *ambima krama angumbar singa pralaya;* § 10, *angumbar wisa pralaya buta mangrupa sadhu*; § 11, *anggora-ga(n)da krama, bahud tan weruh ing baya.*

10 Suwarno, *Dictionary*, no. 1325.

11 It constituted the main point of the accusations levelled against a high-ranking Cirebon minister in 1696, i.e., State v. Ki Aria Marta Ningrat, Hoadley, *Selective Judicial Procedure*, p. 25-26.

in surpassing the ideal eight rubrics. Their actual number ranges from five in the *Arya Dilah* to twenty-one in the *Pepakem Tjerbon*. As shown Appendix I. 'The Problematic *Pepakem Tjerbon*', the latter's attribution to the *Jaya Lengkara* is not substantiated by the contents of the titles at our disposal. For clarity's sake the first paragraph of the *Jimbun Slokantara I* can be reproduced in skeletal form.

> § 1 These are *padu* criteria:
> *trakah*, one who orders (*akon*) a *durjana*,
> *kartah*, one who behaves (*tumandang*) as a *durjana*,
> *isakah*, one who gives shelter (*kaenggenan*) to a *durjana*,
> *sapratikah*, one who knows the actions (*weruh sapolah*) of a *durjana*,
> *sabojaka*, one who eats and drinks (*amangan anginum*) with a a *durjana*,
> *gotah*, one who receives [goods] (*anampani*) from a *durjana*,
> *tatra*, one who gives weapons (*awah gagaman*) to a *durjana*,
> [*sacodekah*, one who same as *sabojakah*]
> *Sacarakah*, one who is family (*sapanduluran*) with a *durjana*,
> These are termed the *astha corah*.

The terms are repeated with minor variations by § 30 of the Yogyakarta *Surya Alam*, thus standing outside the standard 144 *prakara*. They are also found in the *Jimbun Slokantara I*, § 16, the Berlin *Surya Alam* and the van der Hout translation (§ 22), that of Yasadipura (XII, canto 26), and even the *Luwangan* (§ 44). As was the case with the *tatayi*, the *Luwangan* adds respective *sinalokan* for the first five *corah* acts, namely, *anglingga praya madaka tan wruh ing baya*. Yet for showing the way, arming, and accompanying a *durjana* it gives an ostensibly stronger *sinalokan* expressed in semi-Sanskrit terms as *dhustem culikem kapramané*. While the first *sinalokan* is the same as *aksara kilat* (LOr 7440, f. 213) a variant is found in several instances. They have defied translation.

In contrast to the irregular number *corah* of the titles, the *Pepakem Tjerbon* in expanding the original eight to some twenty-one is unexpected. The first seven in Javanese generally correspond to those quoted above. Moreover, all the paragraphs in the *Pepakem* add specific penalties for the offences. For example, § 1 for *teta/trakah* gives as punishment (*kukumanipun*) canning (*sapasuh*), branding (*kabirat*), and terms on the Surakarta [?] chain gang. The following fourteen, thus outside the original ideal eight, deal with aiding and abetting *durjana* as active support (§ 8), not fully confessing (§ 9), swearing support (§ 11), giving clothing (§ 12), etc. The respective paragraphs in the *Pepakem* assign varying types of punishments for these categories, as well as ruling whether the miscreant is to be released and, if so, when. Without going into the details, it can be observed that the punishments seem to be innovations called forth by encroaching Dutch legal concepts. The terms, and one assumes respective punishments, do not belong to the Javanese repertoire as found in the contents of the law texts. Their employment, along with strangling posts and gibbeting of the remains are draconically well documented by the Dutch records.[12] In any event, the reference to a Surakarta chain gang seems out of place. More commonly the chain gangs, i.e., the *modderjavaan* or *moddenaars*, were transported to Batavia where they were set to work cleaning the canals.[13]

Cendhala-Sanggraha

Unlike the *dustha-corah-tatayi* with their venerable terminology harking back to the Hindu legal world, the *cendhala-sanggraha* [*sic sanggama*] category has neither. Moreover, what seems to be the core meaning is not recorded in the Javanese text of the *Pepakem Tjerbon* but is developed further in an area that seems to have little connection with that of the contents of the titles used here. The most reliable reading of *cendhala* comes from the Berlin/van der Hout *Surya Alam*, backed by equivalent paragraphs in the variant *Jaya Lengkara* of LOr 7440, § 9 as a parallel to *Slokantara* I, §§ 6-7.

> This is a padu case, five affairs, namely *istri cendhala*, *astha cendhala*, *sabda parusa*, *sagerah* [*sanggraha, sic sanggama*] *wirotama*, *istri sanggraha*, and *sanggraha wacana*, their meaning:
> *istri cendhala*, reciprocal bad mouthing (*pala-pinaha*) between women,[14]
> *sabda cendhala*, 'female quarrel using rude words' (*pisuh-pinsuh*),
> *astha cendhala/curiga*, lit. 'an evil hand' or 'people who fight against and torture others',[15] alternatively reciprocal bad mouthing (*pala-pinaha*) between men,
> *sabda parusa*, 'male quarrels using rude words (*pisuh-pinsuh*)',[16]
> *sageraha/sanggraha wirotama*, 'person accosting (*amala*) a woman not a relation',

12 *Ibid.*, pp. 99, 108-109.

13 Hoadley, *Towards a Feudal Mode of Production*, p. 106.

14 It is also a modern proverb, see Suwarno, *Dictionary*, no. 1355.

15 *Ibid.*, no. 163.

16 In a set of alternative provisions *sabda parusa* involves men insulting women. If the action is not acceptable to the latter (or their husbands, fathers, or *wakil*) a suit could be brought before the *karta*. The case of Ni Guna v. Pun Tarka is reported in the *Raja Niti* of RAS 33, ff. 99-100 and the *Kuntara Manawa* of LOr 2125, pp. 129-30 and discussed in above, Chapter 7.

istri sa(n)ggraha, 'a man takes a woman into his house (*anyékél*) as if she is his wife' i.e., illicit sexual intercourse,[17]
sa(n)ggara wacana, man making advances (*jajawat*) to a woman not related to him,[18] For these it is allowed for the king to confiscate goods [and the freedom of wife and children are forfeited].

Noteworthy is the fact that three of them have become idiomatic expressions in modern Javanese. In one of them, *astha cendhala/curiga*, there is a discrepancy between the title's intention and the modern Javanese. The former holds itself to the subject at hand, i.e., verbal violence (*wak parusa* of the *Agama* type of law book and illicit sexual advances); the modern version has been broadened into a general category of violence. This interpretation supported by terming it 'bad hands',[19] meaning those who resort to blows in scuffles or quarrels. As is the case with the Thirty *Prakara* considered in Chapter 6, this tends to be characteristic of the transition from *sloka* phenomena specifics to the generalities of proverbs. Here the *Pepakem Tjerbon* is unhelpful. While the Dutch text lists *sabda, astha candala* [*sic cendhala*], and *sabda parusa,* as well as the *istra* and *astha sanggraha,* with translations equivalent to those cited above, it is not supported by an equivalent Javanese text. Not only is the exact wording lost, but with it the chance of confirming that the Dutch was a translation of the Javanese.

While *cendhala* (contemptible, shameful) seems clear, its extension to *sanggraha* is problematic. The *Pepakem Tjerbon* (p. 60) uses *sanggraha/ sanggraha* in a different manner. The Dutch text claims that the five articles deal with *overlast* (annoyance, nuisance, molestation). In contrast the Javanese meaning here is *sanggraha* or sexual intercourse, a term somehow derived from Sanskrit *sanggama*. In another place (p. 92) the context concerns seemingly unrelated agricultural misdeeds, destroying of graves, and scoffing. Here it would seem that this is a spelling error for *sanghara* 'to destroy, smash, annihilate.'[20] 'Destroying the land' for *sangraha* (*sic sanghara*) – more usual is the *prakara* '*amok punggung*' (Table 6.1) – is done by someone building a house, cultivating it, or burying someone in it without the permission of the owner (*tanpa krama*) and so on. Parenthetically, the claim of the *Pepakem* that they originate from the *Jaya Lengkara*, as with so

17 Suwarno, *Dictionary*, no. 414.
18 *Ibid.*, no. 370.
19 Ngafenan, *Paribasan*, p. 20.
20 Prawiratmoja, *Bausastra Jawa-Indonesia.*

many others, cannot be confirmed from the texts at our disposal. Outside of the *Pepakem* the provisions are unknown.

The point is not as trivial as it may seem. *Sanggraha* in its regular meaning forms a special group of provisions within the titles. While these may seem to tax credibility, in that they deal with extremes in maintaining distance between the sexes, they are textually well-established within many of the titles. Possibly indicative of puritanical tendencies, the major sources are the Kartasura and Surakarta *Surya Alam*. They are also found in the West Javanese *Luwangan*. Paragraph 20 of Berlin 402, backed by the equivalent section in the van der Hout translation, reads:

> Concerning *sanggraha*, three [*sic* five] points (*prakara*):
> First, a man talking to a woman not related or married to him, outside the context of buying or selling and this is unacceptable to her family; the fine is *catur wara* [termed *kasela-baya*].
> [Second] a man conversing with a woman not related or married to him [i.e., illicit social intercourse] in the street or alley and this is unacceptable to her family, the fine is *catur wara*, *kamarga-baya* is its name.
> [Third] a bachelor picking up a flower or the like on the street and not knowing that the flower is from [the hair of] a woman and this is unacceptable to her family, if the accused is not brought before the government's *hakim* (*jaksa*), he is fined *catur wara*, *kakembang-baya* it is termed.
> [Fourth] if a woman comes out of the bushes where she has relieved herself and a man not related or married to her comes from relieving himself in those same bushes and this is unacceptable to her family, then the fine is *catur wara*, namely the *sloka* of *katahi-baya*.
> [Fifth] if a male guest asks his host's wife to wash a change of clothes and this is unacceptable to her husband, then there is a fine of *catur wara*, namely the *sloka* of *kasa(n)da-baya*.
> All of these *padu* cases concerning men and women are termed *sanggraha*. (§ 20)

In describing the five cases of *sanggraha* the Yasadipura verse version employs more elegant expressions (Canto X, verses 14-18). The *Luwangan* goes a step further in setting *sinalokan* to four of them. For *kamarga-baya* it is the *sinalokan, kirdah maha sahasa kalinggan rondané pinetik wite baud, tan weruh ing baya,*[21] for *katahi-baya* that of *sanggraha lindung ing wana* (adultery in the shadow of the forest), for *kembang-baya, ina krana*

21 *Maha kirdah* = adultery, Suwarno, *Dictionary*, no. 801.

astha-lena candala baud tan weruh ing baya (lowly/despicable because a careless hand brings one under *candala*), and for *kasanda-baya* the same as for *kamarga-baya*.

The provisions seem almost too radical and/or provincial to be believed. As such further explanations seem futile. Here one can only note that the approbation of talking together in an isolated place not connected with buying or selling merchandise, in Java mainly a woman's task, picking up a dropped flower, washing a bachelor's cloths, etc., would provide the opportunity for *sanggraha*. Yet, so would many other phases of normal village life. Curiously, only the *katahai-baya* ('in the pooh') has come down to the present, but in a sterilised version. It has been interpreted as 'to be accused of carrying out wickedness (*jahat*), alternatively 'to be struck by an accusation'.[22]

Witnesses

Judging from modern collections of proverbs and idiomatic expressions, two legal concepts particularly productive of *sloka* expressions were those concerning witnesses (*saksi*) and legal responsibility for witnessing, i.e., reporting, known crimes (*sidhem pramanem*). Categories of acceptable and unacceptable witnesses are straightforward. This may be explained the fact that witnesses played a crucial role within these texts and, for that matter, in legal practice as well. According to the *andhih-andhihan* cited by virtually all the titles, witnesses' relative weight before the law was higher than that of *tarka* (suspicion) and *patra* (documents), but below *bukti* (that coming from the defendant), *cina* (that coming from the plaintiff, as well as *satmata*, *nymana*, *ubaya*, and, of course, *parusa* (Table 4.4). Support for the observation comes from the contents of the *Pepakem Tjerbon*, which sums up law toward the end of the Independent Kingdoms period. Hierarchy in the weight of respective witnesses' testimony attests to the inequalities existing in Javanese society of the time based upon status, capacity, and gender.[23]

A typical enumeration of high status witnesses, the *maha téja* (great aura), i.e., village chiefs, as well as retired *mantri*, children and grandchildren of the same, *ngabèhi*, etc., come from the *Pepakem Tjerbon* (p. 42) citing the *Raja Niscaya*. Also cited as especially trustworthy witnesses are *lebé* (village mosque official), *modin* (*muezzin*), '*priester*' [*ulama*?], rich and powerful persons, advisors to the crown, etc.[24] Contemptible witnesses

22 *Ibid.*, no. 447 and Ngafenan, *Paribahasa*, p. 63, *Ibid.*, no. 636.

23 Hoadley, 'Narrative and practice in gender'.

24 *Ibid.* citing the *Jaya Lengkara*.

included itinerate vendors, *dhukun* (healer, practitioner of black magic), *dhalang* (*wayang* master), metal workers of copper or bronze, etc. (*Ibid.*, 39ff). The latter again cites the *Jaya Lengkara*, which fits only with the LOr 7440 variant version, and the *Jimbun Slokantara I*, §§ 10, 11. One assumes that these professions disqualified witnesses by the nature of the activity, which rendered persons untrustworthy. Some of them seem to reflect Hindu prejudices against professions seen as ritually unclean. As such they would seem to fit better with legal texts belonging to Java/Bali purporting to reflect conditions of Old Java than those of the Independent Kingdoms period. To the unacceptable witnesses come the more expectable ones of persons whose physical or mental handicaps debarred them from witnesses before the *karta*, i.e., deaf, dumb, blind, sick, etc.

When it comes to eliminating potential witnesses a greater source of inequality comes from the fact that some fifty percent of the population was barred from witnessing regardless of status, profession, and credulity. Female witnesses were not so much debarred as eliminated. They simply are not mentioned by the titles. Stronger still the titles indicate contempt for female witnesses. One of the fundamental reasons for losing a case is apparently explained by *panca watidiya* 'having a woman as a witness'.[25] Yet the most demeaning view of women testifying is contained in the *sloka* found in the *Jaya Lengkara.*

> *Éstri nancah* (from *pancah*, (to contradict, answer back)), *adi nancah, anyabawa kusuma nancah, uda wicate, dramara puspa wicati granayaga wicate* or women contradict, water bends, roads are crooked, plant stalks are bend; there is no woman just in her speech, Classic *Sloka,* no. 19.

In summary it can be noted that a modest number of idiomatic expressions are built around *saksi*. These range from *saksi aji* (to have a king as witness) through *saksi kulina dharma* (a witness with good habits) to *saksi angiwak-iwak* (a witness who is like a fish = knows only from the litigating parties), and ultimately *saksi maha ciri* (a disgraceful witness = *saksi asor*).[26]

Failing to witness

While demands for acceptable witnesses were many, not witnessing to what one sees or knows of a criminal act had even more serious consequences. This is the phenomenon known as *sidhem pramanem*. In modern terms this is

25 The *Pepakem Tjerbon* citing the *Raja Niscaya*, p. 39.

26 Suwarno, *Dictionary*, nos. 1381-1393.

> to conceal or eliminate something quietly; to keep secrete a case involving serious bodily injury or death.[27]

Like the *saksi, sidhem pramanem* has given rise to modern short phrases or expressions.[28] Common to them is responsibility to report to the proper authorities anything seen as (or turns out to be) criminal, alternatively as belonging to the prerogatives of the sovereign. In this respect Dora and Sangkara in the opening vignette of the *Jugul Muda* were guilty of *sidhem pramanem*, but not specifically enough to warrant sovereign reprisal. More specifically, the villagers and their chiefs in the Boga-Andrawinah vignette discussed in Chapter 7 were expressly guilty of the crime/sin, which resulted in punishment by the king as expressed as a *sinalokan*. More common for the time was not reporting the finding of a 'bedewed corpse', i.e., a body discovered in the early morning which had not been there the evening before, the work of an unknown assailant. The reason is not far to seek. Those whose property bordered such a discovery were collectively responsible for the *wergeld* to the deceased's family, if not also a fine to the sovereign.

27 *Ibid.*, no. 1185.

28 *Ibid.*, nos. 1449-1456 and Ngafenan, *Paribasan*, pp. 124-125.

Abbreviations

Ar. = **Arabic**
Jav. = **Javanese**
Skr. = **Sanskrit**

Adat	Ar. Customs, customary law
Alun-alun	Jav. Grassy square in front of Sultan's palace
Angger-angger	Jav. Rule, regulation
Catur manggala	Jav. Four chief officials of the realm
Demang	Jav. regional official
Dhalang	Jav. Narrator and puppeteer of the *wayang* shadow-play theatre
Dhendha	Skr. Punishment, fine (lit. = rod)
Den-taywajana	Jav. the twenty letters of the ha-na-ca-ra-ka Javanese alphabet
Drigama	Jav. Experience ('written *adat*'), tradition (alt danger, dangerous hindrance)
Jaksa	Jav. Assessor-at-law
Jayapattra	Skr. 'Certificate of victory' (in the eighteenth century a *surat kukudung*)
Kali-yuga (alt Dopara/Dwapara Age)	Skr. 'Age of deceit'
Kanduruhan	Jav. Treasury official
Kitab	Jav. Book, religious or legal text
Larangan	Jav. Royal reserve, something forbidden
Mantri	Jav. Javanese governmental official
Muarrar [Mouta]	Ar. Islamic law book by Abu Kasim al-Rafei
Musawarat-mupakat	Jav. 'Mutual discussion-collective decision'
Pangadilan	Jav. Law court (from adil = just)
Pangulu (alt pengulu)	Jav. Village official, religious functionary
Patih	Jav. King's chief councillor
Pégon	Jav. Javanese written in the Arabic script
Pepakem	Jav. A summary or concise version of a known story or narration
Prajanji	Jav. Promise, treaty
Sidhem Pramanem	Jav. 'The crime of silence'
Sengara (alt sangara or sangkara)	Jav. curse, solemn oath (not to do s.t.)
Tata Tantrem	Jav. Peace and order
Ubaya	Jav. Agreement, summons to appear before a court

Sources Consulted

BKI Bijdragen tot de Taal-, Land-, en Volkenkunde van het Koninklijk Instituut.
TBG Tijdschrift voor Indische Taal-, Land- en Volkenkunde van het Koninklijk Genootschap van Kunsten en Wetenschappen.
VBG Verhandelingen van het Koninklijk Bataviaasch Genootschap van Kunsten en Wetenschappen.
VKI Verhandelingen van het Koninklijk Instituut voor Taal-, Land- en Volkenkunde.

I Unpublished Primary Sources

A Mainstream titles

Raja Niscaya. LOr 7410, ff. 2v-8v; Add 12303, ff. 35v-38r.
Jugul Muda. LOr 7440, ff. 315-401; LOr 7410, f. 71v-113v; RAS 6, ff. 23-52;
Jaya Lengkara. Add 12 303, ff. 19r-31r; LOr 7410, ff. 27v-40v; RAS 38, ff. 4-98.
variation: LOr 7440, ff. 208-248, (ff. 215-231 = *Jimbun Slokantara* I §§ 1-14).
Undhang-Undhang Luwangan. LOr 7440, ff. 264-315; LOr 4710, ff. 47v-57v.
'*Undang-Undang Mataram*', *TBG* vol. 17 (1869), pp. 349-355.
Surya Alam.
Combi-RAS 6, ff. 71v-77r (§§ 1-9) plus Add 12303, ff. 4v-18v (§§ 10-37) and Add 12329, Add 12323, IOL 99.
Kartasura. Berlin 402, ff. 397-1 (*pégon* numbered back to front).
Yasadipura. Soeripto, R.M. *Ontwikkelingsgang der Vorstenlandsche Wetboek*, *Bijlage* IV. Leiden: E.J. Brill. 1918.

B Minor titles

Adilulah. LOr 7440, ff. 117-131; LOr 7442, ff. 1-21.
Arya Dilah. LOr 7440, ff. 146-164; Add 18398, f. 63v-67v.
Cacad. '*Cacad ing wong apadu dan sarsila*', LOr 7440, ff. 174-201.
Jimbun Slokantara I. LOr 7440, ff. 100-117 (LOr 1832, ff. 220a-253 [1-67]; Add 18398, ff. 94r-94v.
— *II*. '*Slokantara, Raja Nista* [sic *Niscaya*], *Wadigun* [*Wangkara*]' LOr 7440, ff. 131-140; LOr 7410, ff. 15r-18r; Add 18398, ff. 55v-56v.
Wadigun Wangkara. Add 18398, ff. 60r-62v; LOr 7440, ff. 181-188 (in *Cacad*), 140-142.

C Titles 'Left Out' (Appendix III)

Niti Sruti, LOr 7440, ff. 1-37.

Niti Praja, Ibid., ff. 37-72.

Sunduk Prayoga, Ibid., ff. 72-100; Add 12303, ff. 35r-v.

Kuntarakara kalawan Adilulah, Add 12303, ff. 31r-35r.

D Jimbun Era titles

Gajah Mada, RAS 33, ff. 1-84.

Raja Niti. Ibid., ff. 86-175.

Jaya Lengkara, LOr 2125, ff. 1-40.

Kuthara Manawa, Ibid., ff. 41-171.

Undhang Sénapati Jimbun, Ibid., ff. 172-299.

Kitab Toepah. Keyzer, S. (ed.). *Kitab Toepoh, Javaansch-Mohammedansch wetboek*. The Hague: E.J. Brill, 1853.

E Internet sources.

Niti Praja. (http://kandjengpangerankaryonagoro.blogspot.com/) downloaded 17 March 2015

Suluk Sloka Jiwa. (www.jawapalace.org/suluksaloka.html), Ahmadi 2002, downloaded 17 March 2015

II Published Primary Sources

Adatrechtbundel I, 'Adatwijzer, houdende practische wenken bij onderzoekingen naar het Adatrecht', pp. 16-20, first published by the Commission on Adat Law in 1910.

Berrett-Jones, Antoinette M. *Early Tenth Century Java from the Inscriptions. VKI* vol. 107. Dordrecht: Floris Publications, 1984.

Brandes, J. 'Eenige officeele stukken met betrekking tot Tjerbon'. *TBG* vol. 37 (1894), pp. 449-488.

Carey, Peter (ed.). *The British in Java 1811-1816. A Javanese Account.* Oxford: Oxford University Press for the British Academy, 1992.

— (ed). *The Archive of Yogyakarta, vol. I, Documents Relating to Politics and Internal Court Affairs.* Oxford: Oxford University Press for the British Academy, 1980.

Carey, P. & Mason C. Hoadley, (eds.). *The Archive of Yogyakarta, vol. II, Documents relating to Economic and Agrarian Affairs.* Oxford: Oxford University Press for the British Academy, 2000.

Van der Chijs, J.A. (ed.). *Nederlandsch-Indische Plakaatboek,* 17 vols. The Hague: Martinus Nijhoff, 1885-1900.

Hazeu, G.A.J. (ed.), 'Tjeribonsch wetboek (Pepakem Tjerbon) van het jaar 1768 in tekst en vertaling uitgeven', *VBG*, vol. 55, pt. 2 (1905), pp. 1-187.
Hoadley, M.C. and Hooker, M.B. *An Introduction to Javanese Law. A Translation of and Commentary on the Agama.* Tucson: University of Arizona Press, 1981.
—. 'The Law Texts of Java and Bali', in M.B Hooker (ed.). *The Laws of South-East Asia. Volume I: The Pre-Modern Texts.* Singapore: Butterworth & Co. (1986), pp. 241-346.
Holle, F.K. 'Bijdragen tot de Geschiedenis der Preanger-Regentschappen'. *TBG* vol. 17, no. 3, (1869), pp. 163-167.
van der Hout '*Surya Alam*'. *BKI* vol. 10 (1863), pp. 1-57.
Raffles, Thomas S. *A History of Java*, 2 vols., Appendix C, pp. xxxviii-xlvi. London. 1817.
Rani, Sharada. *Salokantara, an Old Javanese didactic text.* New Delhi: International Academy of Indian Culture, 1957.
'Robson, S.O. 'The Serat Arok'. *Archipel*, vol. 20 (1980), pp. 281-301.
— (ed.). *Désawarnana (Nagarkrtagama) by Mpu Prapanca.* Leiden: KITLV Press, 1995.
Serat Angger: Jugul Muda, Solo: Stoomdrukkerij 'De Bliksem', 1929.

III Secondary Sources

A Articles

Ayang Utriza Yakin. '*Undhang-Undhang Banten.* A 17th to 18th century legal compilation from the *qadi* court of the Sultanate of Banten', *Indonesia and the Malay world*, vol. 44, no. 130 (2016), pp. 365-388.
Creese, Helen. 'Judicial process and legal authority in pre-colonial Bali' and 'Old Javanese legal traditions in pre-colonial Bali', *BKI* vol. 165, nos. 2-3 (2009), pp. 241-290 and 515-550 respectively.
Hardjasaputra, A. Sobana, 'Bupati di Priangan. Kedudukan dan peranannya pada abad ke-17–abad ke-19', pp. 9-65 in *Bupati di Priangan.* Bandung: Seri Sundalana, no. 3, 2004.
Hoadley, Mason C. 'Continuity and change in Javanese legal traditions: the evidence of the *jayapatra*', *Indonesia*, vol. XI (1971), pp. 95-109.
—. 'The Role of Law in Contemporary Indonesia'. Working Paper in Contemporary Asian Studies, Lund University, No. 4, 2004.
—. "Why 'You Can't Go Home'; The Legacy of Law and Indonesian Public Administration," Department of Sociology, National University of Singapore, Working Papers, No. 164, 2004.

—. 'Institutional Inequalities: Indonesian *Adat*', SSAPS-Lund Conference Papers, 2003.
—. 'Sanskritic Continuity in Southeast Asia, the *Sadatatayi* and *Astacorah* in Javanese Law'. in Lokesh Chandra (ed.), *The Art and Culture of South-East Asia,* New Delhi: International Academy of Indian Culture (1991), pp. 111-124.
—. Japlak and Awas. 'Literature as Law: the case of pre-colonial Javanese texts', Papers from the 3rd International Seminar on Southeast Asian Literature, Kuala Lumpur, 2004.
—. Practice and narrative of gender relations in early-modern Java', *Historia. Journal of Historical Studies,* vol. VIII, no 1 (June 2007), pp. 1-15.
—. 'Javanese case law. Textual, didactic, or actual', in progress.
Hoadley, Mason C. and Neelambar Hatti. 'Notes on Corruption and Morality'. *Social Science Spectrum,* vol. 1, no. 4, (December 2015).
Jaspan, M.A. 'In quest of new law: the perplexity of legal syncretism in Indonesia', *Comparative Studies in Society and History,* vol. 7, no. 3 (1965), pp. 252-266.
Keyzer, S. 'Een verzameling van Javaansche spreekwoorden en spreekwardelijke uitdrukken', *BKI* vol. 10 (1863), pp. 161-201, 221-237.
Kooria, Mahmood, 'The Dutch Mogharaer, Arabic Muḥara, and Javanese Law Books: A VOC Experiment with Muslim Law in Java, 1747-1767', *Itinerario* vol. 42, pt 2, (August 2018), pp. 202-219.
Naerssen, F.W. Van. 'Astadasavyavahara in Old Javanese', *Journal of the Greater India Society,* vol. 15 (1956), pp. 113-114.
—. 'De Saptopapatti', *BKI* vol. 90 (1953), pp. 239-258.
Ricklefs, M.C. 'The Yasadipura problem', BKI vol. 153 (1997), pp. 273-283.
Rouffaer, G.P. 'Vorstenlanden' in *Encyclopaedie van Nederlands Indië, 4* vols. (1931), pp. 582-683.
Soebardi. 'Raden Ngabehi Jasadipura I, court poet of Surakarta. His life and works', *Indonesia* 8, (1969).
Winter, J.W. 1902. 'Beknopte Beschrijving van het hof Soerakarta in 1824'. *BKI vol.* 6 (1902), pp. 15-172.

B Monographs

Ayang Utriza Yakin. *Undhang-Undhang Bantên et Fakih Najamuddin: Etude de l'Histoire du Droit sur Les Archives du Grand Juge Islamique au Sultanat de Banten, à Java, du XVIIème au début du XIXème Siècles.* Unpublished PhD thesis, Sorbon, Paris, 2009.
—. *Undhang-Undhang Bantĕn: Étude philologique de la compilation des lois du Sultanat de Bantĕn (Indonésie) aux 17e et 18e siècles'* (Philological Studies

on the Compilation of Laws of the Sultanate of Banten (Indonesia) in the 17th and 18th centuries), École des Hautes Études en Sciences Sociales, Paris, France, 2013.

Ball, John. *Indonesian Legal History, 1602-1848*. Sydney: Oughtershaw Press, 1982.

Crawfurd, John. *History of the Indian Archipelago Containing an Account of the Manners, Arts, Languages, Religious Institutions and Commerce of its Inhabitants*, 3 vols. Edinburgh & London: Constable, 1820.

Darmasoetjipta, F.S. *Kamus Peribahasa Jawa dengan Penjelasan Kata-Kata dan Pengartianya*. Yogyakarta: Penerbit Kanisius, 1985.

De Casparis, J.G. Indonesian Paleography, *A History of Writings in Indonesia from the beginnings to c. AD 1500*. Handbuch der Orientalistik, Leiden: E.J. Brill, 1975.

Florida, Nancy K. *Writing the Past. Inscribing the Future. History as Prophecy*. Durham: Duke University Press, 1995.

Fuller, Lon L. *Anatomy of the Law*. Harmondsworth: Penguin Books Ltd. 1968

Gonda, J. *Sanskrit in Indonesia*. New Delhi: International Academy of Indian Culture. 1963.

Graaf, H.J. and Pigeaud, Th. *De Eerste Moslimsche Vorstendom van Java*. The Hague: Martinus Nijhoff, 1974.

Haan, F. de. *Priangan*, 4 vols. Batavia: G. Kloft, 1910-1912.

Haar, Barend ter. *Het Adat process der Inlander*. Amsterdam: A. H. Kruyt, 1915.

—. *Adat Law in Indonesia*. New York: Institute of Pacific Relations, 1948.

Hoadley, Mason C. *Selective Judicial Competence. The Cirebon-Priangan Legal Administration 1680-1792*. Ithaca, New York: Southeast Asia Program, 1994.

—. *Islam dalam Tradisi Hukum Jawa dan Hukum kolonial*. Yogyakarta: Graha Ilmu, 2009.

Holleman, J.E. *Van Vollenhoven on Indonesian Adat Law. Selections from Het Adatrecht van Nederlandsch-Indië*, 2 vols. The Hague: Martinus Nijhoff, 1918, 1931.

Kern, R.A. *Javaansche Rechtsbedeeling, een Bijdragen tot de Kennis der Geschiedenis van Java*. The Hague: E.J. Brill, 1926.

Lingat, R. *The Classic Law of India*. Berkeley: University of California Press, 1973.

Lavelle, Lise. *Amerta Movement of Java 1986-1997. An Asian Movement Inprovisation*. Lund: Centre for Languages and Literature, 2006.

Mertono, Soermarsaid. *State and Statecraft in Old Java*. Ithaca: Cornell Modern Indonesia Project, 1968.

Niel, Robert van. *Java under the Cultivation System. Collected Writings. VKI* vol.150 (1992).

Pigeaud, Th. *Java in the 14th Century,* 5 vols. The Hague: Martinus Nijhoff, 1963-65.
Raffles, Thomas Stafford. *The History of Java.* 2 vols. 2nd edn. London: John Murry, 1830.
Ricklefs, M.C. *Jogjakarta under Sultan Mangkubumi, 1749-1792. A History of the Division of Java.* London: Oxford University Press, 1974.
—. *The Seen and Unseen Worlds in Java 1726-1749. History, Literature and Islam in the Court of Pakubuwana II.* Honolulu: University of Hawai'i Press, 1998.
—. *Modern Javanese Historical Tradition. A study of an original Kartasura chronicle and related materials.* London: School of Oriental and African Studies, 1978.
Robson, Stuart (ed.). *Desawarnana* (*Nagarakrtagama*) by Mpu Prapanca. VKI, vol. 169, 1995.
Schacht, Joseph. *An Introduction to Islamic Law.* Oxford: Clarendon Press, 1964.
Seto, Ario. *Netizen, Activitism and Online Community Transformation in Indonesia.* Singapore: Palgrave Macmillon, e-book, 2017.
Sinduhana, Gabriel Passenti. *Putri Cina.* Jakarta: Gramedia Utama, 2007.
Soeripto, R.M. *Ontwikkelingsgang der Vorstenlandsche Wetboek.* Leiden: Eduard Idjo, 1929.
Vollenhoven, C van. *De Ontdekking van het Adatrecht.* Leiden: E.J. Brill, 1928.
—. *Het Adatrecht van Nederlandsch Indië.* 10 vols. Leiden: E.J. Brill, 1918.
Winter, C.F. [1858]. *Javaansche Zamenspraken,* vol. I, Taco Roorda (ed.). Leiden: E.J. Brill, 1911.
—. *Javaansche Zamenspraken,* vol. II, S. Keyser (ed.). Amsterdam: Johannes Müller, 1911.

C Bibliographies and Reference Works

Behrend, Timothy E. *Katalog Induk Naskah-Naskah Nusantara, Jilid I. Museum Sonobudoya.* Jakarta: Jambatan, 1990.
—. 'Small collections of Javanese manuscripts in Indonesia', *Archipel,* fol. 35 (1988), pp. 23-42.
Darmasoetjipta, F.S. *Kamus Peribasa Jawa dengan Penjelasan Kata-Kata dan Pengartiannya.* Yogyakarta: Penerbit Kanasius, 1985.
Ekadjati, Edi S. *Naskah Sunda. Inventarisas dan Pencataten.* Bandung: Lembaga Penelitan Universitas Padjadjaran & Toyota Foundation, 1988.
Eringa, F.S. *Soendaas-Nederlands Woordboek, med gebruikmaking van eerder door R.A. Kern bijeengebrachte gegevens.* Dordrecht: Foris Publications, 1984.

Florida, Nancy K. *Javanese Literature in Surakarta Manuscripts*, vol. 1, *Introduction and the Manuscripts of the Kraton Surakarta;* vol. 2, *Manuscripts of the Mankunagaran Palace.* Ithaca, New York: Southeast Asia Program (SEAP), 1993, 2000.

Gonda, J. *Sanskrit in Indonesia.* New Delhi: International Academy of Indian Culture, 1977.

Hariwijaya, S.S. *Kamus Idiom Jawa.* Jakarta: Eska Media., 2004.

Margana, S. *Kraton Surakarta dan Yogyakarta 1764-1874.* Yogyakarta: Pustaka Pelajar, 2004.

Mohammad Ngafenan, (ed.). *Paribasaan, Begasan, lan Saloka.* Solo: Aneka, 1995.

Pigeaud, Th.G.Th. *Javaans-Nederlands Handwoordenboek.* Groningen: J.B. Wolters, 1938.

Prawiroatmodjo, S. *Bausastra Jawa-Indonesia*, 2 vols. Jakarta: Haji Masagung, 1992.

Prijohoetomo, M. Javaansche Spraakkunst. Leiden: E.J. Brill, 1937.

—. *Javanese and Balinese Manuscripts and some Codices Written in Related Idioms in Java and Bali: Descriptive Catalogue.* Verzeichnis der Orientalistichen Handschriften in Deutschland, vol. 31. Wiesbadan: Franz Steiner Verlag GMBH, 1975.

—. *Literature of Java: Catalogue raisonné of Javanese manuscripts in the library of the University of Leiden and other public collections in the Netherlands,* 4 vols. The Hague: Martinus Nijhoff, 1967-80.

Robson, Stuart and Singgih Wibisono. *Javanese English Dictionary.* Hong Kong: Periplus Editions, 2002.

Ricklefs, M.C. and Voorhoeve, P. *Indonesian Manuscripts in Great Britain. A Catalogue of Manuscripts in Indonesian Languages in British Public Collections.* Oxford: Oxford University Press, 1977.

Suwarno, Peter. *Dictionary of Javanese Proverbs and Idiomatic Expressions.* Yogyakarta: Gajah Mada University Press, 1999.

Uhlenbeck, E.M. *A Critical Survey of Studies on the Languages of Java and Madura.* The Hague: Martinus Nijhoff, 1964.

Zoetmulder, P.J. *Old Javanese-English Dictionary*, 2 vols. The Hague: Martinus Nijhoff, 1982.

Index

For Product Safety Concerns and Information please contact our EU
representative GPSR@taylorandfrancis.com
Taylor & Francis Verlag GmbH, Kaufingerstraße 24, 80331 München, Germany

www.ingramcontent.com/pod-product-compliance
Ingram Content Group UK Ltd.
Pitfield, Milton Keynes, MK11 3LW, UK
UKHW020012200926
475702UK00014B/1852
* 9 7 8 1 0 4 1 1 8 8 3 1 5 *